Eamonn O'Hara was born in Belfast in 1964. His family moved to his father's birthplace of Knocknacarry, in the parish of Cushendun, County Antrim, in 1973. Eamonn was educated at St MacNissi's College, Garron Tower, and at the University of Ulster at Coleraine, entering sports journalism at the age of eighteen. He worked for numerous newspapers, including the now defunct *Sunday News* and the *Belfast News Letter*, for several years as a freelance reporter before joining the staff of the *Irish News* in 1990. He is married to Patricia, and they have a son, Callum.

RINTY

RINTY

The Story of a Champion

Eamonn O'Hara

THE BREHON PRESS
BELFAST

First published 2008 by
The Brehon Press Ltd
1A Bryson Street
Belfast BT5 4ES
Northern Ireland

ISBN: 978 1 905474 22 6

Cover design by Jake Campbell

Printed and bound by J.H. Haynes & Co Ltd, Sparkford

For Tricia and Callum,
for all those lost weekends over the last couple of years

Acknowledgements

MANY KNOWLEDGEABLE AND ENTHUSIASTIC PEOPLE deserve to be thanked for their greatly appreciated interest and help in putting this book together.

The decision to delve into Rinty Monaghan's boxing career was initially agreed with Damian Keenan and Brendan Anderson. Once the research started it was soon clear that, while revered for his remarkable achievements as a flyweight fighter, there was much more to Rinty. Shining a light on the other aspects of his life was only possible due to Rinty's only son, Sean, who embraced the idea and arranged for me to question the Monaghan family. Sadly, Sean, or 'Spike', as family and friends affectionately referred to him, passed away during the early months of research. Initial contact with Sean followed a few discussions with an old Italian friend of his, Freddie Fusco, whose family once owned a thriving café business in an area of Belfast known as 'Little Italy'.

My thanks to Freddie, a night watchman at the *Irish News*, for some wonderful insights into what the city was like in the 1940s, as well as his memories of both Rinty and Belfast boxing which, at that time, was hugely popular with small hall promotions taking place most weeks in all sorts of venues.

Sean also put me in touch with Rinty's two surviving brothers, Patsy, who lives in Belfast, and Tommy, who divides his time between his home in the US and his native city. I would like to thank both for their immense contributions, and also to acknowledge those of Rinty's sister, Marie, and his daughters Collette, Martha and Reta.

Thanks also to George McCullough, whose brother Eddie was one of Rinty's main sparring partners over the years, and Gerry Storey, the coach of the Holy Family Golden Gloves ABC, and lifelong friend of Rinty's, and not forgetting gym veteran, Vincent McGurk. All were extremely helpful in providing me with anecdotal recollections of the golden days of the fight game, in evoking the city life of the era, and in sourcing both pictures and contacts from the old cabaret scene that Rinty was part of for a great part of his life.

Thanks also to Jerome Quinn at BBC Northern Ireland for help with sourcing archive material, interviews, and old fight commentaries; to Adrian Logan at UTV for archive footage; to the staff at the Central Newspaper Library, where many days were spent poring over microfilm; to Dublin boxing writer Patrick Myler; to Belfast boxer Eamon McAuley, the grandson of Rinty's eldest sister Sarah and Rinty's brother-in-law and ex-sparring partner, Harry McAuley; to Scottish boxing writer, Brian Donald; to Rinty's final employer, Phil Moley; to Liam Burns, whose father played in the early 1950s showband 'Rinty and the Rintonians'; to Brian Kearney and Hugh Russell of the *Irish News* for assistance with pictures and illustrations; to former Irish News picture editor, Brendan Murphy; to Belfast photographer, John Kelly, who grew up a few doors away from the Monaghan family, for his many hours of research and work on old images; to Harry Fitzsimons and Mickey Kelly of Dockers Amateur Boxing Club for the sourcing of pictures; to Danny Walsh for his recollections of the Belfast cabaret scene and early showband years; and to anyone else who helped in any way with pictures, programmes and other archive material.

Last, but by no means least, a special thanks to my editor Nicola Pierce for all her good instincts regarding various aspects of the book, and her perseverance in seeing it through.

Prologue

IT IS APPROACHING 8.30PM ON THE night of 23 March 1948, and the shadowed streets of Belfast are empty and still. The city's inhabitants are holding their collective breath because this is no ordinary Tuesday night. On the wireless the BBC is broadcasting live from the King's Hall, where Rinty Monaghan, from 32 Little Corporation Street, is boxing for the undisputed flyweight championship of the world. The diminutive fighter is already a world champion in the eyes of many: on the waterfront, within his adopted Sailortown community, his city, his country, as well as America. Tonight is almost a formality, concerning some loose ends that need to be tied and Rinty is hell-bent on binding them as tight as the callused hands of a dockworker would knot a rope.

Doors are unlatched around the city's docklands. Front rooms and public houses are crammed with people anxiously following this momentous event on the popular Light Programme as Rinty takes on Scotland's rival title claimant Jackie Paterson. From house to house the same two voices dominate—Raymond Glendenning, the famous sports commentator, and W Barrington Dalby, his inter-round summarizer.

Belfast's world champion, winner of the US-based National Boxing Association's title, is battling with the British Board of Control's claimant before an estimated 16,000 sell-out crowd. This winner-takes-all championship clash is making history: it is the first time a professional world title bout has been staged in the city or anywhere else in Northern Ireland. In fact, it's the first fight of its kind on the island of Ireland for nearly twenty-five years. There are four titles down for decision—Rinty's NBA, Paterson's world version, along with his British and Empire flyweight crowns.

Rinty sends a right hook crashing into Paterson's jaw. Facial nerves ablaze, his senses in misty orbit and balance gone, Jackie lurches backwards. Punches rain all around Paterson and his head jolts wildly right and left, the sweat spraying off his opponent's glistening black hair as Rinty applies the last anesthetic shots. Paterson is down for the last time. The count is academic and the Irish fans are going wild.

'...eight, nine, ten.'

With the ding of the bell a city unites in celebration. Glendenning relays a dramatic knockout sequence that finishes the fight in the seventh round. In less than half a minute of mayhem Rinty leaves his Ayrshire opponent slumped against the bottom rope.

1

MARTHA MONAGHAN KNEW THE UNCERTAINTIES THAT surrounded bringing a child into the world; she had already lost her first-born, Kathleen, just weeks after giving birth to her. Infant mortality rates were frighteningly high in the early 1900s. Her second child, Sarah, was not yet two years of age when Martha went into labour again in the late summer of 1918. She gave birth to a boy at her home in Lancaster Street on Wednesday, 21 August. She and her husband Thomas named their new son John Joseph.

Two years earlier Martha had nearly lost Thomas in the Great War. Luckily he made it back from sea. Blood was still being spilled throughout Europe that summer but thankfully the end was in sight. The Kaiser's forces had fought three long years for domination. However, by the end of August 1918, the Allies were turning the tide. On the day John Joseph was born, they delivered a significant blow on the killing fields at Flanders when Marshall Foch's strategic assault pushed the German enemy into retreat. The Kaiser's forces would be repelled, broken and surrendered before the end of the year.

Closer to home, Virginia Pearson, a popular actress of the time, was playing the lead in a Scottish-based production at the Panopticon Picture House, alongside Pathe newsreels about the battlefields in France. The title of the drama, *The War Mother*, was an appropriate one for Martha and thousands of other women. Martha had been born Martha Wilson into a family of staunch Protestants who lived within the close-knit community of the lower Shankill Road. At the age of sixteen Martha decided to go on a religious retreat with her best friend, Sarah. The retreat made such a deep impression on the young girl that she was impelled to make what must have been an earth-shattering decision to relinquish her parents' faith for Catholicism. A year later, in 1913, she and Thomas Monaghan were wed.

Also diverting people's attention from the First World War in the week of her son's birth were the exploits of the 'Boston Tar Baby', a Canadian boxer who, some twelve years earlier, had challenged Jack Johnson, albeit unsuccessfully, for the world 'coloured' heavyweight title. Prior to tackling Johnson, 'Baby', or Sam Langford, had captured the National Sporting Club of England's world middleweight title. He eventually won a heavyweight 'coloured' prize in 1908. Slugging Sam also claimed a French Federation-sanctioned world title in 1913 against Jean Jeanette, as well as titles in Spain, Australia and Mexico. Loss of sight in both eyes forced an end to a brutally tough career.

The Monaghans' kitchen-house home was situated in the heart of the city's industrial district. A quarter of a mile along the huge mills and factories which lined York Street brought Tommy to his place of work in the docks. Jobs did not pay well in those days and Tommy's was no exception. His weekly wage was less than £2 for grafting on the wharf, after his latest commission with the Merchant Navy. A fortnight or so after John Joseph's arrival, his parents registered his birth with the General Register Office for Northern Ireland. Assistant Registrar, Mr J Harkness, signed the official certificate for the 'District of Belfast Urban No 2' on 12 September. This documentation clears up the first bit of confused, contradictory detail about where and when John Joseph was born. It has been claimed erroneously that he had been born in Thomas Street in years varying from 1919 through to 1921 which resulted in the often-repeated assumption that he made his boxing debut a month after he turned fourteen.

He was two months old when the declaration of surrender silenced the death and destruction throughout Europe. After the war Tommy spent more time at home and got a better paying job as a foreman at Roden's Store. However, it was not long before the sea drew him back. The challenging life of the sailor was in the Monaghan gene. Years earlier, Tommy's father Robert had introduced him to the Merchant Navy and both father and son served on merchant vessels during the war.

Another killer lurked in the air that summer. In 1918 the continent and surrounding islands were swamped by a flu epidemic which became known as the 'Spanish Influenza'. It was a form of pneumonia which was capable of taking life within hours of the symptoms being identified. Over the next two years the deadly virus developed, and was responsible for a massive loss of life worldwide. Troop movements during the last number of months of the war may have contributed to it spreading so rapidly. By 1920 the death toll was estimated at forty million. Good fortune spared the Monaghan household from the flu. Another Belfast family that escaped its clutches was that of leading rabbi, Dr Isaac Herzog, who lived in the north of the city, close to the Cliftonville Road, at Clifton Park Avenue. In 1918, the Herzogs were also blessed with a baby boy, whom they named Chaim. Like John Joseph, Chaim would also follow a fighting trail, but not always as a boxer. Nevertheless, he did box in his youth and won an Irish title at bantamweight. Dr Herzog took his family to live in Palestine and it was there that his ambitious son blossomed. Chaim served with the British Army in World War Two, even assisting in the 1945 capture of Nazi Gestapo chief Heinrich Himmler. Later on, he was made head of Israel's intelligence in the 1967 Six Day War and, in 1983, this Belfast native became President of Israel.

Meanwhile, the Monaghan brood was expanding and Thomas and Martha decided to move into a house on Thomas Street. Sarah was soon joined by sisters Martha and Peggy; three more brothers—Patsy, Charlie and Thomas junior—followed by 1928; then a third sister, Noreen, arrived in 1931 and, finally, Marie came along three years later. Typical of the time, Martha experienced the sadness of losing another child, Kevin, shortly after he was born, and she also suffered a number of miscarriages. Had all the pregnancies been successful there would have been fifteen kids instead of a mere nine.

Marie, the baby of the family, has only fond memories of life on Thomas Street: 'It was a lovely place to live, a lovely home. Daddy was a strict man, worked hard, and mammy was really a very quiet woman. Mammy would have done anything for anyone. She was also a very religious woman, had a great way with her, and if people were ill she would be called on to help them. She was lovely that way with neighbours who were sick, or friends.'

It was not a big house: there were only two rooms upstairs, one of which was a 'return room', just large enough to get a bunk bed into. Kids slept head to toe. Marie said it was always a lively house with plenty of people about the place, and lots of singing, a favorite pastime of her parents, especially her father. He taught all the children to sing.

'Back then that is how families entertained. There was always a bit of music or a song in our house. Daddy encouraged all the kids to sing and he would play the accordion. In the evenings the house would be full sometimes with family and friends. They were happy times, very tough times, because there was not much money about in those days, but I enjoyed my childhood.'

Marie's big brother, John Joseph—all 5'4" of him—has his grandmother Margaret to thank for what was to become his more famous name. In the autumn of 1918, on the Western Front of France, a group of American troops met up with some kids who gave the soldiers their precious toy puppet as a good luck charm. The puppet had been christened 'Rintintin' by the children. When one of the soldiers, Lee Duncan, was searching through the rubble of a bombed-out building, originally a kennel, in Lorraine, he found a tiny, frightened German Shepherd pup. It was love at first sight for Duncan and he decided to take the dog with him, eventually bringing him back to his home in Los Angeles. Lee named his dog after the children's puppet and spent hours training him to perform all sorts of tricks. The dog was soon the centre of attraction at a local fair, and had acquired a reputation as a keen high-jumper: it was claimed that he could jump over thirteen feet. The repertoire caught the eye of a Hollywood film producer, none other than Darryl F Zanuck, who immediately offered Duncan payment to put the dog on the silver screen and this, in turn, led to the start of a career in the movies for 'Rin Tin Tin'. The canine was given its first minor role in 1922 and went on to star in twenty-nine motion pictures, including *Man from Hell's River* and *Shadows of the North.* He also had his own long-running radio show, *The Wonder Dog,* which ran until his death in 1932. Duncan decided to honor Rin Tin Tin's heritage by returning his body to France for burial at Cimetiere des Chiens, a famous pet cemetery in the Paris suburb of Asnieres-sur-Seine. However, the popular canine star's grandson kept his memory alive by starring in ABC Television's 1954-1959 hit series, *The Adventures of Rin Tin Tin.*

John Joseph Monaghan loved the early Rin Tin Tin films, and he worked hard to imitate the wily dog. He once recalled in a radio interview, 'I used to be very fond of a dog. The dog was very famous. It used to jump from wall to wall, from out of a car into a van or something, and I used to practice this all the time.'

Since he was fast on his feet and always up to some trick or other in the street, John Joseph was soon nicknamed 'Rin Tin Tin' after his idol. Then, one day, his grandmother was calling him to come in for his dinner but he was nowhere in sight. Margaret roamed Thomas Street and the surrounding area shouting the three syllables of his nickname until she tired of it and spontaneously shortened it to 'Rinty'. The clipped version stuck. Later it was discovered that Lee Duncan also had a pet name for the real Rin Tin Tin: 'Rinty'.

A striking feature of Rinty the boxer would be his flattened nose. He explained the look was not due to repeated blows from rival fists but the result of an early incident that almost killed him. 'I used to be very fond of the catapult. I was a dead-eyed dick with it, could hit a thruppenny bit with it fifty yards away. I used to sit on this roof, on the ridge tile, and this big woman used to sit down washing the step. She had a big bottom on her. I thought I would get this catapult, put a pea in it, hit her and laugh. But, didn't I lose my grip and away I went through the roof. I saw the first ceiling and I closed my eyes.'

When his father arrived home from sea he found the boy badly broken up, covered in bandages, and lucky to be alive. Tommy, or 'Ta', as he was affectionately known, was horrified at the state of the wee scallywag. Rinty was sore and feeling pretty sorry for himself. There was not much to him.

He was like a twig, little and weak, and he remembered the scene when he came round in a hospital ward not fit to move. Martha and his granny were anxiously sitting by the bedside when he awoke to find himself covered in plaster of Paris. 'There were two little slits for my eyes. I was looking out, peeking at them and my arm was up on a sling. The doctor said I was very lucky and that they had to give me an awful lot of blood.'

One feature on little Rinty's face would be changed forever by the accident. Boxers usually need a few years to develop the flat nose bridge, beaten in by the pressure thuds of ramrod jabs or hooks smashed against it, but young Rinty was left with a ready-made boxer's nose by the time he left hospital.

'I was awful thin, skinny, when I came out of hospital. My nose was all twisted and I talked awful funny and no matter where I went for a message the people didn't know what I was saying.'

Ta decided the kid had to be taken in hand once he was well enough. He had trained as a boxer and had regularly fought for the Merchant Navy at lightweight. He understood the benefits of a sensible diet and plenty of exercise. First he bought a rope and taught Rinty how to skip. Then he made his fragile son a punch-bag so that he could build up his strength.

'He took me to this barn, put up a bag and said, "I am going to teach you something," and he started teaching me to fight. I was very skinny after the fall and I was very weak. The wind would have blew me away and Papa said he would build me up, so he gave me exercises to do. I kept training and kept taking raw eggs and milk—goat's milk—and I kept taking that all my life until I gave up boxing.'

Rinty proved willing to try anything to make him stronger. One day in school he was told that warm cow's blood would help build his strength. With no reason to disbelieve this, he determined to try it out.

'I never mitched school really, not deliberately, until this week this man told me, "I have something for you," and it will do me good. I had to go down to the market, get more than a pint of blood in a jug. It was nice and warm, lovely. I took it all the time. I think it done me good as well.'

2

TOMMY'S FATHER, ROBERT, NEVER KNEW HIS grandchildren. He died in May 1916 during the greatest sea engagement of the First World War, when the naval might of the British fleet took on the battleships of Germany's Kaiser Wilhelm II in the icy waters off the northern coast of Denmark. Tommy wasn't too far away, aboard another vessel as the famous Battle of Jutland unfolded in the Skagerrak, a stretch of North Sea close to the south-east of Norway. When reports of a British ship being hit filtered through to Belfast, Martha and her mother-in-law, Margaret, were told to come down to the docks to wait for news. It transpired that over six thousand personnel had been lost at sea, and the Monaghan household, like so many others, braced itself for the worst.

Marie Monaghan remembers her mother recounting the events of that sad day when wives, mothers, sisters and girlfriends stood anxiously at the water's edge and waited. 'My daddy and my grandfather were on sister ships during the Battle of Jutland. One of their ships was torpedoed. When word came through down at the docks, they did not know at the beginning which one of them was dead, whether it was daddy or his father, and which of them was alive. It took a long time for the information to come through. They were called to go back down to the docks again and it was then they were told that Robert's ship had been hit by a torpedo and was lost. Mammy talked of that day a few times and obviously it was an awful time for the family and countless other families.'

Tommy made it back safely to Belfast afterwards. He left the sea for a time but kept being lured back. All of his sons eventually took to the sea. Patsy and Thomas junior had careers with the Merchant Navy, both serving during the Second World War, as did their father. Their brother Charlie opted to join the King's Own Tank Regiment and served in India. Rinty tried out with the Merchant Navy but it was not to be. In fact, he ended up shipwrecked in Ballyholme Bay, off the County Down coast, which gave his father no end of amusement. Tommy took to calling Rinty 'Sinbad the sailor' and made him repeat the story at every family gathering.

'It was a little coaster and we went over to Scotland twice a week. It was a very slow boat, five or seven knots, when the weather was good. We used to sing all the time, coming into the harbour or at the seaman's bar. This particular week we came from Dublin to Belfast to have the compass fixed.'

The sea trials did not go according to plan. Rinty was standing on watch as a gale suddenly whipped up. The choppy sea flooded cabins, forcing the boiler to be shut down, and the captain decided to try to bring the boat out of the bay towards the relative safety of the Irish Channel and away from the shoreline. However, Mother Nature had other plans and the force of the waves detached the anchor, setting the boat adrift and back towards the merciless rocks that tore at its hull. The boat didn't have a chance and duly sank to a watery grave. Fortunately, nobody was hurt and the entire crew made it to dry land.

Patsy served long haul, travelling great distances to South America, the West Indies and to western African ports with cargoes of aircraft fuel and supplies. He was a keen boxer and took part in tournaments in Trinidad and Buenos Aires or wherever the opportunity presented itself. His brother Thomas ran the gauntlet of wolf packs of U-boats that terrorized the North Atlantic and the North Sea. Many incidents from the Second World War were to be made into films, including the notorious Murmansk Convoy, in which Tommy was involved while serving with the Norwegian MV *Herband* from 1943. He had worked the supply lines from New York to Avonmouth and Liverpool before his ship signed up to the convoy to Murmansk and Archangel.

US long-range aircraft support, incorporating improved radar technology and intelligence work regarding code deciphers that could detect torpedoes, provided the 34-strong convoy of merchant vessels and support ships with cover. *Herband* made it, along with the other fuel tankers; the support ship *Kite* was the biggest loss. Tommy joined with other crews at the port of Kola for the return crossing to Loch Ewe in Scotland. The Murmansk operations claimed more than one hundred ships. The sinking of the *Tirpitz* and *Scharnhorst* battleships was crippling for the German sea forces.

Tommy's old vessel finished up as scrap in the British Iron and Steel Corporation in the 1950s. Rinty's brother recalled, 'My first commission was as a galley boy. I worked on a number of tankers that carried oil supplies, and on British freighters. The Russian convoy run I remember. A lot of people lost their lives.

'When the war finished I moved to America with my wife Rita in 1948. I have lived there ever since. In later life I have split my time between America and Belfast. I never gave up working on boats. Until I retired I worked on Lake Michigan, on the ferries between Ludington, where we lived, Milwaukee and Manitowoc. Loved the life. Rita was originally McWilliams and we met while I was training with Rinty at the gym in Hardinge Street. It did not have any water supply so we used to go to the houses near to the gym to get bottles of water filled. Rita lived in one of them and that is how we first met up.'

Patsy dodged his way into the Navy at fifteen, a year under the legal age, thanks to a friend of his father's. He had been working at Hugh Wilson's shop in Great George's Street for seven shillings and six a week and was eager to broaden his horizons. Upon joining the *Empire Bronze,* he did not 'see daylight for about twenty months' when he ended up in Aruba after stopping off in the US for a cargo of fuel for military aircraft.

'The *Empire* carried about twelve thousand tons. From Aruba we would convoy across the Atlantic to ports in Africa. Once we were diverted for safety reasons and ended up at Ascension Island. From a very young age I just wanted to be at sea. All my family was at sea. It was in the blood so I was not happy until I managed to sneak into the Merchant Navy a year before I was supposed to. I never regretted the decision. One of the lads I worked with on trips to places like Buenos Aires was Gerry Fitt. He attended the same primary school, St Patrick's in Donegall Street, as us. Gerry worked in the engine room of the ship. Of course, like John, he became quite famous in later life.'

When back in Belfast Patsy worked out with John. Boxing, like the navy, was a passion of his. He and Tommy fought each other as amateurs at Peter's Hill in the Ulster Championships.

While 'Sinbad' did not stick with the sea life, his first job was on the waterfront at Victoria Wharf. He was taken out of school in order to get a job. This was the 'Hungry Thirties', and the economic markets were in meltdown. People scratched a living out of whatever they could. Those who worked around Belfast's docks or in the many factories for the most basic of wages did not have it easy. Life was a constant struggle for every household in the community, keeping one's head above water, above the absolute poverty threshold while trying to resist the troublesome 'helping hands' of the moneylender. Housing conditions were very poor, and vulnerable to the cold and damp. As a result, illnesses were rife.

Ta's wages were just not enough to support his large family, so he and Martha decided that their eldest boy would have to finish with school and do what he could by way of boosting the family income. His big sister Sarah was already working at one of the flax mills that employed women and young girls to produce linen. Rinty was brought to the docks and, after a bit of bartering, a job with Workman Clark, one of the city's main shipbuilders, was secured.

Yard tasks were difficult and dangerous, and industrial accidents were common. About this time the *Regina*, a steel steamer, much like the type of vessel Rinty's father had worked on, had been built and fitted for the Havana's Cuban Molasses Transportation Company. For years the company thrived with contracts from the Montreal Steamship Company, Allan Line and Norwegian shipping firms. Then the monetary downturn began hitting the waterfront's chief employers hard, and by the time Rinty started work, the order book was being squeezed, and narrow margins of profitability trimmed to break even or worse.

He was about thirteen years of age when he was hired as a catch boy. The job would bring in an extra nine shillings a week but, for it, he risked certain minor injury. His uniform was a pair of heat protection gloves and a small shovel. The catcher worked down in the skeletal stomach of ships under construction, where his task was to catch furnace heated rivets in the shovel and pass them on to the person placing the rivets into the steel plates. It sounds easy enough, and it was—except for the too frequent occurrence of roasting hot chips of scale finding their way inside the gaping gloves. The first aid box was regularly called for. The catcher could also help other work groups for what was termed 'blood money'. There were a few shillings to be made if you dedicated yourself and your hands were not too badly scorched.

In spite of how important the job was for the Monaghan family's finances it did not last. A bit of messing about was to cost Rinty his first contributory role to Martha's meagre budget. It was just as well he was a strong swimmer.

'It happened all the time. Every year, like there is always a bit of uppity about people coming up around the Twelfth. Somebody replaced the coke with clinker and steel and this stout fella and three others were caught on. A few punches were thrown. They started throwing rivets at me and I had to make a run for it.'

Rivets flew about his head, splashing into the harbour waters around him; the odd one caught a piece of skin. One cracked the side of his head as he swam for it. When an old man over at the Harland & Wolff yard helped retrieve Rinty from the soup he was covered in jellyfish, his skin reddened with stings. His working days at Victoria Wharf came to a dripping, bloody end.

Less than a year later the yard was closed due to a financial downturn and falling orders. Within twelve months of Workman Clark's gates being shut for the last time, their former catch boy had switched his sights to something completely different—something that had nothing to do with red-hot rivets or scorching metallic scale. Rinty Monaghan's heart was now set on becoming a prizefighter.

3

HARRY HANLEY WAS A MATCHMAKER, A key player for managers and boxing promoters in the late 1920s and 1930s. He was the man they dealt with if they wanted a fight made and matched as evenly as possible. He also did some promoting, but he worked primarily in the city's professional arena sorting out under-card contests as support attractions to main events. The Labour Hall on York Street staged fortnightly boxing and cabaret bills on Saturday afternoons. Harry arranged the fights, which were a mixture of professional bouts and novelty acts that included a boxing exhibition, with or without a comedian, involving characters who could sing, dance or just clown around. He also ran his own shows, often at the Oval and at the York Rangers Club, which was close to where the Monaghans lived.

The Labour Hall was just around the corner from Martha and Ta's place and was an obvious attraction for Rinty and his friends. After a hard morning of kicking a football around the streets, they headed for the boxing arena. There they would try their luck with the 'Hey, mister' routine in the hope that someone would pay their entrance fee into the hall to see the show. One Saturday the pavement shuffle eventually caught the ear of an obliging neighbour who asked for Mr Hanley, as Harry was the man to see if the boy was allowed in. Harry looked down at the wee nipper and asked him if could sing. Rinty happened to know a few songs his father had taught him, and he was a keen listener to the wireless with a love for music. This was his big opportunity.

'He got me inside and took me through to the dressing rooms and there is this little boy all dressed up. He had lovely shiny hair and everything and the matchmaker said, "Do you think you could fight that boy?" and I said, "Yes," so they put the two of us in the ring. But before they put me in they had trouble finding pants.'

A large pair of blue bloomers was found and Rinty had to be literally tied into them with a piece of twine. They came to below his knee in length but into the boxing ring he boldly went to try out as a pugilist.

'We went out and fought three one-minute rounds and the boy I fought was a lad called Pimple McKee. The fight was a draw. We never hit each other. We just jumped around the ring and when it was over he [Harry] says, "Can you sing?" and I said, "Yes." I sang a song called "Sally". That was Gracie Fields' song and after that I sung "When Irish Eyes Are Smiling". Then I got paid.'

Up until then the only payment John received was in Spanish oranges. His uncle John ran a greengrocers' and hardware stall near Great George's Street, from where he supplied the communities surrounding St Patrick's Church in Donegall Street with its fruit and vegetables, coal and timber. The orange trail led to Tommy O'Hare's backyard in Lancaster Street. Mr O'Hare was an avid boxing fan and enjoyed showing Rinty and his friends how to throw a jab or a hook, duck a punch and defend themselves. Mini bouts were organised for a bit of fun in the backyard and the winner's prize was an entire orange, with half an orange being presented to the loser. Rinty's younger brothers followed the trail of Spanish peel in later years. Patsy knew Tommy's place well.

'Way before we were brought to McAloran's gym, anyone down our street into boxing, or not too into it but just [looking for] something else to do, would go to Mr O'Hare's. He was great into the boxing. His idea was that it would not do us any harm to learn how to box. There was not too much to do so it was good fun. John used to go there. I think most of the boys around our street learned about boxing from Mr O'Hare. He was a character and boxing in his backyard is a very clear memory I have from growing up.'

The Labour Hall was one of many boxing venues scattered about the city. What were called 'small hall shows' were promoted regularly all over Belfast, the most famous venue being Chapel Fields where Mrs Clara 'Ma' Copley ran frequent tournaments in the fair arena's booths. Over twenty venues were in regular use in the city alone, including Celtic Park, the Palladium, Queen's Island, the Rialto, St George's Market, the Oval, Solitude Football Ground, Warner's Saloon and St Peter's. There were also promotions held at the North End Stadium, the Blue Saloon and at halls in Hawthorn, Tamar and Crimea Streets. By the late 1920s there were nearly twelve hundred professional boxing outlets across Ireland, England, Scotland and Wales.

It could be said that Harry Hanley's decision to let the nine-year-old Monaghan boy take to the stage was the beginning of the next part of his life. He went down a storm with the punters and, even better, he got paid for it. Any extra shillings were very welcome in the house but Rinty found himself in big trouble with his mum and dad over his collection of 'nobbins', the boxing term used to describe the coins thrown into the ring by the spectators at ringside to show their appreciation for a contest well fought.

'I gets the money and hands it to mum and says, "Mum, look." My mother looked at the money and said, "Where did you steal the money from?" and "Wait till your father hears." As she said that, my father came up the hallway and he says, "What you do mean?" Mum says, "John got money, says he was fighting around the corner."'

The story did not wash with them.

'My father let me have one and my mother lifts me up and says, "Tell the truth, son."' Rinty was frog-marched to York Street to see Mr Gilmore, the promoter, who assured Ta that not only was his talented son telling the truth but that he wanted Rinty back to perform on the following Saturday's bill, if his father permitted it.

Once matters were straightened out to his father's satisfaction, Rinty never looked back. He was hooked, not just on boxing, but on performing before crowds. He loved it and there was some loose change to be made from it too. The promoter was true to his word. The lad returned to the bill and Harry had the idea to showcase him as 'The Singing Schoolboy' in a boxing and novelty act. This type of attraction, supporting the main fights and entertaining the fans, was common. Rinty was on to a winner.

Most weeks he boxed a bit and sang a few numbers either at the Boxing Arena or at another of Mr Hanley's promotions in the nearby York Rangers Club, on the corner of Frederick Street. The bonus here was that the York Rangers had a small gym upstairs; this was put to good use by the tiny singer-boxer and a few of his pals who had been part of Mr O'Hare's backyard boxing brigade.

'The Singing Schoolboy' proved to be very popular with the punters, thanks to his being a useful little fighter as well as a bit of an unashamed exhibitionist. By the middle of the 1930s Rinty's days of begging a neighbour to bring him in to see the Saturday show were long gone. He was now established as an attraction that boxing fans would gladly queue up and pay to see.

4

MA COPLEY'S FAIR AT CHAPEL FIELDS DREW fighting men from all over the city, including the multitude of nationalities working the docks or on shore leave. In the 1920s the most popular aspect of the hundreds of fairs across the British Isles was the boxing booth. In Wales there was also pit boxing, which involved two men being placed in pits up to their waists and slugging it out until one or the other could no longer raise a fist. The great Welsh professional Tommy Farr started out this way, pit fighting to success around the coal-mining communities. Fairs depended on their regular attendees, and fortunately Ma Copley was able to organise a tournament most weeks. Her boxing booth was a much loved haunt of Tommy Monaghan. He was a frequent visitor with his friends and would even take part if the right offer presented itself. When Rinty was old enough, Tommy brought him along to see the show. Then, one day, Ma approached him and asked if his boy would like to box, explaining that a young kid from Scotland was without an opponent after the lad he was due to meet had pulled out. He was about Rinty's age, and roughly the same height, though he was maybe a stone heavier. Tommy turned to his son and asked him what he thought. Not surprisingly he was up for it and willing to give it a go. His father agreed to allow him to fight. He knew that Rinty had been training for a couple of years with his home-made punch-bag and he was very familiar with the basics, thanks to the backyard coaching from Tommy O'Hare.

Rinty's brother Patsy remembers hearing the story from his father. 'John just wanted to take the fight. Even though there was a stone of difference or thereabouts between the two boys, John was happy enough. He packed a bit of a dig even then. Daddy told us John put the Scottish lad away in the first round. He said that it was a thrill to see.'

For the next number of years the Chapel Fields offered young Monaghan the occasional opportunity to work on his skills, just as the Saturday afternoon shows in York Street would, in due course. However, Tommy sensed that his lively lad wanted more. They talked about it and it was clear that Rinty was eager to try his hand, and his luck, at the real thing: he confessed his ambition to become a professional boxer.

Belfast's fight scene was hectic. There were plenty of characters boxing once a fortnight, and each month saw new juveniles starting out in the variety of small hall promotions available. Tommy was determined to place his son's future in the right hands and took time to consider the options. He needed to know if Rinty had what it took to become a real boxer. Watching him at Chapel Fields he recognised that his son was very fast, quite strong, and capable of putting rivals on the seat of their pants. He eventually decided that a local featherweight, who had once been regarded as one of the leading Irish fighters at his weight, was the man for the job.

Frank McAloran ran a busy gym with his brothers, James and Pat, at Hardinge Street, not too far from the Monaghan residence. The two brothers did all the coaching while Frank was the businessman, the manager. He looked after the interests of their fighting stable alongside pursuing his own boxing career. Tommy and Frank spat in the palms of their hands in the autumn of 1933 and shook on the next stage of John Joseph's career.

Locals nicknamed the McAloran gym 'the hut', and it was not much more than that. There were absolutely no frills, not even running water. James was the chief coach but he also doubled as the resident carpenter when the rickety floorboards looked to be in danger of giving way. His kit bag contained a hammer, some nails and a few strips of wood. It was not uncommon for a fighter to suffer injury after a foot disappeared through the splinters.

Rinty took to training with relish. Thanks to his father he was already in the habit of exercising every day. His day began at dawn, pulling on the training sweats and heavy boots, venturing through the morning mist and mills' smog for a daily run before tucking into a bit of breakfast and heading off to do a day's work.

Patsy remembers those mornings well. 'At about 6.30am John would be out the door and you would hear him run up the street. He wore these hobnail boots and they made a racket as he left the street each morning to go for a run. He was an alarm clock to the rest of us, probably the whole street, though a lot of people would be going to work about that time in the docks or at one of the mills or big factories.'

His training route took him down along the Shore Road, and then up and across to the northern stretch of the Antrim Road. Cave Hill provided the most punishing part of the circuit as well as the daily supply of goat's milk that he swore by. The hobnail boots beat their way around Belle Vue, the local landmark climb known as Sheep's Pass, and around 'Napoleon's Nose', overlooking the city's industrial skyline. He then made his way back for a quick scrub and something to eat before going to work at Roden's Store, where he was employed to look after servicing the boilers, and other various jobs and tasks.

James McAloran ran a tight ship and was determined to get the absolute best out of each fighter. Like any gym, the talent varied—orthodox or southpaw, boxers, fighters, grafters; everyone had to abide by the rules James set down. The hardest task he faced was developing the absolute correct way to punch, whereby boxers must plant their feet in the perfect position to get better snap and power into their lefts and rights. James devised a method that involved wearing just one shoe—usually heavy work boots since proper boxing footwear was used only for contests. This was not without its hazards, given the poor state of the floor.

The idea behind it was straightforward enough. James needed to improve their sensory system, their understanding of how to land their shots on an opponent properly. It must have looked peculiar to see boxers working punch-bags or sparring with one foot bare to the world.

George McCullough, whose brother Eddie would play an important role in Rinty's career, was one of those teenaged amateur boxers.

'It was probably a bit funny to look at but it worked. It definitely made a difference. For Rinty, this was part of his training and look where it took him eventually. It was all about learning to throw a punch correctly, properly, with a bit more power and James had this technique he used with all of us.

'I suppose he thought it was the only way to get the message into boxers' heads. I think he had been frustrated with everyone so this day he ordered all of us to take off one of our boots or shoes. Probably looked strange to anyone who watched what was going on. When you threw a punch you felt the sole of your foot plant hard against the floorboards. That got it through to the boxer what James wanted him to do.

'Nowadays you listen to people talking about a boxer planting himself properly when throwing his punches or not planting his foot properly. It was exactly the same for us at the Hardinge gym, though it was risky enough given the state of the floor we trained on. It was not in great shape. Sometimes a board would give way and break. James's routine was interesting and I think it helped produce better boxers, some really good boxers, some better than others.'

Rinty's brother-in-law—Sarah's husband, Harry McAuley—was also part of Frank's stable of fighters and a frequent sparring partner. Harry would in time establish himself as a featherweight of note, winning a Northern Ireland Area title against Billy Donnelly in the early 1940s. This was originally the property of Derry's British and Empire titles winner Jim 'Spider' Kelly.

All of Rinty's brothers went on to train at the gym, with Thomas junior the last of them to join. Nowadays, Tommy, the youngest of the brothers, lives in Sarasota in Florida but, more than half a century after he first trod upon the busted-up boards of 'the hut', the memories of the severity of the Spartan gym facilities are as vivid in his mind as ever.

'It was terrible. The conditions were atrocious, but it was a boxing gym after all, and boxing gyms are meant to be tough places. There is nothing easy about a boxing gym and certainly in those days there were no niceties about it. But the McAlorans had some very fine boxers, some really good fighters; my brother obviously was one of the really good ones.

'Patsy Quinn was one of the good boxers of the era who used to train there. Quinn was a big name about Belfast at a time. There was Freddie Price of Dublin, my brother-in-law Harry, young Eddie McCullough, a top-notch bantam. One thing that stands out for me thinking back to the gym was the sparring. Harry and Rinty sparred a lot and when they got in there it was always worth watching for us younger ones. The sparks would usually fly. There was a bit of rivalry there. Harry could dig, was a tough featherweight, and he was afraid of no one.'

Tommy recalls an incident concerning a reputed 'kayo' puncher from Dublin called John Ingle, who was particularly hard to match. No one wanted to mix it with him for fear of taking a count, or worse still, failing to beat it. 'Ingle was one of the hardest punchers in the country, and had this great reputation but because he was so good, and knocked everybody out, it was difficult for him to get fights.

'People just would not box him. There were three Ingle brothers, all very good, and I remember Frank coming up to our house one day looking for Harry. I was asked to go and get him round to the house as Frank wanted to talk to him about a fight. The fight was against Ingle. He was in Belfast but was having trouble being matched. Frank discussed it with Harry and Harry agreed to go in with John Ingle. That was the type of him.

'I was at it. Ingle caught him with this right hand shot on the chin; he hit him so hard it lifted Harry off his feet. But fair play to him, Harry got up and came back in the third and knocked John Ingle out. It was a big shock at the time. Harry told me afterwards that he was given ten pounds for winning and that was an awful lot of money then.'

Some of the other characters about the gym at that time included the local heavyweight prospect Paddy Slavin, who regularly accompanied Rinty on his morning runs about the tough Cave Hill tracks. There was also Kildare's Frank Hayes, another Dubliner by the name of Frank Parsons, Billy O'Neill, Jim Campbell, Jack Lynch, the McCullough boys, Bertie Todd, Joe McEntee, Sam Thompson, Martin Salmon, Billy Mehaige, Peter Robinson, John Rocks, Bill Townsley, Jim Malligan, the Dempseys, Charlie and Frank, and Jimmy Carson to name but a few.

It was quite a sight when the boxers went jogging together, as if part of a parade, towards the Antrim Road or along the Shore. The children would run alongside the convoy, at least to the end of their own streets. One of them was a wee lad from Artillery Street where Rinty's cousins, the Dorans, lived. Gerry Storey remembers how he would run with 'the hut' crew before he too was drawn into training at the gym. He was still at school when Rinty was making his way as a professional fighter. They became close friends over the years and Gerry developed into a skilful coach for the Holy Family ABC. He familiarised himself with Rinty's training methods which resulted in the top amateurs at 'the Family' treading the punishing Cave Hill route.

'I was about eight or nine, running about the New Lodge, and got to know of Rinty and the McAloran gym about then. I watched them training for years. Knowing flyweights and what they were like, how tough it is to make the weight, I can safely say I have never seen a flyweight, amateur or professional, built like him. Rinty was so strong. He had these great shoulders, all this great muscle definition to his arms, and he certainly was a very powerful puncher. His record shows that.

'I remember Rinty would bring me to where they trained in the Cave Hill, to all their haunts, and over the years all the Holy Family boxers, the Rices and Russells, the Webbs, McStravicks, Storeys, Hamills, and the likes of Sammy Vernon and Patsy McAuley, followed his training plan.

'Hardinge Hill, where the gym was, was close to Artillery Street where I lived and to where the Hardinge Street Christian Brothers' School was. I would go along most nights to watch the boxers training. The gym had this wee fireplace in it and they used to burn the tar of big batteries for heat. That is what they had for coal, I suppose. God knows what the fumes off the tar did to them.

'There was no shower, nothing. The toilet was just the wall outside at the back of the place. It was as rough as anyone could imagine it could be but that is how it was and no one ever complained. It produced some really tough boxing men in its time. I trained there for a few years as well, trained with Jimmy Carson, who was the last major fighter the McAlorans had before the gym closed sometime in the 1950s.'

John Denvir was the man who attempted to massage away the aches and strains of a tough session. Sparring was a distinctly painful ordeal for the more junior members; for one thing, when you were at the lower end of the pecking order, sparring did not include a gum shield. Furthermore, the state of the gloves was dismal, as George McCullough recalls.

'A guy called Bertie Dunlop, who lived over on the Newtownards Road, was there the same time as me. I remember how we sparred with these big gloves, old gloves with leather toughened with hardened blood. That gave the gloves a reddish, brownish colour and they would really mark up your face. You would be pretty sore by the time you were going home to get a bath.

'There were many times when I went home with the face cut off me by them. You did not have a gum shield either. Back then you were only given a shield once you were in training for a contest. My teeth survived that, though Eddie had one of his knocked out not long after he joined the gym. The place had walls covered in old boxing bills from different shows.

'It really was the centre of the community for anyone interested in the fight game. There was not much else to do at that time. Boxing gyms were important places then and always very busy. James and Pat and Paddy Bradley were all good trainers, all very good boxing men. Frank McAloran was a top boxer himself and a real gentleman. There was no messing about with them. If you were good enough they brought the best out of you and there is no doubt they brought out the very best in Rinty Monaghan.'

5

NAT JOSEPHS WAS THE FIRST OF the local promoters to mark the debut of Belfast's brand new boxing arena, The Ring Stadium, in Thomas Street, previously a busy bus depot. Wednesday, 7 December 1932 was the night in question and it was to be a grand affair indeed, with Irish flyweight champion, Jackie Quinn, aka John McGreevy, and Irish featherweight champion, Jack Garland, providing the main attraction. Jack Hinds was Master of Ceremonies while the British Boxing Board of Control sent across Manchester official Tommy Shields to referee all five scheduled contests. A reporter was dispatched from the *Belfast Telegraph* office to cover the fights for the next day's edition. Nat was roundly congratulated for marking the opening of The Ring with 'auspicious circumstances' in a quality programme of contests that delivered 'plenty of thrills'. It also produced two high profile upsets as Nat's two top draws were beaten.

Quinn fought regular Scottish rival Jim O'Neill of Cambuslang, while Garland faced Dublin's George Kelly. Quinn appeared to be hurt by an accidental punch below the belt early in the fight but was 'urged by the referee to continue'. He was unable to produce his well-known wicked body punches while O'Neill's ability to box at length and score with his jab left him 'a comfortable winner on points'.

Meanwhile Garland was involved in a terrific all-action scrap. He was floored by the initial Kelly fireworks but then returned fire in the second round, battering Kelly on the ropes. The two fighters took turns to dominate over the next five rounds. Then, in the eighth, Garland had a chance to finish off the Dubliner but failed to take advantage as Kelly dug in and fought hard to the final bell. Kelly was given the decision, which provoked uproar among the Garland supporters, so much so that an over-excited spectator had to be physically removed from the stage.

Con McCann, a well-rated Markets man, knocked out Belfast rival Davy Barr in the second round. Derry's Dan Canning had a points win over Belfast man Hughie McGahey while Scotland's Kid Johnston was disqualified in the third round of a lively battle with Royston's Tommy Moore.

The Ring quickly gained in popularity as a venue and proved a competitive alternative to Ma Copley's shows at Chapel Fields. In less than two years the former bus depot staged over a hundred professional fight nights. An American-based welterweight from County Down, Jimmy McLarnin, dominated Irish boxing at this time. He took the world title in May 1933, the first Irish man to do so since Ennis-born Mike McTigue in the 1920s. Jack Doyle was also flying the flag as a promising and colourful heavyweight. He had challenged Welshman Jack Petersen for the British title earlier that summer. On the local front flyweight Jimmy Warnock, Jackie Quinn and Derry's Jim Kelly were three of the big draws.

Bill number 107, on Friday, 28 September 1934, is one that is of particular interest because this was when Rinty Monaghan took his first bow as a paid flyweight. His manager Frank McAloran had already made his boxing debut at the new venue, featuring on an Edgar promotion just eight days earlier, when he forced Warrington's Norman Milton into retirement in the sixth round. Sixteen-year-old Rinty shared his first appearance at The Ring with another Belfast rookie, nineteen-year-old Sam Ramsey, who had been signed up by Mr Hanley to fight him. Sam hailed from Coates Street and trained at the McWilliams and McMullan Boxing Club on Ardmullan Avenue. His training partners included Johnny McMullan, Joe 'Gunboat' Smith, Billy Duffy and Frankie Burns. The two flyweight newcomers fought out a draw.

Johnny 'Ginger' McMullan topped the bill. He fought a draw over ten rounds with Morecambe's Kid Dempsey. The supporting cast included 'Machine Gun' McKenzie and 'Hard Hitting' Christie—who were billed as a novelty act—as well as Belfast's Tiger Smith, Tommy Walsh, Jack Sloan and Dunadry's Joe Gale.

On the same night that Rinty and Sam made their unbeaten debuts a future world champion, American Henry Armstrong, nicknamed 'Homicide Hank', beat Perfecto Lopez on points at California's Ventura Athletic Club. Over the next five years Armstrong claimed the featherweight, welterweight and lightweight world titles, against Petey Sarron in 1937, Barney Ross in 1938 and Lew Feldman in 1939.

Rinty and Sam became regular rivals through to July 1937, fighting six times, four at six rounds, with each one of the contests lasting the distance scheduled. Rinty had three wins, young Ramsey three draws. The only time they met outside Belfast was in March 1936 when they fought to a draw in Carrickfergus. Sam—a regular at Chapel Fields, the CYMS in North Queen Street, Harps Hall in the Goats Row area of the Springfield Road, the Philis Arcade, as well as in halls at Divis and Frederick Street—became known as the 'Coates Street Clouter' and went on to fight in eighty contests.

Fourteen days after their second drawn bout, Rinty, now listed as 'John Boy Monaghan', was matched against Jim Pedlow from Whitehouse. It was another four-rounder, each two minutes long, and The Ring's 123rd fight night. Here Rinty had his first victory. He was awarded a decision after having to withstand a few good rights before his gloved fist was raised in victory. The *Belfast Telegraph* reporter noted 'a promising novice' and felt that Monaghan and Pedlow, a newcomer to the boxing circuit, had performed very well as support to Jimmy Warnock, who won over six rounds against Billy Tansy of Leeds.

'A bright display of boxing over four "two's" was contributed by two juniors, Boy Monaghan (Belfast) and J Pedlow (Whitehouse). The latter was making his debut and did very well against a more experienced opponent. Monaghan, a snappy little puncher with a useful left, did most of the leading but young Pedlow showed a good guard and at times revealed a right with a sting. Monaghan won on points.'

Warnock's win drew praise for an outstanding performance against the superior Tansy, who had recorded fine wins over the likes of Marvin Harte and Jim Sharpe. Patsy Quinn, another of the big names of the era, beat Glasgow's Freddy Smith on points.

Elsewhere that week Benny Lynch, the Scottish champion, and England's Southern Area title-holder, Tommy Pardoe, a tough character from Birmingham who had won five consecutive English ABA titles as an amateur, were matched for a British title eliminator. The winner would be entitled to challenge the BBB of C's flyweight kingpin, Jackie Brown, who was also Europe's world title claimant, for his British and World Championship belts.

For the moment Rinty concentrated on nurturing his talent, training every day. When he wasn't training or fighting himself he was a spectator at Thomas Street, intent on seeing as many fights as possible. One of his favourite fighters of the day was the classy Derry featherweight known as 'Spider' Jim Kelly. Kelly was a highly skilled boxer, who could have just as appropriately been nicknamed 'Shadow' Jim Kelly, such was his elusiveness in the ring. He was difficult to catch, and could slip punches and out-box opponents brilliantly. Rinty was hugely impressed by Kelly's style and tried to replicate his idol's fleetness of foot. He practiced his moves, drawing sparring partners in before throwing his favoured right hook.

It just so happened that 'Spider' and Frank McAloran were rivals, both highly rated in the Irish and British rankings. In the autumn of 1935, a year after Rinty's debut, they clashed for the Northern Ireland Area title. Unfortunately for Frank, his opponent proved too slick and strong and he was stopped in the fourteenth round. Nevertheless, it was an important fight that broke new ground for Northern Ireland, being the first Area title match of any weight to be sanctioned by the fledgling Northern Ireland Area Council of the British Boxing Board of Control.

Next up for Monaghan was Victor Large, who, like Rinty, was billed as 'Boy'. They met for the 132nd show at the Thomas Street stadium on Sunday, 17 February 1935. Rinty finished the fight with a flourish, earning both a knockout stoppage in round four to stay unbeaten, and a brief mention in the *Belfast Telegraph*. Irish bantam champion Jackie Quinn topped the bill, beating John Ellis from Manchester over eight rounds.

The following month was a busy one for Frank, as a fighter and a manager. He halted Benny Thackeray of Leeds at Thomas Street, while a fee was agreed for Rinty to box 'Boy' Finnegan on 29 March. This was Rinty's first six-round fight but, no matter, he won on points, which gave him an unbeaten record in five contests. His manager, who was fighting on the same bill, wasn't as fortunate. He was disqualified for a low punch against Boyd Burns of Bolton.

In April the British welterweight champion Pat Butler paid a visit to Belfast when he was matched against South African champion 'Panther' Purchase at The Ring. The ability to attract these rival national title-holders was something of a coup and suggested that the Thomas Street venue was thriving. Certainly, on paper, it was a success. In 1933, no less than seventy-six tournaments were held inside a twelve-month period. The former bus depot was home to 150 promotions, chiefly staged by Nat Josephs, Jim Edgar and Harry Hanley, making a grand total of approximately one thousand fights. Nevertheless, healthy profits failed to materialise. Less than three years after it opened, The Ring went out of business. One of the last professional shows featured Jack Mussen, Johnny Collins, Len Rose, Patsy Maguire, Frankie Smith and Al Swaffield, while one of the last amateur events was the 1935 Ulster Amateur Championships for juniors and juveniles, with Hugh Cupples, who boxed for Red Triangle ABC, and Newsboys' Eddie Rice winning Junior Ulster Amateur titles.

The year 1936 opened for Rinty with another fight against Sam Ramsey, this time at Chapel Fields. Their first meeting over six rounds, Monaghan edged it to record his fourth win against Sam. Following this he boxed once a month until May. He beat Felix Brennan, alias 'Young' Josephs, from Carrickfergus at Chapel Fields. He then drew with and defeated Ramsey on 20 and 26 March. Next he beat 'Young' Kelly in Belfast to improve his record to 7-0-3. He fought Felix again on 16 May, gaining his third stoppage win, a third-round victory back at Chapel Fields.

At the Belfast Arena later that month he was matched in his first ten-rounder, against Jack McKenzie. It took place on a Wednesday evening and drew a big crowd, according to a report carried in the *Telegraph*, which described the match as 'a derby'. Rinty came out 'with heavy guns' but found McKenzie 'a wily campaigner capable of slipping some nasty shots while foiling his opponent's best-meant attacks'. The lively affair was scored a draw and those at ringside 'paid cordial tribute to both boys at the finish'.

The headline fight involved local bantam Jackie Campbell and Scotland's Pat Sherry, with a close decision being awarded to Campbell. Jack Higgins, Jack McCleery, Al Swaffield, Sam Lee, Sam Dingly and Johnny Regan all took part that night. The McKenzie bout was Rinty's second in the space of four days; in other words, given the tight schedule, a win and a draw was a decent return.

Over the next few weeks he rested up and did not get back in the saddle until 24 July, less than a month before his birthday. Again he fought Felix Brennan, this time in Larne; the fight was incident-free and scored a draw. It was to be their last meeting. Tragedy lurked close at hand for Brennan, who was diagnosed with diphtheria eight weeks later; he died from complications. Rinty returned to Larne shortly afterwards for contest number fourteen, against Joe Duffy, which he won after six rounds. It was his last fight of the year and he did not box again for another seven months. When he reappeared he met with defeat in Belfast at the hands of Lisburn's Jim Keery. The long lay-off was blamed and Frank decided to tackle the cobwebs by keeping the teenager busy: he fought eleven times over the next twenty-eight weeks. Three of the fights—all victorious—were against Ted Meikle, one of four fighting brothers (the other three were Joe, Billy and Charlie), who trained in facilities they'd put together at a garage in Mount Joy Street. Ted would be a future challenger for the Irish title at bantamweight before moving to New Zealand in the 1940s. The third meeting was part of the first pro bill staged by John Sholdis at the new Sports Stadium at Cuba Street, located off the Newtownards Road, on Friday 17 September. There were also wins over Liverpool's Paddy O'Toole and Glasgow's George Lang; back-to-back victories in Belfast against Mick Gibbons; another win over Ramsey; and 1937 was brought to a successful end with a fifth-round kayo victory against Tommy Allen of Manchester. Rinty's record stood impressively at 19-1-5.

Jimmy Warnock was one of the major players in the flyweight scene of Northern Ireland about this time and commanded a top world rating. Unfortunately, he was denied what many of his supporters and sports writers believed was his due, the world title itself. However, with the emergence of Belfast man Jim McStravick, plans were under way with the British Board's Area Council to organise a Northern Ireland title fight between Warnock and McStravick. Shankill Road star Warnock had firmly cemented his reputation earlier in the season at a packed King's Hall when he defeated the French champion Pierre Louis over twelve rounds. Louis was down for a count of seven in the fourth.

The same event saw one of Rinty's early idols, 'Spider' Kelly, Ireland's featherweight champion, produce a fine win over England's Southern Area title-holder, Dick Corbett of London. McStravick marked time until a Northern Ireland title shot with a win over England's Northern Area flyweight star, Oldham's Phil Milligan.

Meanwhile, Rinty's form was beginning to cause a few ripples after closing out 1937 with three consecutive stoppage victories, all against cross channel rivals, and in less than nine rounds of boxing.

January, February and March of 1938 all delivered stoppage wins. Hartlepool's Alf Hughes was knocked out in the ninth, Jarrow's Pat Murphy in round four, while 'Spider' Allen, also from Hartlepool, was dealt with in less than six minutes—Rinty's twenty-second win to date. Frank decided it was time to broaden the flyweight's horizon, and so Rinty was scheduled for ten rounds against Manchester's Con 'Cyclone' Kelly at Liverpool Stadium. While Kelly halted Rinty's run of stoppage wins that Friday, 3 March, he was not good enough to deny him a win. The fight was great exposure for Monaghan, raising his profile, and the result extended his victory roll to fourteen back-to-back.

On his return to Belfast Rinty performed at a fund-raising concert in aid of the Doctor Barnardo Homes at the King's Hall. The show was hosted by Richard Hayward and Irish heavyweight hope, Jack Doyle, and a crowd of two thousand turned up to enjoy a variety of acts that included Doyle giving a rendition of his favourite songs—'The Rose of

Tralee', 'Sweet Mystery of Life' and 'Mother Machree'. Rinty sang a few songs along with Ireland's 'Shirley Temple', Margaret Maguinness, and Jack Clarke. There was also a wrestling exhibition by local favourite Alec Robinson, who thrilled the crowd with a knockout of Barnsley's 'Stoker' Davies.

Eight days later Rinty and 'Cyclone' Kelly tussled again, this time in Belfast, and Kelly was beaten on points. Joe McCluskey and Peter Peters were then taken care of, Peters falling to a first round kayo cluster of punches. Ivor Neill suffered the same fate, while at the Oval, Rinty scored a distance win over Limerick's Joe Kiely, bringing his record to 28-1-5.

Whispers began to circulate about Rinty fighting for a Northern Ireland title. Frank was certainly keen to switch gears and began negotiations with Glasgow promoter-manager Pat Collins. Collins's protégé, Jackie Paterson, was about to make a dynamic entrance.

6

TEENAGER JACKIE PATERSON WAS BROUGHT ACROSS from the Anderson gym in Glasgow for what was only his second contest in the paid ranks. It was widely expected that he would prove to be no match for the more experienced Rinty and his fierce hard-hitting right hand. Jackie was only too aware of Rinty's having knocked out five of his most recent opponents, including Ivor Neill, Peter Peters, 'Spider' Allen and Alf Hughes.

Rinty's father was ringside, as was his younger brother Patsy. They and the local crowd settled down to watch their boxer score another success. Then came the horrified gasps that accompanied Jackie's knocking Rinty out cold in the fifth round. It was a total shock to everyone, possibly even Paterson.

Afterwards Rinty blamed his own cockiness for the mishap. 'I was beating Jackie. It was only a matter of time, but I was laughing. I had Jackie's eyes cut, his nose as well. I just walked up to him smiling and I do not know what hit me.'

It was a phantom punch, Rinty never saw it coming. When he came to in the dressing room, Frank had some explaining to do.

'Four times I was up and down and afterwards when I came to in the dressing room my manager said, "Bad luck!" and I said, "What do you mean, bad luck? The fight hasn't started yet." I did not know the fight was over.'

Dusted off and under revised coaching from James McAloran, Rinty was sent over to England. Frank needed him to get over the kayo, the biggest setback he had had in more than thirty fights. Accordingly, the manager struck a deal with promoter Johnny Best and set up a fight in Liverpool: ten rounds with Joe Curran, a veteran of nearly sixty contests, more than half of them wins. Fortunately, Frank's decision turned out to be a wise one; Rinty came through it okay. Jackie Paterson had got the best of him this time but Rinty couldn't afford to dwell on his performance; there was another opponent waiting in the wings.

Northern Ireland's first flyweight champion was Tommy Stewart. Three years older than Rinty, Tommy was brought up further along the track towards Gallaher's tobacco works and the famed flax spinning mills on Henry Street. This was a densely-populated industrial horizon that sprouted high chimneys from York Street to the docks, along Belfast Lough, as far as the Falls Road in the west. Chest ailments were rife, thanks to the dark plumes of smoke and toxins that spiralled from the factories' sentry-like stacks. By the 1890s there were almost thirty factories in the general area, and in the 1920s Belfast was renowned for its linen production. Women were often the main breadwinners, finding it easier to obtain positions at the dozen or so mills nestling about the Falls Road district, at Lepper Street, on York Street or at the tobacco factory. Children were also employed by the mills, some as young as ten. The few coins they earned went some way toward supplementing their parents' meagre wages. Rinty's big sister Sarah worked at the mills from an early age, and was duly followed by all her sisters.

After a stint working for Workman Clark, Stewart started boxing professionally some time in the early 1930s. At that time the fight scene in Belfast was particularly intense. There was no shortage of potential rivals, spurred on by their neighbours, however distant, or fellow church-goers. Tommy and Rinty met for the first of their three contests in 1938 as part of Northern Ireland's move towards a first British Board approved Area Championship title promotion. In the late 1930s this organisation was still in its infancy. Then, in 1938, it was decided to formalise an area title for the lightest weight of eight stone. Jim McStravick, from North Queen Street, would meet the winner of an elimination contest, which was set to take place at the Oval on Friday, 2 September.

Stewart, a tough and tenacious fighter, who boxed out of White City's amateur club at Trafalgar Street, had several hundred rounds under his belt from almost one hundred bouts. Meanwhile, Rinty's reputation as a heavy hitter, especially with the right hand, promised a good match.

In the fourth round Stewart's ability to stand up to Monaghan's dig was sorely tested, though he had found a way to Rinty's chin earlier in the lively battle. The Henry Street man was caught several times in round five and even went down at one stage. In the sixth he found himself in another spot of bother but managed to fight his way back by the bell. From there Tommy became the more aggressive, taking the fight to Monaghan at every opportunity, though Rinty boxed solidly in the ninth. A ten round contest, it came down to the last session. The referee judged Stewart to have forced enough of the fight to shade the decision and, with it, Rinty's title chance was put on ice.

The Area Council plan was delivered soon after. At a show in the King's Hall the flax mill district battler proved a shade too strong for McStravick. An onslaught in round eight turned a good, evenly balanced affair Stewart's way. Relentless aggression eventually paid off in the tenth when McStravick was floored. In spite of beating the count the referee decided to wave it off—thus the inaugural championship, and a place in the history books, was Stewart's to enjoy.

Despite Rinty winning two of his three meetings with Stewart, he retained the highest respect for his tough York Street neighbour; Tommy left an impression on Rinty that lasted a lifetime. Many, many years later, when Rinty was asked in a radio interview to name his most difficult opponent, he answered, 'The fight that sticks in my memory as my hardest fight was against a Belfast man, Tommy Stewart. I broke my right hand against him.'

The novelist and poet John Campbell wrote about the district's finest boxers in *Once There was a Community Here*. Regarding the historic Oval meeting, he wrote, 'The decision was a popular one with the spectators and Monaghan proved to be a good loser when he stepped forward and shook Stewart's hand.'

Nevertheless, it was a second major setback for Rinty in the space of three fights. His manager decided it was time for a break and had Rinty take the next five months off. He was still only twenty, with lots of time hopefully to improve and achieve his potential. Careful management was essential for nurturing the young, ambitious boxer. A few more negative results could send his career, and dreams, plummeting from headline attraction to the poorly paid backwaters of the under-card. With thirty-odd bouts against his name and not a title in sight, Rinty could ill afford to finish on the wrong side of many more contests. His next result was crucial. If he wanted to stay in the contender category he had to produce a winning sequence.

Frank decided to seek out Curran again, opting for another trip to England, away from the local spotlight. A match at St James's Hall in Newcastle, in the north east of England, was arranged in preference to a bout on Ma Copley's next BBB of C sanctioned bill at the Ulster Hall in early January, where Belfast heavyweight Tommy Mallon was top-lining against Boston's Larry Hunt. Tommy Madine, Dick Frame, Micky McAloran and Jim Thompson featured in support contests along with Belfast novices Bob Watson and Jim Parlow.

After his defeat by Stewart, the *Belfast Telegraph* printed a list of the top six practitioners in the eight different weight classes—heavyweight, cruiser, middleweight, welter, lightweight, featherweight, bantam and flyweight—as nominated by the British and National Boxing Association of America. Rinty's name was nowhere to be seen.

Alabama's 'Brown Bomber', Joe Louis, was number one in the most illustrious division of all, heavyweight, as he was the world champion. His nearest rivals were deemed to be Lou Nova, Max Baer, Welsh star Tommy Farr, England's Len Harvey and Bob Pastor. Harvey was also listed as the number two cruiserweight next to John Henry Lewis. Fred Apostoli and Jack McAvoy were one and two at middle, while McAvoy was rated three at cruiser. 'Homicide Hank', aka Henry Armstrong, was the main man at welterweight. England's Eric Boon was fourth in this division.

Ireland's highest rating belonged to Derry's Jim 'Spider' Kelly; he was number three at featherweight. Only Joey Archibald and Liverpool's Chris 'Ginger' Foran were rated above him, though Foran's position raised eyebrows in Irish boxing circles as Kelly was British and Empire champion while Foran had recently lost to both Billy Walker and Josef Preys of Belgium. However, Kelly was temporarily missing in action, thanks to a tendon injury which had forced him to cancel scheduled fights against Sunderland's Tom Smith and Billy Walker.

Top British bantams 'Kid' Tanner, the British Guiana champion and number one Empire contender, and British champion Johnny King were third and fifth respectively while England's Peter Kane was where every boxer in Rinty's division wanted to be. Kane was considered the top flyweight, ahead of Tut Whalley, Filipino 'Little' Dado, American Jackie Jurich, Tiny Bostock and Paddy Ryan.

This was the grouping that Monaghan's management had their eye on. It was vital that Rinty's recent form could be turned around quickly. Rinty's stock had to rise and soon, at least in the eyes of the British establishment. He was well down the pecking order now. Even on the domestic front, a title fight looked a long way off. In January 1939, the Council announced a schedule of eliminators but nowhere on the list was the Hardinge Street gym's hopeful. Instead, Jimmy Warnock would oppose Jack McKenzie with the winner taking on Al Sharpe for the right to challenge Stewart. The title, however, lay dormant for the next number of years.

As for the trip to Tyneside, the venture was not without incident. Rinty was an avid cinema enthusiast. When he was not training or working, he enjoyed nothing better than sitting in a dark cinema and watching his favourite movie stars on screen. He particularly enjoyed musicals, which were all the rage at the time.

'Is Rinty Monaghan in the audience?'

The Public Address announcement flashed up on the screen during the song, 'Hang Your Heart on a Hickory Limb'. If Rinty was in the stalls he was asked to 'report to St James's Hall immediately'. On 27 February, once all the preliminaries had been dealt with, Rinty had asked for permission to slip out to the nearest cinema to see the new Universal

Studios hit, *Paris Honeymoon,* starring Bing Crosby. Monaghan immediately realised he was on a sticky wicket. He should have had his hands taped up by this time, his fighting silks on and preparing to go ten unpredictable but very important rounds against accomplished Liverpool man Joe Curran.

The absent-minded pugilist was out of there in a flash as Crosby's 'Sing a Song of Sunbeams' faded behind him. When he darted into St James's the fans were loud with their impatience. They gave him a flea in his ear, slow hand-clapping him into the hall.

'I went round to the pictures about half past three. The picture was so good I over-stayed my time and the next thing there is a big notice comes on the screen. So, I jumped up and says, "Oh gosh, my fight," and I gets out. I forgot about the fight really. I was feeling great, felt smashing. I did get in but I could not get my undies on proper. I was going into the ring still pulling them up.'

No matter, Rinty knocked his opponent out in five rounds. The fight signalled Rinty's return to top form. After back-to-back wins against Sammy Reynolds, Tommy Stewart, Billy Ashton and Africa's Seaman Chetty, 1939 was turning out to be a very good year.

Meanwhile, 1939 was also a turning point on the domestic front. Rinty had met the love of his life, Frances, a few years previously when Ta had secured him the job at Roden's, where Rinty's task was to maintain the boilers. Frances had been already working for Roden's, and Rinty was immediately taken with her. The feeling was mutual and the ensuing courtship resulted in the couple getting married at St Patrick's on Boxing Day in 1938.

When Frances gave birth to a girl, Martha, on 20 April the following year, it was to the delight of grandparents, Thomas, Martha, Samuel and Susan. One of three daughters, Martha was to spend a good part of her life in the United States where she raised a family, only returning to Belfast in the late Seventies when her mum's health started to fail. Nevertheless Martha never forgot her Little Corporation Street childhood, where neighbours' front doors were left open and a pot of tea was always on hand.

'Compared to the houses now our home was small, had really tiny rooms, but daddy and mammy loved the place. Daddy never left there, never moved away. That was a special place. Everybody just loved it. Daddy used to say when he looked at other people moving away from the street to live in bigger newer houses that they would have to carry him out of there.

'He loved the district, loved the people. He also loved it because there was a bookie's shop close by. Daddy loved a wee bet on the horses. Mammy was fun to be around but a nervous kind of person. She chain-smoked one cigarette after another but was also a great cook. She was always in the kitchen and had a habit of bringing the beggars in off the street, poor people who did not have anything, and cook them a meal.

'I would walk in the door after school and there was someone sitting on the stairs with a plate on his knees, knife and fork, eating fried bacon and eggs. She never turned away anyone. The door to our house was always open. Everyone was made welcome. Little Corporation Street was a lovely home, a great place to live as a child. I have nothing but great memories of number thirty-two.'

After Martha was born Rinty's boxing commitments eased. The next few years would be consumed by the war with Hitler's Germany, the effects of which would stretch as far as the vulnerable streets of Belfast.

***

Joe Curran was one of those boxers who was well thought of, no matter how he scored in a fight. The kayo in Newcastle set him back for a few years; he went on to lose twenty-seven of his next fifty-two contests before boxing Monaghan again, on 18 October 1945. Just before meeting the Belfast man in Merseyside, he lost to Mickey Jones, who had lost seven previous contests in a row. Curran had also under-performed to hand novice Tim Mahoney a first win before losing to the 78-fight veteran Norman Lewis. Earlier in the year he had been beaten by tough campaigner Sammy Reynolds.

Curran badly needed a win. And he got it ten rounds later when Rinty was nursing the seventh defeat of his career. For the Mersey boxer the October result brought a remarkable change of fortune. Nine months later he was fighting his 147th contest, at Glasgow's Hampden Park, in front of tens of thousands of Scottish fight fans for the biggest prize in flyweight boxing—the undisputed Championship of the World.

Joe's jumbled box of infrequent wins and frequent losses had not prevented him from being offered the chance to challenge Jackie Paterson. The sport with all its politics, behind-the-scene characters and deals, occasionally threw a golden opportunity to a grateful fighter. Curran's nearest previous brush with a title had been in 1944 when he knocked out his old adversary, Joe Lewis, in the eleventh round of a British eliminator.

So here he was, in the dusk of his career, hoping to return to Liverpool as the new world champion. The odds on him doing so were enormous and the outcome was as expected. However, Curran did not let himself or his supporters down. Paterson was taken the full fifteen rounds before he was finally announced the winner. Joe had to settle for having taken a terrific shot at pugilistic paradise; at least he had given the gates a good rattle. It was more than could be said of some.

7

UNDER COVER OF DARKNESS THE GERMAN Luftwaffe dropped its deadly cargo of destruction throughout the months of April and May 1941. The screams of more than two hundred metric tons of incendiaries, bombs and parachute landmines filled Belfast's sky. One of the deadly arsenals smashed into the cobbles of Concord Street, near the Monaghans' house, leaving behind a crater. Other bombs wrecked homes, killing many huddled inside, and demolished factories. Marie, the youngest of Martha and Tommy's family of nine, and older sister Noreen were lucky to escape with their lives. They were upstairs when a nearby bomb ripped away the front of the house, causing the roof to cave in. It was their brother Patsy who managed to find them in the rubble and drag them to safety.

'When I was about five-years-old mammy and daddy moved house from Thomas Street to Concord Street, where they were bombed out during the Blitz and were very lucky to be alive to tell the tale. For a child, what happened during the war was very frightening and only for Patsy I do not think my sister Noreen and myself would have survived the bombing.

'I remember the family was all about the house, downstairs that day, when the Blitz started. Someone said that the two youngest, Noreen and me, should be put up the stairs in one of the bedrooms thinking that might be safer if something happened. Patsy took us up and not very long after we were put upstairs a bomb landed in the middle of our street.

'The next thing was Noreen and me were trapped as a big wardrobe and the ceiling had fallen on top of us. The whole front of our house was blown away. The front door was not there anymore. Luckily Patsy managed to get to us, move the stuff off us and get us out before any more of the house collapsed or went on fire.

'The stairs were gone. There was nothing left of them. Patsy put one of us round the front of his neck, had the other hanging off the back of his neck, and somehow managed to get down to the ground and get us out. I do not know how he managed to. He was quite young at the time too but he found a way. I have always said, mentioned it to Patsy many times, I believe we would not be here today but for him. When I would bring up the subject he would just look at me and he would smile.

'He does not talk much about it. But I remember it well, just as if it happened only yesterday. The memory never leaves you. It was a very frightening time in our lives, terrible for Belfast. There were many other people who lived close to mammy and daddy's house who did not make it through the bombings. I think we were very, very lucky.'

More than nine hundred people were killed, thirty in a single incident when people seeking refuge in a designated shelter at Percy Street were caught up in the Luftwaffe's raid. The dead were ferried by whatever means available to the city morgue, and when that was filled beyond capacity, relatives were directed to the public baths on the Falls Road and St George's market place. The heart of the docklands was the prime target; therefore, the wharfs and surrounding districts were subject to a barrage of attacks. Fatalities were high as the bombing raids devastated whole streets and families. The Harland & Wolff yards were badly damaged, as was the Victoria shipyard, Queen's, Clarence and Alexandria Works, the Abercorn yard and Gallahers' tobacco factory. One large mill in York Street disintegrated under the bombs, crushing over forty homes nearby.

Patsy Monaghan was thirteen-years-old at the time. He remembers the extensive damage on the New Lodge, the Antrim and Lower Shankill roads, the harbour and east of Belfast. One of his best friends, Joseph McAuley, whose house stood at the end of Concord Street, was killed during the air raids.

'That was a very, very frightening experience and a very difficult time for people living in Belfast. Looking back at what happened in the Blitz, and all those people who lost their lives in it, I am just so thankful we somehow managed to come through it. It is very sad to think of the people I knew who were killed. There were people about our street, about the next few streets, I knew. I knew their faces. They were there one day and gone the next. The destruction was awful. When you walked down the streets there were bits of shells from the German bombs scattered all about the place.

'Where our house was damaged we were very fortunate to get out of it because other houses near to us were completely demolished. The thing I remember clearly is going to get my little sisters, Noreen and Marie, out of the wrecked house. Once we made it out on to the street my brother Charlie, who was on leave, was there in his bare feet pulling people out of the rubble.

'One of the girls was hurt. Noreen said, as I put her around my neck, that there was something wrong with her legs. I could feel the stickiness and once we got out I managed to take her to one of those ARP places used in the air raids to shelter people to see about first aid. I was told there was nobody able to see to her injury because a landmine had hit the church. It killed all the wardens and lots of families who were in the place. What you could see about the streets as we made our way to the Mater Hospital was terrible, half bodies, bits of people all over the place. I will never forget it. You can't forget something like that. Entire families were just wiped out.

'My mate was killed. The McAuleys lived at the end of our street. I was told that the family was huddled together when the bomb fell on Concord Street. A large piece of masonry fell on top of them and Joseph was hit and died of his injuries. Fortunately the rest of his family survived. There was another family close to us who were almost totally wiped out. Only one of them was not killed.'

Noreen and Marie were evacuated after the Blitz. Initially, the family was split up, the boys sent to the Glens of Antrim, the girls to a house in Newry. However, when Noreen became very homesick, Martha decided to take a house in the country where she and the children could see out the rest of the war. Charlie returned to duty with the Army, eventually going on tour to fight in the Far East with the King's Own Tank Regiment. Meanwhile Rinty stayed in Belfast working for the Air Raid service, driving an ambulance and working when he could for ENSA, the entertainment wing of the Allied Forces.

ENSA, or the Entertainments National Service Association, had been founded in 1939 by the actors Basil Dean and Lesley Henson, and was considered to be an important morale boosting vehicle in both the theatres of war overseas as well as on the Home Front. Sometimes referred to jokingly as 'Every Night Something Awful', the organisation nevertheless attracted contributions from entertainers and actors as diverse as George Formby and Laurence Olivier.

Formby, in particular, inspired Rinty when the Belfast man toured garrison theatres and Allied officers' clubs with him. The popular English singer and comedian, renowned for his blundering Cockney clown routine, and famous for such popular ditties as 'When I'm Cleaning Windows', was a frequent visitor to Belfast during the war years and was even known to attend various boxing promotions whilst in the north of Ireland.

Another regular contributor to the ENSA programme of light entertainment was the Queen of the British comic monologue, Joyce Grenfell, who was later to enjoy some cinematic success in the *St Trinian's* series of films. She was involved in the ENSA tour of Northern Ireland in 1942, participating in various productions staged in military hospitals across the province.

An example of the risks which these performers, and many like them, took can be found in the tragedy which befell Belfast operatic star Helen Gilliland, who was lost at sea when the ship which was taking her to an ENSA engagement in the Far East was targetted by the Japanese Navy and sunk, with no survivors. Such risks were clearly not alien to Rinty, whose involvement with ENSA took him to such places as Norway, Gibraltar and, in 1944, less than forty-eight hours after the D-Day landings, to Normandy where he entertained the soldiers of the Expeditionary Forces with his song and dance routine.

The war effort restricted all aspects of everyday life. Time to train became a luxury of sorts for anyone who was involved in sports. Promoters were hard-pushed to put on any worthwhile bills, thanks to the black-out regulations—not to mention the risk of bringing a lot of people together in one place in case there was another air raid. After a points defeat to Jimmy Gill in Newcastle, in the north of England, in March 1940, boxing sank to the bottom of Rinty's priorities for the foreseeable future. He understood that whenever he was able to concentrate on his boxing career again, it would be a long haul back to a position where he would be considered as a challenger for any level of championship belt. Towards the end of 1942 it was arranged for him to take on one of the Mount Joy Street boxing brothers, Joe Meikle, to keep his hand in. He had previously fought Joe's brother, Ted, three times in 1937, which added some spice to the proceedings. While wife Frances did not much like boxing at the best of times, she probably liked it even less when she heard the date of the fight—26 December, the day of their fourth wedding anniversary. Luckily, at least, the match went well and Rinty earned an eight rounds decision on points.

Harry Rodgers had fought Eddie 'Bunty' Doran six weeks earlier for the Northern Ireland flyweight title, the second Area Council title bout in just over a month. On 3 October Jim McCann beat Charley Brown at featherweight. Unfortunately for Harry, he was unable to tame Bunty and suffered a knockout loss in the sixth round. As it happened he was Rinty's next comeback opponent in March 1943. Rinty was well out of practice, and struggled to deal with Harry, only managing a draw after eight threes. The result was his first shared contest since the 'Young' Josephs bout in Larne, almost seven years previously.

Frank, always thinking ahead, had a dream fight in mind. He reckoned that fans would flock in their droves to see Bunty defend the Northern Ireland Area Championship title against his cousin, Rinty. However, the manager also knew that it was premature to think about tackling someone as good as Doran. Rinty needed to put in a lot of work first. His inactivity since 1940 had moved him right off the radar, while Bunty, in contrast, was the stellar flyweight of the moment. He was the north's number one and also highly rated on the British and European circuit. There was plenty of speculation about him as a potential world title challenger. Rinty had his work cut out for him to merit a mention in these types of conversations.

Frank's initial task was to position his prospect, and a deal with promoter Bob Gardiner opened a window of risky opportunity. Gardiner had secured the prized catch of British lightweight title-holder Eric Boon to headline a big show at Solitude Stadium, home of Cliftonville Football Club. This promotion would take place the day after the Twelfth of July celebrations. Gardiner anticipated one of the largest crowds for a professional boxing event in the city for years when he announced that Irish welterweight champion Tommy Armour would be Boon's next opponent. The show promised to be a perfect promotional event for boxing. Despite Rinty's lack of profile and general slump over the last couple of years, Frank convinced Bob his prospect was ready to box another Northern Ireland title eliminator. It must be remembered that Rinty wasn't exactly a novice; he had already shown himself to be a talented counter-puncher and was, on his day, capable of challenging at domestic championship level. Bob duly agreed to match him on the Armour-Boon bill, against Ike Weir. The Area Council sanctioned the fight as a final eliminator, thereby placing Rinty just one win away from challenging his cousin. This was the closest that Rinty had come to challenging for the title in almost five years since his 1938 knock-back against Tommy Stewart.

As the Solitude show was being organised battles continued to rage across Europe with the fight for the Italian island of Sicily at Syracuse and Agrigento. The Belfast public was, no doubt, grateful for any distraction from the constant news of war. The asking price was three shillings, with sixpence being charged for the outer ring, and one pound and one shilling for a ringside seat. Gardiner reported he was seeing strong ticket sales at his Newtownards Road office and forecast a record attendance for the Tuesday afternoon card.

Bunty was also engaged to box, as was Rinty's brother-in-law, Harry McAuley. Doran was matched against city rival Jack Mussen, a former

Northern Ireland champion at bantam, who won the original title in 1938 against Jack Bunting. Harry would square up to Clonmel feather Jimmy Smith while Charlie Meikle faced the noted Dublin puncher John Ingle.

Boon's manager, Jack Solomons, a big player on the British boxing promotion scene, attended the Cliftonville Football Club bill but he didn't enjoy it. The main fight ended in controversy when Armour knocked out Boon in the fifth round. The match, made at 10st 7lbs, saw Armour nail the number one British lightweight with a cracking left hand. Boon went down for a count and Jack claimed that his fighter was punched repeatedly while on the canvas. Then, when he thought Armour had been disqualified, he signalled to Eric to get up, only for Tommy to rush in and send disoriented Boon down again. Boon struggled to rise a second time only to be met once again with punches. Tommy inevitably connected with the sleeper punch and Boon suffered the first knockout defeat of his career since winning the British title five years earlier. Jack left Cliftonville furious. He claimed unfair tactics and lodged a protest with the Board of Control.

Nevertheless Armour's triumph was a sensation. Bunty was on form too. He only needed three rounds to see off Mussen, but there was no joy for McAuley and Meikle. Harry lost on points, Charlie by a sixth round stoppage. Rinty also failed to succeed, and for the second time in his career he let slip a chance to fight for the Northern Ireland title. Weir fought a smart fight and his timing exposed Monaghan's lack of competitive rounds since the Jimmy Gill contest in 1940. However, it wasn't all plain sailing. Weir had to remain alert to avoid catching a haymaker on several occasions. For the most part though, Rinty's overall boxing was just not up to scratch. All in all, it was still a good fight, even exciting at times.

It looked as if the cousins' duel would be postponed indefinitely. Ike Weir had his chance to challenge Bunty but Doran proved too strong and knocked him out in less than three rounds.

For Rinty, it was back to the drawing board. Weir had highlighted areas he needed to work on. His counter-punching was lacking and this had to be rectified if he hoped to advance himself. The defeat at Solitude extended the poorest run of his career. Since January 1940 he had fought just six contests—three were lost, one drawn and two were successful. It was pretty unimpressive compared to his standing when he beat Seaman Chetty in England at the end of 1939. His dream of challenging for a world title seemed as far off as ever.

8

THE WAR DOMINATED RINTY'S 1944 AND it was not until early October that a match, the only one he fought that year, was arranged against his old foe Joe Meikle. For the tenth time in his career he sparked out an opponent. Ten months later, in July 1945, he met Dublin's Joe Collins in the Irish capital, a match which he won on points. Then, on 13 September, he had a good ten round points victory over Tommy Burney in Liverpool. With a bit of rust knocked off his timing, and an overall improvement in sight, Frank McAloran presented him with another fight in Merseyside. Unfortunately, this one did not go so well and he dropped a decision to Joe Curran. Meanwhile, back home, the word on the street was that Rinty was preparing to meet his cousin, Bunty Doran, flyweight champion of Northern Ireland and rated among Europe's top eight-stone boxers.

Monaghan's management sorted out terms and, despite the fact he had boxed only six times since December 1942, a date was agreed for 6 November 1945. Belfast badly needed the distraction of an attractive title fight what with the newspapers being dominated by stories of labour disputes, strikes and general post-war depression. Leading boxing promoter, Bob Gardiner, negotiated the deal to match Doran and Monaghan, with an offer of £80, and placed the terms for the title clash at the offices of the British Boxing Board of Control. Frank was confident in his boxer and believed the time was right for the fight. He was in the minority. Bunty was regarded the best boxer in the division; he had not lost a bout in his home city since his February 1941 meeting with Jack Kiley. As far as everyone was concerned he was the clear favourite against Rinty.

After eleven years as a professional boxer, part of which was interrupted by the war, this would be Rinty's first championship contest in Belfast. Like any major opportunity, there was a huge risk involved. Rinty must have had his own concerns about the clash but he was not going to dwell on them. The show had to go on. His 1943 defeat to Ike Weir had forced him and his trainer James to reassess his method. They reckoned they should concentrate on his counter-punching skills. Rinty had long admired the punching style of 'Spider' Kelly and he sought to incorporate big punching into his training regime.

Bunty had won twenty-seven of his last twenty-nine fights. This impressive sequence of results included a kayo of Ike Weir and stoppage wins over highly respected opponents, Jimmy Warnock, Norman Lewis, Scotland's Alec Murphy, Joe Collins and Harry Rodgers. The latter win earned Bunty the Northern Ireland title as vacated by Tommy Stewart. He had fought sixty-four times in total, losing a mere five times. On the other hand, Monaghan had only lost six of his fifty fights, his most recent loss being to Curran three weeks earlier. The biggest problem facing Rinty was that he had done very little boxing over the past two years and certainly none at all against someone of his cousin's calibre.

A large crowd was expected despite money being extremely tight for luxuries like boxing matches. Local man Vincent McGurk remembers the excitement surrounding the battle of the cousins. He paid his half crown along with a group of friends to see it.

'Everyone you met on the streets around the Ulster Hall talked about Bunty, how he was fighting his cousin. He was number one at that time and a big favourite to beat Rinty. All the talk was of Bunty challenging for some of the major titles. He was tops, but Rinty was dangerous, a good puncher, had a great right hand. Everyone knew he was very strong and could put opponents away if given the chance.

'Bunty was said to be in line to fight for the European title, so it was really a massive fight, the biggest in Belfast for years, probably since before the war. People wanted to see it and I think as many as they could get into the Ulster Hall were squeezed in to see Bunty and Rinty that night. I was glad to be able to get in. It was probably the best half crown I have ever spent on watching boxing.

'It turned out to be really sensational. The place was packed, the atmosphere was brilliant, as both of them had a big following, and to be fair Rinty had not received the credit he deserved before that fight. That was maybe to do with the way he liked to box. Even though he was very powerful, he liked to fight on the retreat, counter-punch and wait his chance. Rinty was clever at waiting for an opening. Then he would go for his opponent. When he landed a big punch they certainly felt it.'

On the morning of the fight one newspaper posed the big question on everyone's lips, 'Can Monaghan wrest the title from Doran?' By Tuesday night fight fans were virtually unanimous about who would prove triumphant. The formbook declared Doran to be the favourite, an opinion which was broadly shared outside the Hardinge Street gym. Boxing columnists and the general public were singing from the same hymn sheet, all reckoning that Doran could not be beaten.

Bob Gardiner had undoubtedly scored something of a coup in setting up the much anticipated bash. He played all his marketing cards to create more hype, even going so far as suggesting to the local media that the current world champion, Rinty's old foe Jackie Paterson, was the ultimate target he envisaged to meet the winner.

Rinty stepped up his training at the gym, working long hours with James and Pat.

Every morning before breakfast, he could be seen pounding the pavement in his heavy boots, taking steep muscle-aching steps up to Bellevue, the Sheep's Path, pushing himself physically and mentally. The McAlorans were well aware of the possibilities for Rinty should he beat his cousin. A win would hopefully inspire his backers to push his name forward in the right places, which would result in an opportunity to challenge for a British or Empire title, maybe even a much-desired world title fight with Paterson. It was a long shot, but the only way of furthering

Rinty's claim was his beating Doran. The stakes had never been higher. In short, he had to beat the best to be the best.

Doran was renowned for being a sharp tactical pugilist. General opinion was that he packed the better range of punches, the greater sting, and his record suggested he was more than capable of stopping Monaghan with either hand. Bunty's left had sparked out quite a few rivals in his time, as had his right. Yet Rinty had already proved himself as a talented boxer and Bunty could not afford to underestimate him. Rinty was equally noted for being very fast about the canvas; he was an intelligent boxer who could comfortably box on the back foot, prove awkward and elusive, with the smarts to stay slippery as a bar of soap. It was also a fact that when he executed his offensive strategy to perfection, he could deliver a sledgehammer right hook. He had not been stopped since Paterson scored against him at Glentoran Football Club in 1938.

On 6 November, the boxing correspondent in the *Irish News* summed up the general feeling:

'As both are anxious to have a tilt at Paterson's world title the result of this contest means a lot and each will be out to win. Regarding the prospects of these two clever Belfast boys, opinion is very much divided. Doran is the stronger of the two and carries a damaging punch in either hand but Monaghan, who is fast and clever, will not be easily stopped.'

Rinty had a pre-fight ritual, which Bunty may have caught a few bars of before they made their way to decide which of them would leave the Ulster Hall as the Northern Ireland champion.

'Playing my harmonica just before a fight has a tonic effect on me and my opponent is left wondering what sort of man I am who plays a mouth organ a few minutes before the start of an important battle.'

As expected, Rinty was happy to fight on retreat, trying to stay elusive, slipping the shots and waiting for a chance to strike back. Fast on his feet, he skirted the ropes, using every inch of space available, avoiding Bunty's attempts to short circuit his ambitions. Patience was his motto—wait, bide time, look for a mistake and then pounce. Doran dominated from the first bell. He was reportedly well ahead on points after three rounds, but his boldness of approach—the flailing all-out attack—was not a wise one.

There were plenty of big names in the crowd that night, including the Governor of Northern Ireland, the Earl of Granville, and the Northern Premier, Sir Basil Brooke, who was sitting ringside beside Bob Gardiner. Further back in the half crown seats Vincent McGurk and his pals watched the unthinkable unfold.

'For the first four rounds of the fight with Bunty, Rinty fought the same, boxing on the retreat, waiting for an opening because Rinty could punch when the opportunity was offered to him. He was dangerous that way. Bunty was a great boxer, he really was, and a lot of people thought Rinty was taking on too much too soon. Most thought Bunty would be too good for him. It turned out to be some fight. It did not last too many rounds. Rinty delivered a hell of a knockout. People talked about what happened for years afterwards.'

Rinty had played it cute, allowing the title holder to dictate terms, throw plenty of punches, miss with plenty, and eventually be drawn to take bigger risks. When his guard was left open to a surprise counter, Rinty struck with the timing and sting of a scorpion. As Doran blasted away, trying to close out the fight as quickly as possible, he ignored his defence, even after being caught in round two by an ominous hard right hook. Then, in the fourth round, his title was snatched away in terrific style.

'It was Doran's impetuousness and his carelessness in rushing around the ring after Monaghan that lost him the fight. Had he been wise, like Monaghan, and kept at a safe distance and allowed Monaghan to go on the offensive occasionally the result might have been different,' a reporter observed.

The champion had banked on a quick finish. Instead of being patient and working out what Rinty had to offer, Doran abandoned his usual approach and chased after Monaghan. He set about pressurising Rinty all over the canvas, trying to nail him with big shots at every turn, swinging in left hooks and crosses around the challenger's head.

The finish was absolutely jaw-droppingly good from Rinty's point of view. Bunty worked in the lefts, pressed, got careless time and again, and then, wallop! Rinty hit a classic home run Babe Ruth would have been proud of—precise, powerful, right on the money—a real peach of a right hook. His cousin's knees gave way and the title fight was hurled into its final dramatic act. One commentator described the finish:

'It was during one of his rushes at Monaghan that he took the right hook that put him down for a count of eight. It was a strong punch and weakened Doran considerably. When he beat the count he was practically out on his feet and Monaghan had very little trouble in finishing the contest with a terrific right hand punch, which put a completely unguarded Doran down for the final count. Monaghan supporters created a scene. They were all on their feet cheering and shouting so loudly that the M.C.'s appeal for order through the megaphone was useless. After some time order was restored and Monaghan, the new champion, crooned a song.'

The next day's *Irish News* headline summed up the evening's dramatic events with 'Belfast Boxing Sensation' and 'Monaghan Knocks Out Doran in Fourth Round'. Their correspondent opened the ringside report:

'Rinty Monaghan (Belfast) created a first-class sensation at Bob Gardiner's big boxing tournament in the Ulster Hall last night when he knocked out "Bunty" Doran in the fourth round of a contest which 90 per cent of the boxing patrons of Belfast expected Doran to win with ease.'

Gardiner's show was hailed as a success. The completely unexpected result was the biggest break in Rinty's boxing career and provided his manager with a bargaining chip to use in future negotiations aimed at reeling in Paterson.

According to a glowing review, the main event and a top notch card of supporting fights was said to be 'the greatest boxing thrills that have been witnessed in Belfast in half a century'. Fiji Islander Ben Valentine stopped Chris Cole, a former Irish heavyweight champion, in the seventh round. Jim McCann and Charlie Meikle fought out a thrilling featherweight bout, McCann shading the decision. This bout was rated one of the best seen in years.

In other contests Jackie Holland of Belfast beat Derry's Paddy Harkin on points, while former Northern Ireland welterweight champion Tommy Armour knocked out Scotland's Billy Ross in the third round. Rinty's brother-in-law Harry McAuley, the Northern Ireland featherweight champion, lost out on points to a former Empire title holder, Jim Brady of Dundee. Brady had lost his bantamweight title two months earlier to Jackie Paterson in Glasgow in front of one of the year's biggest boxing crowds, of some 39,800 spectators. This type of popularity, plus three prized titles, highlighted Paterson as a prime target for both Bob Gardiner and Frank McAloran, who hoped to be able to broker a deal with Paterson's manager Pat Collins. However, the Scottish man was hard to pin down, particularly at eight stone, for while he was the undisputed world champion Paterson campaigned mostly at bantam. He had fought thirteen times since winning the flyweight title in 1943 from Peter Kane in front of almost 49,000 people after a match that lasted just over a minute.

As Rinty boosted his profile, Jackie was at the Queensberry Club in London's Soho district, boxing bantam, defeating Wolverhampton's Sammy Reynolds inside three rounds. Reynolds had lost twice previously to Monaghan. A news agency report the day after the Ulster Hall shock stated that Reynolds had suffered a 'merciless beating'; he was floored twice at the start of the third round before the fight was stopped.

Meanwhile, Bunty's ambitions for title fights with Paterson at flyweight were vanquished and he decided to move up, switching his sights to bantam—Paterson's long-time hunting ground—though the big name everyone was after at this level was world champion, Manuel Ortiz, who, unfortunately, remained just beyond Bunty's reach due to injuries. In 1947 Doran took the Northern Ireland bantam title from Tommy Madine, and also won the Irish Championship against Joe Collins. However, both British and European title chances slipped by because of badly timed injuries—Ortiz was always a couple of steps ahead of him. Bunty retired in the early 1950s after fighting 101 pro bouts.

Patsy Monaghan had to settle for listening to the fight on his wireless because he was at sea, aboard the *Empire Dickens*. He had trained, however, at the gym during shore leave just before the fight and remembers Bunty was the hot ticket with the Belfast bookmakers.

'Bunty was beating everybody at that time and was four-to-six in the betting. The bookies were no mugs. Bunty was the clear favourite. But I was confident John could win. I remember I got even money in the bets on ship, with the skipper, a man called Kerr from Islandmagee. Everybody wanted money on Bunty and by the end of the trip I had ninety pounds built up in winnings from Rinty's beating him.

'I was getting paid £30 a month then. I had my rating then, so the bets on Rinty at that time were worth three months wages to me. That is one of the fights I was not going to forget. It was a big, big win for Rinty, really important for his career, so I have great memories of the time he won the Northern Ireland title.'

Rinty's fortunes were seriously on the up. As for the fighting cousins, they were never to meet again inside the boxing ring. They pursued their goals at different weights from then on, although there is no doubt that Rinty owed much to his shock win over Bunty. If it wasn't for the peculiar risks Doran decided to take, Rinty's career might have turned out very differently indeed.

9

A LITTLE FRENCH FLAIR APPEARED ON the horizon of Rinty's career after an exceptional year in 1946, at the end of which the ratings commission of *The Ring* magazine installed the Belfast man as their choice as the world's number one flyweight. It was a prestigious position, making Rinty a divisional king in the eyes of *The Ring*'s respected writers and analysts, even though the actual trappings of the title of undisputed champion of eight stone boxing still belonged to Glasgow's Jackie Paterson.

By this stage Paterson was preoccupied with the pursuit of bantam success. He had won the Empire Championship against Jim Brady in front of 39,000 at Hampden Park the previous September in what was Glasgow's first big boxing event since the end of the war, before reversing a loss in Paris to Theo Medina and a defeat by Bunty Doran over ten rounds in Dublin with a victory against Medina for the vacant European title.

Everyone was keeping a close watch on Rinty's progress. He opened 1946 with an eight round win over Tommy Burney in Liverpool in the first week of April before proceeding to beat the top-rated Scot Alec Murphy on points in Glasgow. His season finished back home with an eighth round disqualification win over Sammy Reynolds. Sandwiched between these victories was a showdown, on 7 June, with Paterson during which Rinty extracted revenge for his previous defeat at the hands of the Scot at the Oval. It had taken eight years to start to settle that score, with Rinty finding the measure of Jackie to stop the then world champion in a non-title affair inside six rounds. A cut ended Paterson's challenge, although Monaghan's superiority on the night was virtually total.

The accumulative impact of an unbeaten 1946 season, added to two title wins the previous year against Joe Collins and Bunty Doran, pushed Rinty to the top spot in *The Ring*'s world renowned rankings—a huge boost to his campaign to get a shot at the world title. It was also an interesting assessment of the division, and Jackie Paterson's standing in it, beyond Great Britain.

Matched at 8st 4lbs, the prospect had whetted everyone's appetite for the main deal to be struck. Jack Rutherford, writing in the popular periodical, the *Ulster Sports Gazette*, reflected that Rinty 'really hit the world set-up' when he stopped Jackie in stunning seven.

'Local fans got quite a thrill in the first round of the contest when Rinty connected with a fast right cross which was just a little too high. The crowd gasped as Paterson fell back against the ropes, but getting into a shell, the champ survived the round.'

Rutherford considered the weight issue, with the fight pitched four pounds over the flyweight limit: 'Had it been at 8st, Rinty's natural fighting weight, it might have been curtains for the finely trained Scot in that first exciting session.'

Rinty was labelled a 'singing leather pusher' who carried in his right glove a punch to provoke an opponent to 'sleep', that is, to knock him out cold. Rutherford noted that this colourful reputation was proving increasingly difficult to sell to other promoters and boxers within the BBB of C network. At the top end, people were protecting their positions, which was only to be expected. More money was required to feather deals to attract the fights he needed.

The stoppage of Paterson had everyone talking. The win sparked speculation in the local media and the London press about Monaghan's contender rights—he now seemed to be the ideal domestic match, plus a genuine test, for Paterson. Surely now a world title fight could not be too far away. Speculation did not pay the bills, however. Options for McAloran and Gardiner to work on were limited. There were no British takers, so it had to be Emile Famechon. The French knew that a win over the Belfast man, who had not fought in four months, could be their ticket to a world title shot for their man.

Frank was anxious to step up Rinty's profile, and word was that the new sensation of French flyweight boxing, Emile Famechon, could provide the type of publicity they were after. As far as his fellow countrymen were concerned Famechon had world champion potential. His scalp would provide extra leverage to convince the European governing body to support Monaghan's claim to meet Paterson. They were finding it tough to get Rinty decent matches since he'd fought Murphy and Reynolds the previous September within the space of thirteen days. Rival contenders, both flyweight and bantam, were understandably managed with care to protect positions.

Monaghan's manager reckoned he had a deal sorted with the French star's advisors. If his man could defeat Famechon it would do him a power of good, publicly and privately. Negotiations were tweaked here and there and the game plan played out perfectly, as it transpired. Famechon, they were told, would not be ready for a few more weeks. Almost six months after beating Sammy Reynolds, the delays were unhelpful. They needed to avoid a further month without a contest to alleviate the problems of inactivity, ring rust in pugilistic parlance. Another Famechon, André, entered the mix, indicating he would face Rinty on 11 March.

Then André got cold feet, as did Gallic bantam Jean Jouas, both at the eleventh hour. Yet again a fight deal was verging on collapse, which would be detrimental to Frank's plan regarding Paterson. Fortunately, there was still wriggle room left to repair the bill in time. Until the curtain goes up on any given night everything is fenced with uncertainty. Late changes to the bill are rife and this London event was no different. The saviour turned out to be an emerging English fighter based in Islington, who went by the assumed name of Terry Allen.

Allen was born Edward Albert Govier. A former amateur of note, with more than one hundred bouts to his credit before turning pro, his early professional career was fought as E A Govier. Then, during the war, Edward Albert went AWOL from the navy, concealing his identity by taking the ID card of a Terry Allen. Unfortunately for him his escape plan was foiled when he was arrested. He was duly reassigned and posted to northern Africa, finishing out the war in Egypt. Here, boxing was a perfect outlet for him. His new station, the strategic supplies port of Alexandria, was the location for regular boxing shows that provided entertainment for Allied troops involved in the conflict with Hitler's North African Corp. Govier's boxing career flourished, and he boxed fifteen times between May 1944 and December 1945. Furthermore, he did not lose a single bout and knocked out no less than six of his fifteen opponents of unknown quality.

When the tour of duty finished Govier was posted back to England. Five days after knocking out someone in Egypt, by the name of Hocine Rabath, inside a single round, he signed up to fight leading British title contender Alec Murphy in London, who slammed the brakes on his wartime winning streak with a sixth round stoppage. Govier decided to make a serious go of boxing. He took on the name Terry Allen again to pursue a professional boxing career and four wins followed the loss to Murphy. He agreed at short notice to risk his 34–1 record against Rinty. After all, it would be one hell of a feather in his cap if he could upset the odds and beat the highly-rated boxer.

Rinty warmed up for Allen with an exhibition bout against his sparring partner, bantamweight prospect Eddie McCullough, on a Bob Gardiner promotion in Belfast. A full page in the programme hailed him as 'leading contender for the world's flyweight title'. The four three-minute round workout was in support of a card headlined by former Northern Ireland welterweight champion Tommy Armour and Lurgan's Gerry McCready. Also on the bill were welter rivals Paddy Bonner (Derry) and Mickey McAloran (Belfast), featherweights Jim Irvine (Belfast) and Jim McCambley (Lurgan), another McCambley boxer, Fred, against Belfast's Jim Robinson in a lightweight rematch, and an appearance by former Ulster amateur flyweight champion Jackie Briers and Portadown's Frank McCoy.

Rinty was in superb condition for Allen. Experienced from forty-four wins in fifty-six fights, he pulled the rug from under the Islington man's quickly disoriented feet. Before Allen could say 'Jack Robinson'—Rinty's favourite punch-line—the punches hammered in and it was all over before the bell ended the first round.

Terry had never experienced anything like it. For Rinty, however, it was a terrific return to action after almost six months of twiddling his thumbs, waiting for someone to fight him. London's media were frothing about it. The big English hope for the world title was taken apart and the same English writers who had built up Allen, with whispers of a possible meeting with Paterson, now lavished praise on the Northern Ireland champion. They gushed about how he knocked Allen out, and reckoned he could go places in the flyweight division. Even if they were getting a bit carried away, it was good publicity. The first round knockout would make Paterson sit up a little straighter and take note and recall the hard clips Rinty had delivered the previous summer in Belfast. Generous comparison was made with one of the greatest of all early 1900s flyweights, the mighty Welshman Jimmy Wilde. Jack Rutherford wrote:

'Within ninety seconds Allen had landed on the canvas for counts of six, eight, seven and nine when the referee stopped it. Following this display a famous English sports commentator wrote of Rinty, "I expressed the opinion that we should never again see a Jimmy Wilde. Well, I withdraw that phrase to say we have one who should follow closely in the Welshman's footsteps and who will win a world flyweight title."'

The British Board and the National Boxing Association in America now regarded him as the emerging boxer at eight stone. Emile Famechon agreed to meet him on 1 July 1947. Famechon was good, knew his way about the ring, but he found Rinty too clever, too elusive. A patient performance, sharp when he needed to be, off-loading some heavy shots, gained Rinty a points win after ten competitive rounds. It was a good result, and it rang the right bells in America with the NBA. Five days later Reuters filed a report from the USA, which stirred up the prospects of a world title fight before the year was out. The drift net on Paterson was closing. At least, that is how it looked.

Although he did defend the world flyweight belt in Glasgow in the summer of 1946, shortly after losing to Rinty, by agreeing to meet Merseyside's seasoned domestic campaigner Joe Curran with the EBU bantam title also on the line, the Scot worked the rest of the year at the higher weight. He engaged Jimmy Webster, scoring a fifth round kayo, and closed the year with a third meeting with Theo Medina. That contest, the final bout of a trilogy spanning eleven months and two EBU Championship bouts, cost Jackie the European title when he was knocked out for only the second time in his career.

Monaghan's management believed that their boy would be next to face Paterson, especially in the light of the three knockdown blitz of Terry Allen, which had given the British Board plenty to think about in terms of sanctioning a Paterson-Monaghan world title fight. The expectation in Belfast was that the US body would nominate Rinty. It was bewilderment, therefore, that rained down on Rinty's team when, in New York, the NBA instead used its influence to nominate not Rinty but a relatively unheard of Hawaiian by the name of Salvador Dado Marino.

Paterson had switched up twice to bantamweight to contest titles in the previous few months, losing the European rematch to Medina before beating 222-fight veteran Johnny King for the British Championship after the Curran fight. Rinty's claims were cast-iron, but alas, in boxing, politics is a card often played on the backroom tables. Rinty had been nudged sideways again in favour of someone who had never fought on the mainland United States, and who had boxed exclusively in Hawaii against competition impossible to evaluate. The NBA reckoned the British Board had used their option in allowing the Paterson-Curran encounter and now they looked to have their own wish list attended to. Thanks largely to the industrious and visionary manager, Sam Ichinose, working on Marino's behalf, the NBA made their call.

Despite the disappointment in the Monaghan camp, Paterson himself appeared cornered by the NBA. He had to defend against Marino in July in Hampden Park and, given Jackie's on-off health problems, things were fraught and officials were, naturally, worried. Reuters in New Jersey outlined details of a communiqué sent from A J Greene, President of the NBA, to Charles F Donmall, Secretary of the British Board, on the evening of 6 July, in which the Americans stated their position ahead of

Paterson's second defence of the undisputed championship. Rinty Monaghan was to be awarded the slot of next-in-line contender. The situation was now bubbling along nicely. The communiqué contained a lot more of interest, not only for Rinty and his management and promoter Bob Gardiner, but also for the London promoter, Jack Solomons.

Rinty's credentials could not be ignored. No less than *The Ring*, after all, had rated him above Paterson, above Marino, and had him perched at the top of their flyweight listings; surely he deserved a title shot? He had won seven fights in a row, not losing once since dropping a ten-round decision to Joe Curran. The NBA's take on the flyweight issue was encouraging all the same. Rinty was not to know at this point that, just 111 days following his fine win over Emile Famechon, he would be confronting the one man that stood between him and the biggest prize of his career.

David Kui Kong Young, a top-notch bantam, who had extended world champion Manuel Ortiz for the full fifteen-round distance in May 1947 in a title challenge, but had lost on points, was the only notable name on Marino's record. They had fought twice, in 1943 and 1946, and Young won both times. Nevertheless, Sam Ichinose convinced the NBA to support his man in a quest to seek out Scotland's world title holder and bring the crown back to Hawaii. He put together a European tour, took his stable of fighters to New York to train at Stillman's Gym, and set about convincing the American officials to side with Marino rather than the world number one-rated Monaghan.

The Honolulu deal-maker had worked for years to position Marino, a boxer he first saw in island plantation tournaments, in range of Glasgow's top gun. In late February he had matched him in Honolulu with Gus Rosa (0-3-1), where Marino won on points, a fifth successive win since losing to Young for a second time. He would not fight in Hawaii again until the summer of 1948.

Meanwhile, travel permits for Europe were finalised and passages to Scotland, London, and a training camp in France, with a brief stint in Belfast, were secured for Ichinose's band of travellers. Sam's man was on the verge of becoming the first overseas challenger to an undisputed flyweight champion based in Europe since the Italian-American 'Young Zulu Kid' had travelled from America to London to take on Jimmy Wilde in 1916. It was a task of immense magnitude. For one thing, no one outside of England had ever fought Paterson with the world title at stake. For another, no boxer outside of Europe had managed to lay claim to the flyweight belt for sixteen years. Frankie Genaro of the USA had been the last fighter to achieve this goal.

Now that the NBA was rowing in behind the Hawaiians, intensive talks were fast-tracked to thrash out a date and venue, with Glasgow's Hampden Park chosen to stage the proposed contest. Ichinose, Marino and the rest of the team arrived at Prestwick Airport in early May and attended Jackie's contest against Emidio Cacciatori on the fifteenth. Paterson knocked out the Italian in the third round—a warning shot delivered in style to the visitors, though the contest was made at eight pounds above the flyweight limit. Freddie Price, a stable-mate of Rinty's at the Hardinge Street gym, gained a win by disqualification over Scotland's middleweight champion Jake Kilrain on the same bill.

Ichinose, Scottish promoter Charlie Black, and Paterson's manager Pat Collins had settled on 11 June for the title bout, although Rinty's promoter Gardiner was working behind the scenes to upstage matters by offering Paterson a huge purse, in the region of several thousand pounds, to switch his sights to a title defence in Belfast. Others were on fishing expeditions too but with less than a month to go, the main concern became whether the illness-prone champion could actually be brought to the weight by his coach, Johnny Rafferty. Paterson fell ill a couple of days after the Cacciatori bout. His condition, identified by an outbreak of boils and sores, was diagnosed on 31 May as a form of blood poisoning.

The British Board moved the date of the fight to 9 July. Training was interrupted and fresh doubts over Paterson's ability to prepare were growing. Having spent so much of the past four years at bantamweight, it was dubious whether Jackie could safely make it to eight stone while remaining healthy and strong for the unknown threat Marino posed. Concerns intensified by the week regarding whether or not the fight would take place at all.

A report filed by Reuters confirmed what the British boxing press, especially correspondents attached to the main Scottish newspapers, the *Glasgow Evening Times*, *Citizen* and *Express*, suspected. In it, the agency relayed the worries of the NBA and outlined American thinking on the situation. What they were proposing, if the British authorities agreed, would move things on significantly for Rinty if the champion failed to show up at the designated hour. Irish and British commentators picked up on it and it was generally reckoned that, even if the fight were to go ahead, Paterson could not, in the time he had left to prepare, be strong at the weight. Precious weeks of necessary training and conditioning for core stamina, strength, sharpness and ability to absorb the punches of his opponent, had been lost. Jackie was in dire straits with the unstable sands of time shifting beneath his feet.

One school of thought proposed that, if it came to the bit, his only way to retain his title, were he to beat the scales, was to stop Marino early. What power and fitness he had needed to be used quickly since he would surely lack the stamina for fifteen rounds. Paterson was renowned and feared for his southpaw right, a technical lead weapon which commentators considered to be his ace card. Meanwhile, no one in the European media could assess what exactly the Hawaiian Marino would be bringing to the battle.

What sort of fighter was Salvador Dado Marino? What were his strengths? In fact, Marino's career was a bit of a mystery. What was known was that no flyweight from the Hawaiian Islands had ever won a world title. A professional since 1941, having boxed amateur to begin with, not even mainland USA knew much about him.

Salvador's journey began on the volcanic island of Maui, where he was born in 1915. His father was an accomplished fighter, who boxed at the turn of the century, at a time when it was prohibited on the Hawaiian Islands by local law. Those who wished to box were compelled to go underground to do so. Salvador's father competed in banned tournaments of what became known as 'bootleg boxing'.

As a teenager, Salvador was sent to work on the island of Lanai, on the sugar cane and pineapple plantations. Long working hours were plentiful, the greenback dollars much less so. A side attraction for the plantation workers was boxing and regular tournaments were organised, where

Marino proved to be skilful with his fists. The young Maui lad was convinced that he had a proper future in boxing. It was during one of these plantation tournaments that he was discovered by 'Sad' Sam Ichinose. The manager had been nick-named thus thanks to his habit of presenting a hangdog expression in interviews when one of his fighters lost.

Ichinose ran a thriving enterprise on Hawaii and based himself at the Pan American Club, which was later renamed the 49th State Athletic Club. Sam became involved in the legalised fight game when the ban was revoked in 1929 and had started out managing a fighter called Freddie Gomez of Mexican and Irish extraction. Ichinose convinced Marino to cut his teeth in amateur boxing. After establishing himself on Hawaii, Salvador began to make some noise across the US. He was soon regarded as a top amateur talent and Sam brought him to various cities on the American mainland to compete. Salvador delivered a variety of tournament wins, including prestigious Golden Glove titles.

Seven years after Rinty turned professional, and three years after Jackie Paterson made his debut at Greenock against Joe Kiely, Sam decided it was time for Salvador to embark on the professional scene with Stanley Ito as his trainer. Marino vindicated the move by chalking up fifteen wins in a row in his first eighteen months, gaining a reputation as a wicked body puncher. The left hook to the body was his favoured weapon.

Details are vague regarding the quality of his early opponents. Marino's first ten-rounder was against Adolph Samuels, whom he fought three times in one year. Samuels' record after the third of those meetings was 0-12-3 but it is impossible to determine the accuracy of this record or any other. This applies similarly to Rinty's famous York Street rival Tommy Stewart, for example, who fought a vast number of times more than his 'official' listed record implies.

It also appears that Marino had fought for a world title, or at least some sort of localised version. His first loss was incurred in May 1943, at bantamweight to David Kui Kong Young, in a contest sanctioned as a version of the World Championship, recognised by the Pacific's Territorial Boxing Commission. To the world at large, only Manuel Ortiz held a world bantam title.

Just as the outbreak of the Second World War slowed down Rinty's and Jackie's careers, Salvador's too was put on hold as he enlisted with the US 7th Air Force serving in the Pacific hotspots of the Marshall Islands and Guam. He fought the occasional boxing contest during his enlistment and, with a forty fight record, sporting thirty-four wins, he set sail for Scotland in the late spring of 1947.

Unfortunately there was a real danger that the journey from Hawaii to Hampden would be made for absolutely nothing. June at Hampden Park soon gave way to early July; Jackie's condition was being closely monitored while time ticked on. On 7 July, two days before the British Board's deadline for the world title bout to take place, further dismay hit when it was announced that Paterson's skin had broken out again in boils and sores. It was obvious that he was in no condition to fight the local greengrocer never mind a wicked body-punching boxer.

The NBA stated that, as far as they were concerned, Monaghan was next in line to challenge for the belt. It now seemed that Rinty was within touching distance of the greatest prize imaginable.

10

THE TITLE FIGHT WAS OFF. THE latest bulletin from Ashton Road in Glasgow was grim; Jackie Paterson was under sedation and confined to bed. Reporters from various agencies and newspapers assembled at the champion's home where his wife Helen explained the circumstances of her husband's illness along with the fact that there was no chance of him meeting Dado Marino.

Boxing officials now found themselves in a bit of a pickle, a sticky situation of their own making. It was true that Paterson was a no-show but the bigger problem had nothing to do with him. A curious decision had been made the previous week to order the stand-by opponent, Rinty, to stand down. Had officials kept him on call he would have been in training, and therefore, ready and waiting to substitute for a sick man. As it was, he had not trained for ten days. With his diet regime returned to normal there was no way he could now be called upon, not for a World Championship contest. Making eight stone correctly at a few hours' notice would not be entertained.

So there would be no world title bout, no top of the bill, and the nonsense left organisers in a quandary. Meanwhile, Hampden Park was expecting a crowd of twenty-five to thirty thousand boxing fans who had paid for tickets to see Paterson fight the Hawaiian. As if that wasn't bad enough, Glasgow's gun-metal grey skies sent down rain in torrents on top of all the fans faithfully converging on Hampden. The promoter and various boxing authorities involved—the British Board and America's National Boxing Association—were facing a huge fiasco.

For months health issues and doubts surrounded Paterson. Key personnel had somehow missed or ignored the warning signs. For several weeks he had been monitored by Dr Crawford Barclay, medical officer for the Board, who regularly assessed his health, weight and training. Helen and his trainer John Rafferty told reporters that Jackie had been examined just a few days earlier and, in a last desperate throw of the dice, he attempted some type of training at their Ashton Road home. A bad decision all round. His condition quickly deteriorated until he was on the verge, it was suggested, of some sort of breakdown.

The truth was that he had rarely been close to the flyweight limit since winning the title from Peter Kane during the summer of 1943. Officials knew this. They were aware that Jackie had mostly campaigned at bantam or in catchweight bouts since then. He had fought at bantam in May in a warm-up with Italy's Emidio Cacciatori for the now cancelled title bout at the lower weight.

The peculiarity surrounding Rinty's premature release from training heightened when Jackie's wife acknowledged during an interview that Jackie's own training had suffered severely for at least five weeks. The skin inflammation had prevented him from working to anything like the intensity required for a championship bout. As she spoke Jackie drifted back to sleep. His coach also revealed that the boxer was two pounds over the weight limit on the morning before the weigh-in. It did not make a lot of sense that on fight day there was no stand-by ready to take his place.

Officials knew Rinty was somewhere in the city since he had planned to be part of the 30,000 watching the match, and someone suggested he be located. This was quickly done, resulting in a very frustrated Rinty being asked to take the fight with Marino at virtually a moment's notice. This was not how he, or any other serious boxer, conducted his career. Yet, despite everything, he agreed to box. There was one proviso, however; he refused point blank to wear any boxing silks or tooth protector which were not his own. John Caughey, a correspondent for

Belfast paper *Ireland's Saturday Night*, who published his pieces under the alias 'The Timekeeper', remarked that 'so unexpected was the call that they had to send a plane specially to Belfast to fetch his gum-shield, boxing kit and dressing as he would not take the ring with anybody else's gear'.

Meanwhile, the Paterson conundrum left the Board with some thinking to do. The American reaction was loud and clear; they wanted Paterson removed as champion and stripped of the undisputed World Championship. The situation as it stood was unacceptable to the NBA as the division had been practically suspended for four years since 1943. The NBA wanted their number one, Marino, and Rinty Monaghan to fight for what they understood to be a vacant title, and for the Board to support them on this. The Board also had to decide on the fairest way to censure the stricken Ashton Road man. An important point was that his inactivity, however unhappy it made the officials, and no matter how much they cried foul over it, was actually defendable. The flyweight issue did not look too bad when compared to how many title fights had taken place in other divisions—in particular during the war years when severe restrictions were imposed on travel permits and boxers had to sign up for military service. It was the same situation at heavyweight, the premier division of professional boxing. Only two contests had been staged during the same length of time that Paterson was below par: Joe Louis had knocked out both Billy Conn and Tami Mauriello. It was an undeniable fact that the logistics of promoting title bouts in wartime ran from exceptionally difficult to downright impossible.

Consider the other major title situations: at light-heavyweight just one contest had taken place between 1943 and 1947—England's Freddie Mills versus Gus Lesnevich in New York in 1946, a fight which Mills lost. Middleweight produced little more, and there were two bouts at welterweight, none at light-welterweight, while the light division fared better. Sammy Angott, Beau Jack, Bob Montgomery, Mexico's Juan Zurita and Ike Williams were involved in a total of ten contests. One was Williams' ninth round kayo of Welshman Ronnie James at Cardiff. This was for an NBA approved title. At featherweight Willie Pep, Phil Terranova and Sal Bartolo kept the title interest relatively busy.

The sticky issue for the NBA was not inactivity; Paterson had fought twenty-five times since the quick-fire over Kane—just not at flyweight. Joe Curran, the Liverpool veteran of over 140 contests, fifty-eight of them losses, and a few of these to Rinty too, was the only person Paterson had scaled down to fly for since Kane. Five of the bantam bouts had been for British, Commonwealth or European titles. The Americans had run out of patience. Paterson had let the cobwebs gather on the World Flyweight Championship for four years and the NBA were not going to tolerate it any longer. The sick note for the Marino bout was the final straw. Even *The Ring* had lost interest in Paterson, which was evident when it rated Rinty number one in the world. British Board officials had to determine whether Paterson was to be afforded another opportunity to beat his health problems, or whether his time was up.

The NBA stance was uncompromising. A J Greene's cable on 6 July, regarding a no-show by Paterson, left the Board in no doubt. Paterson was out of the game as far as the Americans were concerned. Britain's administrative stewards decided they were in agreement with the Americans and formally stripped Paterson of his British and Empire titles, the latter of which he had only defended once since 1943.

***

Moses Deyong, one of the most renowned professional boxing referees at the time, had been booked to supervise a world title fight, and instead found himself in charge of a 'face-saving' international flyweight contest in front of some 25,000 rain-drenched fans. (Much later, in his autobiography, *Everybody Boo*, Moses, or 'Moss' for short, described how a London Jew from Petticoat Lane made it all the way from humble beginnings to the main stage in the sport.) The rain was so heavy that sawdust had to be generously sprinkled over the canvas to help the boxers maintain their footing.

Moments into the non-title fight, and Marino experienced what it was like to sit on saturated wood chippings as Rinty caught him with a terrific right hook. The leather had barely warmed when it crunched into the Maui islander. Fortunately for him, the count was short but the fight was further delayed to allow for the sawdust to be wiped off Marino's gloves. By the third round Rinty's work had become ragged. He steadied his aim and launched attack after attack, throwing punches from all angles, sometimes wildly, but his opponent's good defence dealt with much of what came at him. At close range, Marino was quick and powerful with body hooks, thus forcing Rinty to hold on—much too often for Deyong's liking. The referee lectured him twice for holding and Marino also complained about the waywardness of Rinty's head. The Hawaiian was cut in the fourth after another clash opened a gash over his left eye.

Lacking any training in the week prior to the fight, and with good Glaswegian fare consumed just hours beforehand, it was no surprise that Rinty sought to conserve energy. He would open up only sporadically. Behind on points, he was still strong and unfazed. In the fifth and sixth rounds his work was good and it was clear he still posed a threat. Despite the sawdust the conditions were far from ideal; the heavy rain was very uncomfortable for both boxers. Just trying to keep balance was a chore while getting a foot gripped to offload punches properly was hellishly difficult. It was inevitable that the pace of the fight was slowed down considerably.

In round eight, the Hawaiian walked into a storm of another kind. Rinty got a good combination together and Marino was down again from two hard shots. The crowd sensed a dramatic end in sight, then, within seconds, the fight turned on its head as Marino refused to buckle and hit back. He caught Rinty flush, a superb right hook, sending the Belfast boxer into the sodden sawdust for a count. Rinty very nearly did not make it back to his feet. Deyong's count reached eight before he managed to rise. Thankfully the sawdust bought him more time, just as it had for Salvador, as officials allowed his corner extra seconds to wipe his gloves clean. Once sorted, he in turn blazed back, landing a hefty right over the top of Marino's guard. The round was by far the most exciting of the contest and opened up the fight once again.

Rinty burst into action, as did his opponent. They tangled, traded, held on now and then, grappled a bit to the disapproval of the referee and suddenly Moss took centre stage. The Englishman accused Rinty of holding too often and, to the genuine amazement of the boxers and soaked spectators alike, he firmly disqualified Monaghan. Everybody booed.

Rinty was in shock, pierced by the irony that he had helped save the show. There would have been no top bill event except for him kindly agreeing to ignore his lack of immediate training and heavy dinner. And now, with less than two rounds to box, the referee felt compelled to disqualify him. Yet, he did not complain. He merely accepted Deyong's decision and, when interviewed afterwards, said that he had 'no excuses to make'. What he stressed was that fairness be shown to him when correspondents reported on the fight: 'It must be remembered that I was a last minute substitute.' With that he left for Belfast, confident in the knowledge that talks were under way to match the pair again, and this time he would be good and ready.

The fight at Hampden Park had given him a crucial insight into the skills of Salvador. Whatever about the injustice or otherwise of the referee's decision, the result was largely unimportant. The next one would mean everything. Discussions were quickly up and running. The British and American sanctioning bodies had a few things to iron out, deciding that a vacant world title fight between Monaghan and Marino was to take place before the end of the year, preferably some time in the autumn. Just weeks earlier, Marino had arrived in Scotland a virtual unknown. Now, he was a household name to Rinty, officials, promoters, and at least 25,000 boxing fans. This would help sell a world title fight to one of the country's leading promoters. In other words, the NBA's decision to nominate him ahead of Monaghan had, to a degree, been vindicated.

Salvador was interviewed following the disqualification and expressed confidence in his ability to mix it again with Belfast's world number one rated rival. He had given away six pounds to Monaghan in weight for the catch fight and did not foresee any problems at eight stone. Interviewed by the Press Association he made the following comment: 'I enjoyed the fight. Monaghan is very strong and I think I would do much better against him if he was eight stone.' In spite of the various factors involved, boxing commentators were in agreement. A rapid punching, tough and diminutive Marino had fought a fine fight. They agreed he was well in front on points when the contest was halted and had shown he was capable of taking a good punch.

However there was a bit of discomfort over the matter. The context of the Hampden bout was felt by some people to have undermined Jackie Paterson. Debate about Paterson's status and his right to the undisputed title continued in the background. Some correspondents moved to distance themselves while others argued that the dynamic Hawaiian could now claim to be the world's number one at flyweight. Rinty, however, remained *The Ring*'s champion.

Given Marino's record, suggesting he was now the best eight stone boxer on the planet was a bit of a stretch. The evidence was inconclusive, and would remain so until the NBA's top two squared up for a second time, this time on level terms. In the meantime, everyone was entitled to an opinion and Northern Ireland commentator John Caughey observed: 'Discount any adverse impression you may have had of his July display against Dado Marino in Glasgow, bearing in mind he took on that engagement as a last-minute substitute and had dropped training a week earlier. But even unfit, he gave Dado quite a lot of trouble, a surprise toss, and a badly damaged eye as proof that he was no pushover.'

On the other hand, Marino's manager had invested thousands of dollars in their European venture and was pretty fed up, what with the no-show from Paterson, the dreadful Glaswegian weather on the night of the fight, and the fact that this had not even been the fight he'd wanted and worked for. Nevertheless, he accepted the invitation to take his team of boxers to Belfast. Accordingly, the Hawaiian team stepped onto the docking wharf in the city the following Monday. Sam also stated his desire to have Marino and Monaghan fight for the title. In fairness to his challenger, he did not want it to take place in Belfast and demanded a neutral venue, saying he would be happy with anywhere in England after the Glasgow fiasco. Not surprisingly, there was massive interest in the Belfast trip and local newspapers ran amok with plenty of photos of the snappily dressed Marino. His manager indicated that they intended to stay in Europe until October. This was the time-frame then for the first Irish challenge for the world flyweight title.

Behind the scenes officials were frantically trying to figure out what to do. Once the sedatives wore off and reality kicked in, Jackie flatly refused to accept that he had lost his flyweight titles, claiming genuine ill health. In boxing circles, Paterson was considered fragile, his champion status severely devalued by July's events. For the next two weeks the BBB of C debated and considered what the best course of action would be. Jack Solomons, an astute Jewish businessman and high profile presenter of professional boxing shows, emerged as a key player in the discussions. He regularly presented events at the Harringay Arena in London, having first developed a foothold in the fight game by transforming an old church into the Devonshire Sporting Club.

Officials were in for a bumpy ride. Jackie was headstrong and refused to be quiet.

He considered taking the legal route and reckoned it to be worth a try. After all he had nothing left to lose by exploring every possibility.

Meanwhile, life went on as normal for everyone else. Bob Gardiner had more than one iron heating in the fire: in July 1947 he also had Bunty Doran primed for a shot at glory. Bob put a £5,000 offer on the table to Manuel Ortiz, who was in his second term as undisputed bantam champion. It was a live possibility. Ortiz's advisors were talking with him and negotiations were at a delicate stage. Earlier that year, Manuel had lost for the first time, as title holder, to Harold Dade, but then retrieved the title against Marino's fellow islander, David Kui Kong Young.

Bob needed to keep Doran in the headlines and keep him active. He would fight again on 25 July at the King's Hall. Marino and his sparring partner, Tsuneshi Maruo, were also being lined up to appear on the bill. The Ortiz-Doran talks continued and Bob was optimistic, hoping that Ortiz would defend in Belfast in early September.

For Bunty, the July show was uppermost in his mind. The challenge of French title contender Jean Jouas, who attended the Marino-Monaghan fight at Hampden, could possibly make the Ortiz deal, or shatter it. Also due in the city for the King's Hall event was top-rated Swansea lightweight Cliff Curvis and former Empire flyweight contender, Kid Tanner. Advertisements appeared in all the local newspapers promoting Marino's appearance on Gardiner's show. He was lined up to fight another Belfast man, Jackie Briers, a future Northern Ireland champion. Rinty would not be taking part.

Bunty did not disappoint, beating Jouas, but his luck was out nonetheless. The win was gained at a price, and punctured negotiations with Ortiz's people. Doran fought with terrific zeal and skill, but unknown to the crowd, he was in agony. It was discovered afterwards that he had fought for most of the ten rounds with a broken bone in his hand, and a damaged wrist. Elusive skills and an ability to pick off the Frenchman left ringside observers hailing the performance as one of the finest exhibitions of boxing ever witnessed at the King's Hall. However, Bunty's injuries put his title hopes beyond reach. The Americans cooled on Gardiner's offer and the £5,000 bid to tempt them to Belfast was rejected.

Ortiz did not return to the ring until December, when he accepted terms to go to Manila and defend against Tirso Del Rosario of the Philippines. Doran's manager, Tony Vairo, switched his attention then to the European title and lodged a £1,000 challenge on Doran's behalf with the British Board to push the European authorities to give Bunty a shot at it. Vairo sought to secure a fight with the winner of September's European title clash at Manchester's Belle Vue. This matched former world flyweight champion Peter Kane and one of Paterson's recent conquerors, Theo Medina of France. Doran fought again that same month, against Belgian champion Joe Cornelius. Incredibly, he was struck with more bad luck after he was severely cut during a clash of heads. His European title fight plan went out the window.

While Bunty's prospects suffered a couple of bad setbacks, Rinty spent a few weeks resting up with his family. He returned to light training with the rest of McAloran's stable of fighters at the Hardinge Street gym. Word was that a world title fight was in the works for some time in the next six to eight weeks, with speculation rife that London would be the venue. In early August the scrum-down to secure the contract got under way and, on the twenty-sixth of the month, it was formally announced that Harringay Arena in London would stage the showdown, with Jack Solomons named as the promoter. Just as Rinty would be the first flyweight from Ireland to contest the championship, Dado would be his region's first world title challenger. In the final week of the month Jack contacted Alex Dalzell, chairman of the Northern Ireland Area Council, to inform him that Marino and Monaghan were signed up for 20 October, a Monday night, and ready to go. Rinty was finally close to realising his ambition.

There was a fascinating subplot to Solomons' plan. He later confirmed that, if judged medically fit, Jackie Paterson would also be part of the October headline event, fighting at his regular bantam limit against Norman Lewis, a useful, experienced fistic tradesman who, in the autumn of 1946, had lost a points decision at Port Talbot to Bunty Doran. It was a perfect opportunity for Jackie to get his career back on track in what was to be a meaningful title fight as opposed to a six or eight-round card filler.

Jackie's British and Empire Championships would be defended as he had been asked to put the titles up following the May stoppage of Italian Cacciatori. He had not defended the Empire crown won against Jim Brady as of yet, and Lewis would also be his first domestic challenger since February's British title win over Manchester's Johnny King. He would prepare for Lewis with a warm-up bout in September against Stan Rowan. Away from the publicity and boxing ring Paterson was also preparing a case with his legal advisors to take before a judge in London.

Back in Rinty's home city, his supporters focused on obtaining tickets and travel permits, which were essential, to see their star man try to make history at Harringay. Bob Gardiner was appointed by Solomons as his agent in Northern Ireland to sell packages from 2 September. At the time Britain's government had a new post-war Super Austerity Plan in place, which dealt with food and petrol rationing. Use of motor vehicles was limited to emergencies and there was a ban on all foreign travel. Fans were grateful to hear that special passes would be made available for the return trip to London. Tickets for the bill were priced between £1'1s and £10'10s.

Boxing was not the only sport in the local news. Golfer Fred Daly had just made history, becoming the first man to take two main British professional titles in the same year. He beat Belgium's Flory Van Donck for the £2,500 *News of the World* Match-Play Championship at Royal Lytham and St Anne's. This secured selection to the international Ryder

Cup team to play the USA at Portland, Oregon, on 1 November—the first Ryder Cup match to be organised since 1937.

Rinty found himself caught up in another big news item when, on 11 September, a seafaring disaster occurred involving the *Reina del Pacifico*. The ship had a close association with Belfast, having been built at one of the city's yards for the Pacific Steam Navigation Company in 1931. She had served in the Second World War and gained notoriety after Britain's first Labour Prime Minister, Ramsay MacDonald, died onboard from heart failure on 9 November 1937. Following a refit the ship ran into severe problems on that September afternoon between the Firth of Clyde on Scotland's west coast and Belfast's Queen's Island. Four of its engines exploded northeast of Copeland Island. The ensuing inferno resulted in the deaths of twenty-eight people, including Leonard Septimus Brew, the Victoria Works Manager for Harland & Wolff. News reports mention Rinty as one of the volunteers who presented himself at the dock to ferry the injured and dead to the Mater Hospital. His training had to be temporarily abandoned.

Less than a month later Rinty was in the final stages of preparation for his world title challenge. An exhibition, six rounds at two minutes each, was arranged with one of his sparring partners, Eddie McCullough, at the RAF base at Aldergrove, which would be refereed by his manager. The airport base show was a relaxing event for both men. Rinty crooned some favourites for the crowd and Eddie, a talented musician tutored in the violin by the Hippodrome Theatre's first violinist Ned Morris, played a few numbers to finish off the night.

Sam Ichinose took a different approach, signing up former world flyweight champion, England's Peter Kane, to put Dado through his paces. Kane, who had won eighty-two of his eighty-seven contests, would, reckoned Sam, provide the perfect workout for his boy. Perhaps Sam should have lowered his sights. When the fight took place in Manchester Kane's expertise nearly turned the pre-Harringay assignment into a dreadful embarrassment for the Hawaiians. A P McWeeney, writing in Dublin's *Irish Independent*, considered the Filipino-American's prospects against Monaghan: 'I have not yet seen Marino boxing and therefore I must discuss his merits on hearsay. By all accounts he is very strong and very plucky but he took a rather severe hammering from Peter Kane and at the age of 31 there is a limit to the number of such beatings a man can take without lasting effect.'

Kane boxed strongly, pressurising the Hawaiian for ten rounds, and gaining the decision. It was a setback that boosted the Monaghan camp, along with reports from Marino's gym suggesting that Dado's training lacked substance. Ichinose wisely decided to put some distance between his team and the media by bringing his boxer to Paris for the final weeks of training.

Earl Granville, Governor of Northern Ireland, confirmed he would travel to London to attend the Marino-Monaghan world title fight. Permits had been finalised and tickets sourced for upwards of one thousand of Rinty's supporters. The demand was so great that five planes had been specially chartered. In an interview with the *Telegraph* Rinty asked his fans not to read anything into what happened in July at Hampden Park: 'Don't judge me by my performance against Dado in Glasgow. I came in as a last minute substitute that time and, while I offer no excuses, I can promise a far different show at Harringay.'

Meanwhile, on 8 September, Paterson and Rowan squared off at Harringay. Unfortunately, Jackie's return to action did not go as he had hoped. He suffered a spectacular defeat which left him facing renewed questions about his well-being and his career. Rowan obliterated Paterson's defence and resilience to hard punches in less than two rounds. The match, made at 8st 8lbs, saw Jackie floored five times in round two. A correspondent for London's *Daily Telegraph* who was at ringside suggested there was 'little sense' in Paterson's forthcoming British and Empire bantam bout with Lewis; 'the prospect of another vacant title is obvious'. In spite of this Jackie remained undaunted.

He made his move seven days before the Solomons promotion. On Monday, 13 October his efforts to bring his case before a judge in London started to bear fruit and he applied for an injunction. On 14 October the *Belfast Telegraph* detailed the previous day's events at the Chancery Division in London under the headlines, 'B.B.B.C. to Hear Paterson Again: Action Adjourned'. Mr Justice Romer listened to what Mr Milner Holland had to say on behalf of his client. The hook the case hung on was a meeting, some weeks before, with the administrative stewards of the British Board. Mr Holland sought on Paterson's behalf a re-hearing with the BBB of C's administrative stewards. They had previously met with Jackie and decided, following much deliberation, to strip him of his titles. Mr Charles Russell appeared for the British Boxing Board. It was claimed the boxer had attended this meeting without legal advice and without medical witnesses—the boxer claimed he had been unaware of the exact nature of the meeting. In the court report it was stated that Paterson 'had asked on more than one occasion to be allowed to appeal' the sanctions. It also highlighted how the decision to pursue the matter through legal channels was made urgent by a recent development—this related to the Marino-Monaghan fight being given the go-ahead.

After some discussion Mr Russell informed the court of the Board's willingness for another meeting with Paterson to discuss the possibility of granting the Scot another hearing. The court decided that a motion be approved; the case would be adjourned for four days. This was considered adequate to facilitate all parties to move the process forward. Mr Russell emphasised that he 'did not appreciate that the meeting before the administrative stewards was a meeting to arrive at a decision in connection with his various titles having regard to his alleged behaviour'.

Counsel for Paterson believed that the officials were on unsteady ground, thanks to the Board's 'construction of its own rules as to whether or not he had a right of appeal'. Therefore, the fairness of the decision could be challenged. Counsel, however, had 'no intention' of suggesting there was any fault attached to the Board as to why Paterson's case 'was not presented'.

The Board duly agreed to soften their position, and announced that they were 'prepared to give Paterson a full re-hearing by the administrative stewards'. That was all very well but the American NBA was having none of it. Their sanction for what was about to transpire at Harringay was air-tight—it was the flyweight World Championship, nothing more and nothing less. If they had to go solo on this, so be it. Since Elky Clark's unsuccessful showdown with Fidel La Barba in Los Angeles in 1927 they had sanctioned eleven world title bouts, including

Benny Lynch's first challenge in 1935, when the young Glasgow fighter, the last Scot before Paterson to win a title, dethroned England's Jackie Brown. Indeed, there had been just seven title fights since Clark challenged La Barba that had gained universal recognition; that is, complete agreement between the main American power-brokers and the British authorities. If the BBB of C relented and reinstated Paterson, the NBA was prepared to fly their own kite for the first time since the 1938 meeting in California between Little Dado and Small Montana.

None of this troubled Rinty Monaghan or Salvador Dado Marino. They would be too busy preparing for 20 October regardless of what the British Board decided. The NBA was backing them and that was all that mattered.

11

JACKIE'S INJUNCTION DEALT A TIME-SENSITIVE blow to Solomons' promotion. It prevented the meeting of Rinty Monaghan and Salvador Dado Marino at Harringay Arena being billed as the undisputed championship. While the National Boxing Association of America had processed its sanction of it, the British Board had been bound by the judge's decision to support Paterson's argument. This was somewhat disappointing, yet Monaghan and Marino would fight for a world title nevertheless; it would simply be classified as a 'disputed' title claim approved by the NBA. Actually, Paterson's lawsuit was of no real consequence. Disputed world title claims were common enough, especially throughout the history of the flyweight division. And anyway, as far as Rinty, his management, supporters, Marino, and Marino's manager, Sam Ichinose, the general public and media were concerned, the London clash was for a world title.

Rinty had every right to be proud of himself: on paper, in *The Ring*, he was the world's highest ranked flyweight, but it was not enough. It was merely a compliment at the end of the day and Rinty did not want to be an uncrowned king like the 1930s star Jimmy Warnock who had beaten the great Benny Lynch of Glasgow, the then world champion, but was prevented from having a crack at the ultimate prize by Lynch's management. Rinty was ready for the real thing; he wanted to wear the silks of a world champion. This would be the night to prove he was as good as most people thought he was. This would be the most important performance of his life; once inside the ropes, once the bell rang out, it was down to John Joseph Monaghan to do what he could to secure the NBA crown.

The NBA had put his nose out of joint somewhat by overlooking him prior to the summer's fiasco in Glasgow when Paterson failed to show. Sam Ichinose had worked smartly in New York to convince the American officials to back Marino as their top choice. Monaghan might have been *The Ring*'s world number one but the NBA placed him as their number two after Marino. Rinty had no shortage of motivation firing his challenge.

Similarly, the gains to be made at Harringay were enormous for the Maui native. No professional from the Hawaiian daisy chain of volcanic island plantations had attained the dizzy heights of winning a world title, at any weight. Dado was a tough little character and a wicked body-puncher, as Rinty knew from Hampden Park. He was also favoured by many who had watched him box in the torrential rain that July as a dangerous customer, and Belfast's contender was acutely aware of the risks involved in taking him on. Marino carried a fair dig in either hand; Rinty would have to mix caution, cleverness, and clout to deal with him.

Every nerve in Monaghan's body jangled as he made his way to the ring that Monday evening. The anticipation and excitement sent his adrenaline pumping through his limbs. It was the same, undoubtedly, for Salvador as Harringay's packed stadium greeted these diminutive bobbing and weaving gladiators. Those unable to attend were glued to their wirelesses, courtesy of The Light Programme on the BBC.

Of course, it could all go horribly wrong. The one punch rule always applied. It only took one great right or left hook or uppercut, one defensive mistake that exposed the jaw bone to devastating assault, and the dream would, in an instant, become a nightmare. Rinty had to box well, box carefully, spike Salvador's strong points, and bide his time. A first class counter-punching display was demanded.

This was only the second world title bout to be staged in England's capital since the outbreak of the Second World War. In May 1939,

The Births and Deaths Registration (Northern Ireland) Order 1976, Article 34

CERTIFIED COPY OF AN ENTRY OF BIRTH

Ref: 076755/01

BIRTHS Registered in the District of Belfast Urban No. 2 BK.128

No. (1)	Date and Place of Birth (2)	Name (if any) (3)	Sex (4)	Name and Surname and Dwelling-place of Father (5)	Name and Surname and Maiden Surname of Mother (6)	Rank or Profession of Father (7)	Signature, Qualification and Residence of Informant (8)	When Registered (9)	Signature of Registrar (10)	Baptismal Name if added after Registration of Birth and Date (11)
13	1918 Twenty First August 23 Lancaster St	John	M.	Thomas Monaghan 23 Lancaster St	Martha Monaghan formerly Wilson	Labourer	M Monaghan Mother 23 Lancaster St.	Twelfth September 1918	J Harkness asst Registrar.	/

CERTIFIED to be a true copy of an entry in a register in the custody of the Registrar General and given under the SEAL of the General Register Office, Belfast

this 27th day of November 2006

£11 70569

The Registrar General shall cause any certified copy of an entry given in the General Register Office to be stamped with the seal of the Office of which judicial notice shall be taken.

CAUTION: THERE ARE OFFENCES RELATING TO FALSIFYING OR ALTERING A CERTIFICATE AND USING OR POSSESSING A FALSE CERTIFICATE. ©CROWN COPYRIGHT

WARNING: A CERTIFICATE IS NOT EVIDENCE OF IDENTITY

Rinty's birth certificate which confirms his year of birth as being 1918.

Sammy Reynolds, Wolverhampton's noted bantamweight (front centre left) and Rinty before their September 1946 non-title bout at the King's Hall. Rinty won in the eighth after Reynolds was disqualified for a low blow. Also pictured are Bob Gardiner, 'Skin' Callahan and Frank McAloran.

Frances Monaghan, pictured in the late 1930s.

Rinty with his mother, Martha.

Rinty and his brother-in-law Harry McAuley (left) working up a sweat while Paddy Slavin looks on.

The Hardinge Street fighters. Rinty sits in the centre with Frank McAloran while others pictured include James McAloran, John Denvir, Peter Robinson, Eddie and George McCullough, Harry McAuley, Freddie Price, John Rocks, Jim Malligan, Hugh O'Neill and Jim Campbell.

Belfast promoter Bob Gardiner stands between Rinty and cousin Eddie 'Bunty' Doran ahead of their NI flyweight title scrap in November 1945.

Frank McAloran keeps an eye on his flyweight star as Rinty goes through his floor exercises. Sparring partner Eddie McCullough is directly behind the manager.

Rinty in caricature by the cartoonist, 'Jock'.

Hard graft at Hardinge Street as Rinty gets into condition for his next contest.

Hawaii's Salvador Dado Marino catches a straight left from Rinty during their Harringay encounter.

A signed photograph of 'Sad' Sam Ichinose (left) and Salvador Dado Marino (right) dedicated to Frank McAloran. The Hawaiians were posing before the planned Marino-Paterson bout at Hampden at which Paterson would not show, opening the door to a challenge from Rinty.

The programme cover for the Monaghan-Marino world flyweight title encounter in October 1947.

Harry Hanley, who first matched Rinty against Sam 'Boy' Ramsey and others in the glory days of Belfast's The Ring stadium.

Jackie Paterson, Scotland's undisputed flyweight champion.

Jackie relaxes at home with his wife Helen before his titles defence against Rinty in March 1948.

Frank McAloran and Bob Gardiner watch on as Rinty signs the contract for his undisputed world title fight in 1948 against Jackie Paterson in Belfast's Linen Hall Library.

Toe-to-toe action between Paterson and Monaghan in the first world title promotion ever to be staged at the King's Hall, Belfast.

Battered and broken, Paterson sits slumped against the bottom rope after his knockout by Rinty in the seventh round of their King's Hall bout.

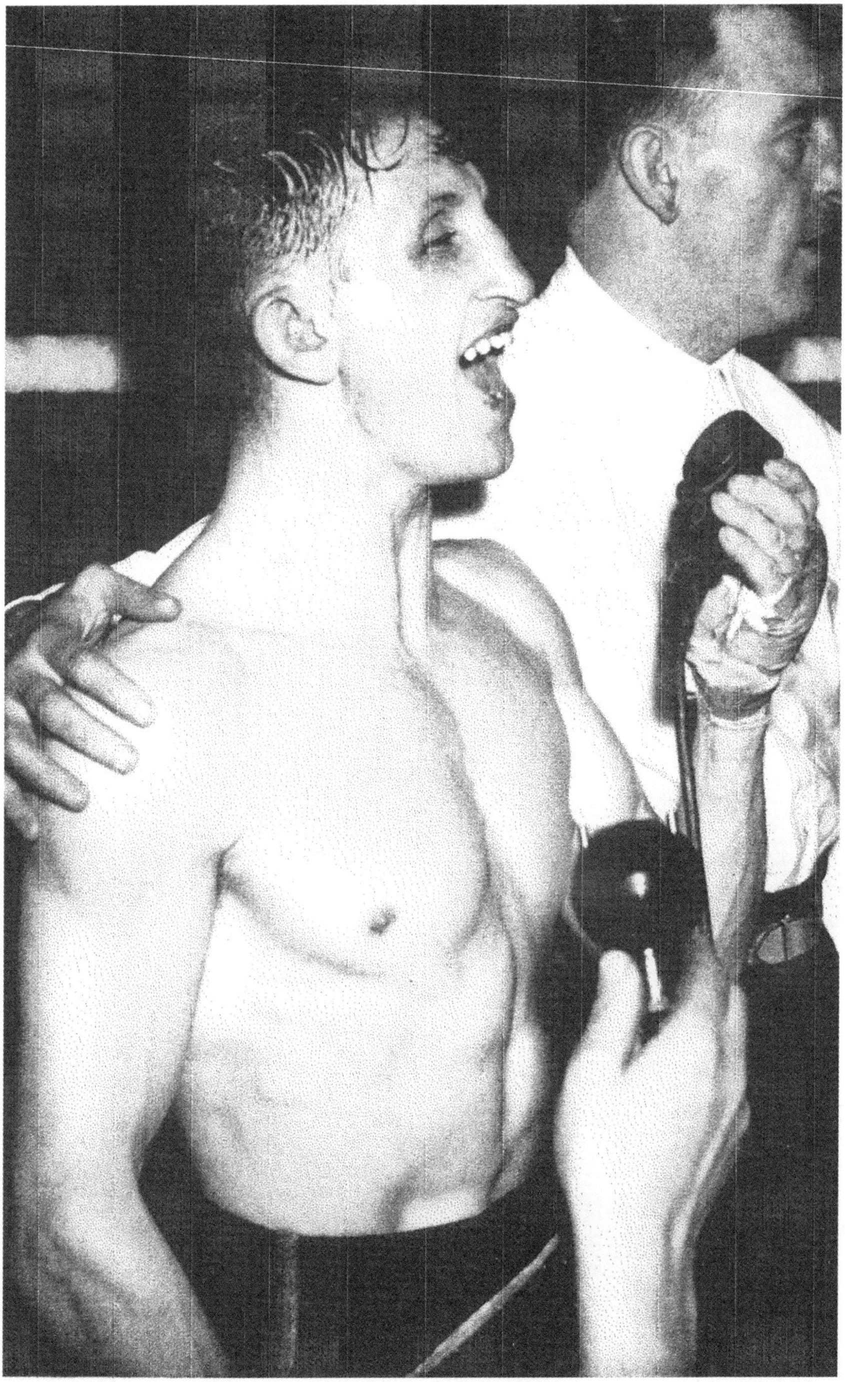

The singing boxer gives the crowd a tune at the end of a match.

Marino, Paterson and Monaghan pictured together in 1947.

The Main Attraction: a newspaper advertisement for cinemas screening the Monaghan-Paterson world title fight.

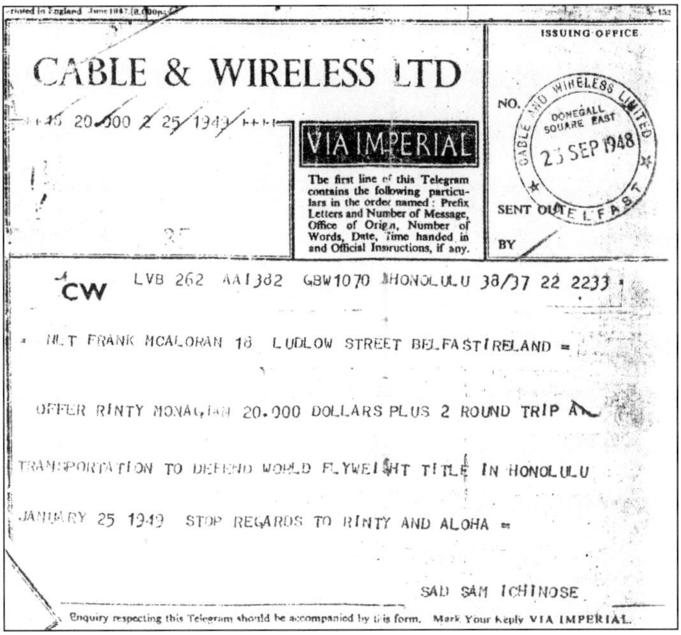
CABLE & WIRELESS LTD

VIA IMPERIAL

The first line of this Telegram contains the following particulars in the order named: Prefix Letters and Number of Message, Office of Origin, Number of Words, Date, Time handed in and Official Instructions, if any.

ISSUING OFFICE

NO.

CABLE AND WIRELESS LIMITED DONEGALL SQUARE EAST 23 SEP 1948 BELFAST

SENT OUT

BY

CW LVB 262 AA1382 GBW1070 HONOLULU 38/37 22 2233

NLT FRANK MCALORAN 18 LUDLOW STREET BELFASTIRELAND =

OFFER RINTY MONAGHAN 20.000 DOLLARS PLUS 2 ROUND TRIP AIR

TRANSPORTATION TO DEFEND WORLD FLYWEIGHT TITLE IN HONOLULU

JANUARY 25 1949 STOP REGARDS TO RINTY AND ALOHA =

SAD SAM ICHINOSE

Enquiry respecting this Telegram should be accompanied by this form. Mark Your Reply VIA IMPERIAL.

Sam Ichinose's offer by telegram to pay Rinty $20,000 to defend his world flyweight title in Honolulu.

Rinty and his youngest daughter Collette.

Rinty's son Sean checks if his father's gloves fit.

Patsy Monaghan poses with his brother's Ring *belt outside the King's Hall, Belfast on the day that the Ulster Historical Society unveiled a plaque in Rinty's honour.*

The poster advertising what would be the final fight of Rinty's career.

'Homicide Hank', America's world welterweight champion, Henry Armstrong, fought the first English challenger at this level, since Ted 'Kid' Lewis lost to Jack Britton in 1921: future European champion, Ernie Roderick. Armstrong retained his title on points after fifteen rounds. During the 1940s, London had hosted just one world championship promotion, for British light-heavyweight stars, Freddie Mills and Len Harvey, Harvey having lost to America's John Henry Lewis in 1936 for the undisputed title. This was for a version of it, matched at 175lbs. Thanks to tight restrictions on travel, world title bouts were almost exclusively located within the United States. They were generally held at New York venues, with occasional contests staged in Los Angeles, Oakland and San Francisco on the west coast, and Detroit and Cleveland. The Mills and Harvey fight was the only exception, with Mills winning inside two rounds.

For an NBA disputed title match, Monaghan's clash with Marino would be added to a varied list of Association-approved contests reaching back over the past twenty or so years. The Greek Anton Christoforidis had beaten American Melio Bettina for their light-heavy belt at Cleveland in 1941, marking the NBA's only single sanction world title event in this division for eight years. Tony Zale, Al Hostak, Solly Kreiger, Freddie Steele and 'Gorilla' Jones had all won NBA promotions in a fractured middleweight scene since the late 1920s. Welterweight had not produced anyone other than an undisputed champion for eighteen years. The NBA had not had to sanction a 'go-it-alone' title fight at light-welter since 1926-1927.

Lightweight was a different kettle of simmering squabbles between rival governing bodies. Since Lou Ambers' win over Armstrong in 1939 the NBA had supported disputed title successes by Sammy Angott, Mexico's Juan Zurita, and Ike Williams. However, this division had settled its differences in August 1947 with Williams' undisputed title victory over the New York commission's nominated champion, Bob Montgomery.

It was a similarly fractured picture at feather. From 1932 to 1946, the NBA and New York officials had followed their own agenda. Sixteen different champions were declared during these years, with the

Californian commission also sanctioning a couple of title claims. The NBA's roll-call of claimants involved Tommy Paul, Freddie Miller, Petey Sarron, Leo Rodak, Petey Scalzo, Richie Lemos, Jackie Wilson, Canada's Jackie Callura, and Phil Terranova. Bantam had served up a few NBA events since the mid-1930s with Puerto Rico's Sixto Escobar and Lou Salica winning and defending titles between 1934 and 1941.

The last six years had been dominated by unification bouts and one boxer: Manuel Ortiz. Rinty's 112lbs division resembled a damaged pane of glass, fine fractures and cracks covering its blood lineage all the way back to 1927, as only five undisputed contests had taken place out of thirty-nine organised. The Monaghan-Marino bill would be the NBA's twenty-second solo promotion in the past twenty years.

It had been a pretty active year so far for world championship boxing, the busiest on record since 1944, when seven title bouts took place with Beau Jack, Sal Bartolo, Willie Pep and Manuel Ortiz all headlining events. Over the past two years four promotions had earned the sport some media coverage. In the first eight months of 1947 there had been five major battles fought, the most sensational of them being Rocky Graziano's stunning sixth-round kayo of champion Tony Zale for the undisputed middleweight title in Chicago, and Harold Dade's shock sixth-round stoppage of Manuel Ortiz at bantam.

Harringay held Ireland's hopes of an historic victory in its hands. The official title of this famous venue, situated at Green Lanes, near to the Tottenham district and Arsenal Football Stadium, was the Harringay Boxing and Ice Skating Arena. Built on the site of a nineteenth-century pottery and kiln, it had been opened in 1936 and had played host to the first boxing match to be televised to a public audience in England, in February 1939, when blacksmith Eric Boon fought Arthur Danahar for the British lightweight title.

As the bright lights shone on the glistening perspiration of two protagonists, could Rinty now make amends for his disqualification at Hampden in July at catchweight? Could he prove that, trimmed to eight stone and fighting fit, he had the strength, skill and class to deny the Hawaiian the coup Sad Sam wanted to finish his European tour with?

Teddy Waltham, a leading international referee from St Albans, presented final instructions to the two men. After the strains of 'It's a Great Night for the Irish' subsided around the crammed arena, and the tumultuous applause diminished, Salvador walked across the ring and placed a traditional Hawaiian garland of orange and white flowers around Rinty's neck.

And then the fight began.

The two darted and danced about the canvas, working every inch, slipping each others' punches, and continued thus, playing it safe. This was not the epic battle that Solomons had hoped for. The frustrated crowd was soon on Rinty and Dado's backs with slow claps and jeers, demanding thrills and spills. 'Experts' called out rapid instructions from the safety of their seats: hit him with this, hit him with that. The first round ended devoid of excitement or incident with hardly a worthwhile punch landed.

The next round jazzed things up a bit. Rinty got his fans on their feet as he threatened to finish it, with a big right hook catching Marino sweet. A solid straight left brought Marino into range and the right sent him lurching across the ring. Rinty followed in, trying to catch him again; nevertheless, Marino managed to see out the round despite appearing to be in trouble. This was more like it.

Unfortunately for the fans, it did not improve much in the third round. Just like the first, hardly a decent punch was delivered. The fourth was not a great deal better. By now, even the referee looked impatient with the proceedings. After six minutes of ducking and diving, with little close contact duelling, Waltham snapped and called both boys in for a chat. At the start of the fifth he made it clear that he wanted to see more action. This was a world title fight after all, not a slow dance at a village hall. He told them to get down to business.

Marino was quickest to react, ripping into Ireland's hopeful and trying to press forward at every opportunity. He began to take some risks, managing to offload a few clusters of punches while he was at it. It was the first time in the match that Rinty had been under any concerted pressure. His counter-punching instincts kicked in. Keeping his head constantly in motion, he used quick feet to evade the rushes and waited for a chance to clip Marino's confidence.

This was the style of fighting that Rinty was used to. He kept a sharp eye and coiled glove on what his opponent was trying to do—waiting for Marino to over-stretch himself, so that he could make a swift and potentially dangerous response. Unfortunately, the fans remained far from happy. At the end of the fifth round there were more slow hand claps, more catcalls, and the arena now rocked to the thud of thousands of feet stamping the floor demanding to see more of a fight. Waltham decided to have another word and made his way to both corners to repeat his instructions to tighten the pace.

Once more his rebukes aroused a bit of aggression. The fists flew from both boxers now and the men showed determination to get inside and work at close quarters, hooking to body and head. The skirmishes were lively and the crowd reacted positively to them. All in all, Rinty seemed the stronger man. His work rattled Marino, who replied well.

In the seventh round Belfast's hope stepped up the tempo of his efforts. It was a good round and an important one for Rinty as the fight was pretty close and he needed to edge a few sessions going into the last third of the contest. He was much more aggressive and sank hurtful shots into Marino's body with a greater intensity and accuracy. As his confidence grew, his caution lessened. It was time to take a few gambles. Rinty stayed with the pace in the next round. He stormed forward at every chance, and was a bit wild with his hooking, resulting in Marino complaining to the referee that some of his punches strayed low.

Rounds nine and ten were blighted by lots of mauling, clinches and holding, much like July's dust-up in the Scottish rain. Back then, too many incidents of holding proved costly for Rinty when Moss Deyong disqualified him. Now Waltham was warning him about holding too, so he had to be extra careful. There was too much at stake for it all to be thrown away by irritating the referee. The mid-section of the fight had generally panned out well for the Irish challenger. He reeled off a few good scoring rounds which could prove crucial if the fight lasted the distance.

The eleventh round almost went disastrously wrong for Monaghan. His supporters were stunned to see him suddenly sent sprawling to the canvas. For a few fleeting seconds the blurred memory of Jackie

Paterson's flooring him at The Oval in 1938—the only time in his life he had been sparked out in a professional fight—raised itself. Rinty was in trouble. Salvador had unleashed a terrific right cross, connecting flush with his rival's nose and drawing blood. Waltham stood over him issuing a count. Marino prayed he had hit his rival hard enough to turn the fight and send him on his way to becoming the first Hawaiian to win a world title. He hadn't, although Waltham reached seven before Rinty got to his knees. The Belfast man had been severely warned—he could not afford to give Marino another opportunity like that.

Meanwhile, Marino began to feel a lot more confident. He had not boxed all that impressively up to this point but now he was prompted to push forward after knocking Rinty to the ground. He wanted to see what Rinty had left and what the punch had taken out of him. Rinty had seemed the stronger fighter over the previous rounds; his punches were harder and cleaner, and he looked to be ahead on points. Nevertheless, his visit to the canvas had invited Marino back into it. Rinty needed to react positively and not get caught again before the bell. He survived the round and listened to what his corner had to say. Taking the sting out of his opponent's attacks was vital in the next session. Keep your distance, stay alert, use the jab, and keep on the move and as difficult a target as possible.

Three minutes of frustration followed.

It was not pretty to watch, but survival tactics and the prize of the NBA's title required Rinty to spoil and stifle, and surely his worried supporters would understand the necessity of it. Three rounds to go. The spectators continued to voice their displeasure with more slow hand claps and catcalls. A draw was a possibility. It was a hard fight to score and no NBA flyweight bout had finished deadlocked since the 1935 meeting in Manchester of England's Jackie Brown and Valentin Angelmann of France.

In the fourteenth, Rinty fully recovered and decided to press for home, showing much more fire and snap to his efforts. Marino looked to be flagging. He had been kept at arm's length since the knockdown, unable to figure out a way to get at Rinty, who began to move forward and let his punches go. The initiative was finally being seized by Monaghan and his supporters, sensing his fresh ambition, jumped to their feet to scream him on. It was a good round but there was still room for improvement.

The boxers stood facing one another for the fifteenth and final round. A grandstand finale was called for from both boys: leave caution in the spit bucket, set eyes on the prize, and let the fists fly with an abandon barely glimpsed during the previous fourteen sessions. This was it.

They did not disappoint. In fact they were both superb. Easily the best round of the entire fight, they hammered in their hooks, tried for haymakers as wild crosses whizzed past jaws and temples. Tired bodies were hurt with shots into the rib cages. However, neither man could summon up that decisive punch—the kayo.

The Hawaiian appeared to come close to it, or so it seemed, as Rinty went down again, but the referee called it a slip and there was no count. That may have been the most significant moment of the fight. Rinty jumped up and rushed back in at Salvador, swinging for all he was worth, or had left to give. This was the last stand. With his fans going crazy he closed out his challenge with a tremendous final minute. He needed it. He had to impress for the sixty seconds and he did, dominating and forcing Marino backwards. In that one minute Rinty perhaps produced the most important passage of boxing skill and determination of his career.

The bell sounded and the weary men hugged.

The decision was now in the hands of Teddy Waltham. A restless ring of fighters, managers and seconds waited anxiously for the result. Waltham made his decision, prompting an estimated twelve thousand fans to throw their hats into the London night air—Rinty Monaghan was declared the winner and the new NBA Flyweight Champion of the World.

There was only one way he knew how to celebrate and that was with a few songs: on the best night of his life there was no way Rinty was leaving the Harringay ring without singing for the fans. A microphone was handed to him and, as he stood there with the Hawaiian garland of orange flowers that Marino had presented to him hanging around his neck, the old anthems were given a fabulous airing: 'When Irish Eyes Are Smiling', followed by a few verses of 'Hello Patrick Fagan'. The fans drifted off delighted, celebrating this magic Monday. The fight may not have been a classic but no matter; their man was the world champion.

Not everyone was ecstatic, however, with the result. Glasgow's former flyweight boxing star of the 1920s, Elky Clark, had watched the match ringside and did not think much of it, which was natural, given the few thrills involved. He also disagreed with Waltham's math: Marino had produced one terrific knockdown. Elky remarked to a press agency, 'It was one of the poorest fights ever seen at Harringay. I thought Marino's aggressiveness at least had earned him the honour. The contest was so poor that any moment it was expected the referee would step in and declare it no contest. Twice the boys were warned to show more action but it had little effect on them. It was a cat versus mouse affair, Marino taking the part of the cat and trying to corner the elusive back-pedalling Belfast boy.'

The *Telegraph* saw things a little differently, stating: 'As a world championship fight, it must be confessed that the duel proved definitely disappointing, but this was due to the crafty tactics adopted by the rivals, who clearly sought to trap each other into a false move that might leave an opening for a knock-out punch. In this battle of wits Monaghan ultimately emerged triumphant. When from the seventh round he elected to stop fighting on the retreat and go forward as the attack leader there was no disputing the fact that he stamped supremacy over the Hawaiian.'

Rinty's wife Frances did not travel to London, preferring to stay at home with family and friends. She treated the world title fight like any other from the days before they were married, when she attended the occasional contest at Chapel Fields. Too nervous to follow the match, she preferred to keep the wireless off and take the kids for a stroll about the docks until it was over. The *Irish News* reporters sent to doorstep the Monaghan home were told she 'was naturally delighted' when she heard the result.

The night sky glowed in Belfast's dockland from bonfires hastily put together and torched. All around Rinty's home the streets echoed with the songs of success, as thousands of local fans converged on Sailortown. His name was toasted from York Street, Frederick Street, Lancaster Street, Thomas Street, and Little Italy to the New Lodge and back again.

On the other hand, Monaghan's win did not exactly leave Jack Solomons glowing with satisfaction. The promoter was more than a little cheesed off with what had been, overall, an uninspiring spectacle. When he was approached by London's *Evening Standard* writer George Whiting to comment about the possibility of promoting a possible Monaghan versus Paterson unification fight, he was in no mood to consider it.

'They can leave me out of any such negotiations,' he said. 'Monday night's affair was a bitter disappointment to everybody. I certainly would not tempt fortune by putting Monaghan in with Paterson. The curious part of it all is that youngsters like Tsuneshi Maruo, Stan Rowan, Mark Hart and Randolph Turpin, whose combined purse was only a few hundred pounds, gave the show a splendid start but the big money merchants were not so good.'

Two days after the fight Rinty revealed that he had actually fought the best part of nine rounds with a damaged right hand, which went some way to explain his lack of killer instinct. He arrived at a post-fight reception held in his honour by Major General W Brooke Purdon, on London's Regent Street, with his right hand heavily bandaged. In an interview for the *Belfast Telegraph*'s 'Timekeeper' column, he explained how Marino ducked to avoid taking a hook which was aimed full at his jaw, meaning that Rinty caught the Hawaiian's head awkwardly, leaving his hand staved.

'This injury proved most painful and gave me a lot of trouble during the remainder of the contest and I had to be careful as I didn't know then whether or not I had broken a bone. The tournament doctor told me later that I had merely damaged a sinew. He advised me, however, to have the hand x-rayed and this I plan to do. I'm still hoping there is nothing seriously wrong.'

Marino, however, had no such excuse and, while Sad Sam was naturally upset with Waltham's scoring, rumours spread that he blamed his boxer for repeatedly ignoring instructions from his corner.

The Hawaiians were already planning to launch another world title bid. It did not seem very likely, what with Paterson's situation still to be resolved, but Sad Sam was not deterred. He was determined on a rematch and promptly secured the services of a representative in Manchester, George Dingley, to negotiate for him, forwarding his wishes for a $10,000-a-side, winner takes all, rematch.

Meanwhile the victor and his team arrived home at 8am on the Thursday after Harringay. A massive welcome had been prepared, despite the early hour, with friends and well-wishers crowding the quayside, all waiting to shake the hand of the man who had put Belfast boxing on the map. Little Corporation Street was a carnival scene, with bunting and flags. Some walls were hastily garnished in graffiti hailing the champion, who was described as 'the mighty atom'. A weary but delighted Rinty walked home accompanied by the well-wishers; he was looking forward to a well-earned rest.

As he told the *Telegraph*, 'The thing I need most just now is an opportunity to enjoy a long undisturbed sleep because I have had practically no such rest since ten past ten o'clock on Monday night last.'

A family holiday was next on his agenda. Then it would be time to think about Jackie Paterson.

12

CHAMPIONSHIP TITLE RULES ARE BOUND BY an eight stone in weight maximum for a flyweight boxer. Therefore, the last week in the gym—the sparring, skipping and conditioning—is critical, while a good diet is essential to develop strength and endurance. Only a combination of exercise and diet ensures that the official limit is met, either just on the button or a few ounces inside the eight. Rinty's five-feet, four-inch frame made him ideally suited to the division, though much of his boxing outside of title bouts was conducted at maybe two to four pounds above this. This eight stone limit had been around for twenty years by the time he took up professional prizefighting.

The obstacles placed in his way during his climb to the absolute summit of flyweight boxing were typical of the politics and power struggles that shaped the first five decades of this division; the flyweight title fight scene was anything but dull. Basically, there were various commissions which claimed to sanction 'world title fights' in their own countries. In England there was the extremely powerful National Sporting Club, which became the British Boxing Board of Control. Then, there was the forerunner to the European Boxing Union, the International Boxing Union in Europe, or IBU. There were two American rivals, New York and the NBA. Of course, compared to modern professional boxing, with the splits that occurred throughout the 1960s and 1970s, this is all very much small beer.

The flyweight division was a relative late starter, only formed and approved at the turn of the twentieth century after boxing became better regulated and moved on from Broughton's Rules (which were introduced in 1743 for bare-knuckle contests). The weight was devised for the safety of smaller boxers who required a fairer playing field. As the fight trade advanced from bared fists to implementing the use of boxing gloves, as standard under rules devised for the Marquis of Queensberry, life for the diminutive battlers and brawlers was constantly fraught with potential fatal injury; no surprise when you consider how men weighing no more than seven stone were regularly matched against rivals who were a couple of stone heavier—that is, bantamweight or featherweight in stature—which was a huge difference in size, strength and poundage. The odds were nearly always stacked against the smaller man. The National Sporting Club of London finally challenged this long-standing irregularity in 1911 when it agreed to introduce a new division, the high end of the weight limit for which was to be no more than eight stone, or 112lbs, for title bouts.

The NSC had sought to establish an eight stone weight for a couple of years. English boxing authorities set their limit at 108lbs (seven stone and ten grams) around 1910, with various American commissions recognising the weight class over the next decade or so through to the middle of the 1920s. The new weight category ended the dubious practice of lighter men beefing themselves up by whatever means possible to fight those at heavier weights, as well as preventing bantamweight characters using the likes of Turkish baths to boil down in an effort to take advantage over a genuine flyweight. The smaller man was provided with safeguards in that at least his opponent would be approximately the same in size and weight, therefore reducing the greatest hazard of all, the risk to his actual life from head trauma sustained in a boxing contest. Previously, any boxer weighing up to 188lbs could compete as a so-called flyweight, and for the smaller man this carried significant risk, sometimes resulting in death. Perhaps the most famous loss of life recorded in a 'flyweight' fight was the death of twenty-one-year-old Mike Riley in 1900. Riley died after being knocked out in the ninth round of an English title bout by Matt Precious.

An earlier tragedy was one of the catalysts for a change to the safety features of the basic boxing ring. In late 1897 Walter Croot and Jimmy Barry met in London for the world bantamweight title fight but, in the final round, the twentieth, Barry caught Croot with a punch to the jaw and Walter fell, hitting his head forcibly on the hard floor space of the ring. Croot never recovered and died a few days after the incident. A trial followed in which the American boxer Barry and officials of the National Sporting Club were charged with manslaughter. The trial concluded with acquittals. Croot's death, however, was not in vain as his misfortune promoted officials to consider ways and means of improving the flooring of the boxing ring. Their deliberations resulted in the idea of introducing a padded area.

Once the agreement on the limit for a flyweight championship contest had been reached the task was now to deliver a champion at the weight. To this end, the NSC set about organising an inaugural World Championship contest. Finding a suitable British boxer was a priority. For the moment they had the support of Europe; establishing American support for the new division was another matter. In 1913 British and European authorities thrashed out consent for Sid Smith, the British champion, and, historically, the original flyweight Lonsdale Belt claimant, to meet Frenchman Eugene Criqui, who was recognised as champion of Europe. Smith was on a boxing tour of America when he heard that he would be meeting Criqui in Paris on 11 April 1913. The bout lasted twenty rounds of unspecified time with Smith awarded the decision on points; Criqui's defeat, unfortunately, also cost him the European title.

Criqui was a remarkable character. During the Great War he served in the French Army when a sniper's bullet shattered part of his jaw, requiring him to have silver plates and wire inserted to hold the bone together. Amazingly, he resumed a boxing career after the war, first wining the French featherweight title in 1921 before going on to win European honours the following year. Then, in 1923, he savoured the glory of winning the world title at New York's Polo Grounds, thus ending the eleven-year reign of world champion Johnny Kilbane with a sixth round kayo.

Smith did not hold on to the new crown for long. He lost the title in his next, and last, contest in an advertised world championship bout against fellow Englishman, Bill Ladbury. The landmark title bout between Smith and Criqui was refused a universal seal of approval as the USA's governing commissions would not accept the English-French alliance. Just as Rinty's original win in 1947 was swathed in dispute, so too was that of the eight stone pioneers.

There were multiple claimants to the flyweight world title in the US and in Europe, with boxers jockeying to secure recognition or acceptance as undisputed champion. At the time of the First World War, Jimmy Wilde, a stylish little fighter from Wales, emerged from the pit and booth-boxing tournaments of the coalmining communities. He revealed a fierce capacity for nailing opponents with 'sleep-tonic' shots with either hand. His power, at the weight, was likened to being thumped with hammers. On St Valentine's Day in 1916 the NSC and European officials matched Wilde with Joe Symonds for what was described as an inaugural undisputed world title bout. Wilde had claimed European success for the IBU title in 1914 against Eugene Husson. The Symonds fight is generally noted as the original 'undisputed' claim to the World Flyweight Championship, though some historians of Welsh boxing dispute this, citing another Welsh flyweight, Percy Jones, who—like Wilde—was trained by 'Peerless' Jim Driscoll, as having beat the exceptional Wilde to the punch on this issue. The argument concerned the NSC and European recognition of Sid Smith as world champion. Smith lost to Ladbury, who, in turn, lost to Jones. The latter was for a vacant British title but, allegedly, the contest was also promoted as a world title fight, a Lonsdale Belt, as well as for Ladbury's European title. Jones won on points. However, in listings published since, over many decades, Wilde-Symonds is noted as the pioneering contest and this appears to have attracted broad acceptance.

The case for Jones, a miner's son born on Boxing Day in 1892 and raised in Porth, continues to this day, however, and he is viewed in some quarters as the first Welshman to become a flyweight world champion. It is claimed he defended this with a win over Eugene Criqui of France. The Great War brought about the end of Jones's boxing career. As a sergeant serving with the Royal Welsh Fusiliers, he was stationed in France, where he was badly wounded, losing one of his legs after more then twenty operations. He was also a victim of poisonous gas. Jones was to die in 1922, on the eve of his thirtieth birthday, from trench fever.

Jones and Wilde had fought many of the same opponents, with Jones winning thirty-nine out of forty-one contests before going to London to challenge Ladbury. The IBU noted in its flyweight listing that, after Smith and Ladbury, Jones was their recognised claimant to the world title. This is all part of the convoluted debate on disputed, unofficial and undisputed claims as to who was champion and when. Given that professional boxing in New York State had its own title recognition problems until the introduction of the Walker Law in 1920, European claims to world titles, arguably, did not have the full support of the USA's multitude of boxing commissions. The Walker Law established the 112lbs weight class in New York State. The NBA and NY State Athletic Commission recognised the 112lbs flyweight championship limit in 1927.

Meanwhile, as far as the Americans were concerned, the terms 'undisputed' or 'world champion' were inappropriate until the best of British and European boxing was matched with a US nomination. Therefore, the status of 'undisputed world champion' was nothing more than a fantastic claim, bereft of reality. Fortunately, Jimmy Wilde's fifth title defence changed the landscape. Wilde, who often scaled well below the limit, in the region of 103lbs, was a phenomenal fighter with a terrific punch. Despite his frail appearance, the former pit boy, nicknamed 'The Ghost with a Hammer in His Hand', raised the bar of flyweight boxing in 1916 when he was matched against 'Young' Zulu Kid. The Kid, of Italian extraction, grew up in the United States and, more importantly, was the American nomination. The title bout would be recognised, it was claimed, for the undisputed bragging rights, and was to be staged at the National Sporting Club in London's Covent Garden.

With American approval now secured this was the biggest fight in the division's formative years. Wilde's wizardry and power battered 'Young' Zulu to an eleventh round stoppage. After three years the new division finally had its first universal stamp of approval for a champion. Wilde and the Zulu Kid had put flyweight boxing, the lightest division available, on the global map. While debate continued regarding Smith, Ladbury and Jones, it was this triumph—on 18 December 1916—that, historically, has been viewed as the most significant.

Wilde's success was sweet and rather short. In a few years he was to become immersed in a private battle against the scales. The eight stone limit proved beyond him and, for the next five years, he campaigned at bantam. It was not until 1923 that he set himself the challenge to trim down to the flyweight limit again for a title defence or, arguably, a vacant flyweight world title in New York, where he was matched against Filipino American star, Pancho Villa. The 'Mighty Atom' had very little left after draining himself to make eight stone. The old dynamite punches were gone. He fought defiantly, with great courage, but had no answer to the brilliance of Villa and suffered a brutal defeat in seven rounds. Villa was hugely popular and came to New Yorkers' attention when his athleticism and speed outclassed American title holder Johnny Buff at Ebbetts Field in Brooklyn. Unfortunately, his popularity did not extend to the National Boxing Association, thanks to his losing the American title to Italian-American star Frankie Genaro (real surname DiGennaro), who had turned pro after winning flyweight gold at the 1920 Antwerp Olympic Games. Genaro also had a big fan-base but promoters opted to match Villa with one of the biggest names in British and European boxing at that time. The NBA was unimpressed, dividing opinion regarding who was the superior flyweight, Villa or Genaro.

The latter had beaten Pancho at Ebbetts Field in 1922 and again at Madison Square Garden. Genaro was too clever for his opponent, too sharp and elusive. Perhaps the risk of losing the claim on the world title, gained after stopping Wilde, explained why Villa side-stepped Genaro and never fought him at world title level. Genaro would have to wait five years to get his chance to win the NBA title.

Sadly, two years after hammering Wilde, Villa was dead. Aged only twenty-three years, his sudden death occurred just two weeks after a non-title fight, on 4 July 1925, against young Irish prospect and future world welterweight kingpin, Jimmy McLarnin, from Hillsborough in

County Down. Pancho had spent the whole fight in agony, thanks to a mouthful of rotten teeth, and witnesses reported him fighting with just one hand as he constantly held one fist in front of his swollen jaw to protect it from his rival's fists. He had three teeth removed in the days following the fight but defied his dentist's instructions to stay in bed, preferring to hang out with his friends. The infection spread to his throat and he collapsed into a coma after being rushed to hospital.

McLarnin developed from a bantam apprentice to full-blown welterweight contender within eight years. In 1933, he knocked out Italy's 'Young' Corbett III, a Californian-based southpaw, born Rafelle Capabianca Giordano in Naples, to win the world title at the bigger weight in Los Angeles. A physical fitness trainer for the state's Highway Patrol, Rafelle gained Californian recognition in 1938 as a middleweight world champion after defeating Fred Apostoli in San Francisco. McLarnin went on to lose two world welterweight title fights and reclaim the championship in the two years following victory over Corbett via a famous trilogy of fifteen-round battles with American, Barney Ross.

So it was that Rinty's career emulated the flyweight successes of Villa and Wilde in October 1947, when the division's history of disputed world champions' claims was re-ignited. He too would settle all arguments and, for a short time, would be the one to unify the division just as the Wilde-Zulu Kid fight had done, uniting British, European and American boxing aficionados.

13

SALVADOR'S SKULL LEFT A LEGACY: RINTY'S win at Harringay Arena had been secured at a bone-breaking price. His victory celebrations were tempered by the painful pangs shooting up his right arm from the hand he'd damaged early in the fight. Behind the smiles and singing he worried about how serious the injury was.

When he arrived home to Belfast, Little Corporation Street was a scene of sheer jubilation. Hundreds of people crammed into his street, all wanting to personally congratulate him. Number 32 was a hive of happiness and boiling kettles as Frances, who was seven months pregnant with their third child, and neighbours kept trays of tea flowing all day.

Rinty's eldest daughter, Martha, has vivid memories of the day her daddy made a hero's return from London.

'I was eight years old when he won the title and I remember all these people celebrating at our house. The street was filled with people as far as you could see. After daddy made it to the house he decided to treat everyone to a few songs but because of the crowd he went up the stairs and, with some help from a few people, actually took out the windows so that he could sing to the crowd.'

The baby of the family, Rosetta, had turned five that April. The sight of hundreds of people celebrating her father's great success was an unforgettable one.

'What sticks in my mind were the windows of our house being taken out and daddy getting a microphone organised at one of the windows where he started singing to the crowd. I remember the crowds of people. There were so many people in the street. Daddy sang away to them. He was always singing. The night he won the title all these bonfires were lit in the street by crowds celebrating.'

Over the next few days Rinty was a busy man. He was inundated with people to see, events to attend, and frequent visitors to the house. He also made an appointment to see a specialist about his hand, which remained badly swollen. Initially, on inspection, at ringside by James, his trainer, it was suspected that the problem was no more than bruised tendons and ligaments. However, Rinty felt that the problem ran deeper than that and, on the morning of 28 October, he attended the Mater Hospital to have the damage scanned. The x-ray plate identified that he had boxed his way to world title glory with a broken hand. There was not a complete, clean fracture involved, but rather part of a bone had chipped off as the awkwardly angled right hook caught Marino's head. A second scan was scheduled for two days later to allow for closer examination of the tendons and ligaments once swelling had reduced.

As news of the extent of the injury became public, the business of managing his interests continued oblivious to the fact the new world champion would be sidelined for possibly two months, maybe longer, depending on how quickly the hand healed. Rinty was highly in demand. His stock had soared and manager Frank McAloran was not short of options and invitations. There was also the ongoing saga involving Jackie Paterson.

Jackie had been the *The Ring*'s number one from 1940 through to 1943, the year he beat England's Peter Kane in front of 48,500 spectators, making him the first southpaw to claim a world title in the eight stone division. However, during 1944 and 1945, *The Ring* decided not to nominate a top flyweight rating. Jackie had made no attempt to defend the world title since June 1943, preferring to box at the easier made weight of bantam. He duly went on to achieve success at this level in

September 1945, when, in front of 40,000 fans, he defeated another highly respected Scotsman, Jim Brady, for the Empire title, a title Brady had held for four years.

With Paterson inactive as flyweight champion *The Ring*'s analysts turned their attention to those progressing on the European and US scenes and the fighter they selected for his impressive record, following a Northern Ireland title fight stoppage of Bunty Doran, was Monaghan. His name was now printed alongside those legends of the other divisions, the top dog of all top dogs being world heavyweight champion, Joe Louis. That Rinty had not yet won a major title outside of Ireland made his recognition by the leading American boxing writers all the more impressive.

Keeping company with Louis in print was light-heavyweight star Gus Lesnevich (the first undisputed champion at feather for seven years); Willie Pep; lightweight rivals Ike Williams and Bob Montgomery; new welterweight title-holder Sugar Ray Robinson; Manuel Ortiz at bantam, and the middleweight man of the moment, Tony Zale. Rinty's rating, the only number one for a boxer not residing in the US, was certainly something to be proud of, although it was not quite the same as owning a world title belt. The win over Marino gave him that. When the listing was issued for 1947 he again appeared alongside Louis, Lesnevich, Pep, Ortiz, Robinson and new middleweight kingpin, Rocky Graziano. Rinty was sought after and it was up to his management to decide what would be his next move, with approval from the Board of Control. The US offer would only be feasible if the Board sanctioned a permit for him to travel.

Jack Solomons' promotion at Harringay had been diluted, to a certain extent, by the judicial gymnastics involving Paterson, a London court and the Board of Control. An injunction had prevented British officials from recognising the Monaghan-Marino contest, which was unsatisfactory to both McAloran and Monaghan, although neither man paid much attention to the legal wrangling.

Rinty was world champion, having earned the title fair and square in the boxing ring, and was widely acknowledged as such on both sides of the Atlantic. Meanwhile, Rinty's standing in the States was going from strength to strength. Frank confirmed to news agencies that he had been approached by the powerful Twentieth Century Sporting Club, a US-based promotional firm which wanted Belfast's stellar flyweight to defend his new world title in New York. His manager was sounded out about making the trip to defend the NBA's World Championship crown at the city's most famous boxing arena, Madison Square Garden. It was one of the first approaches made in the wake of the Marino fight but Frank was determined not to be rushed. He replied that, while obviously interested in showcasing his fighter in the USA, he would keep his powder dry for a while yet. His boxer required a few weeks of rest, not to mention a period of recuperation for his broken hand. Frank indicated he was keeping an open mind on the Madison Square proposal and requested that the Club's representatives put meat on the bone of what exactly they were offering: what were they prepared to cover in terms of travel, training and accommodation overheads, Rinty's fight fee, and so on? The Club was keen on a promotion being staged the following March or April with a second meeting between Monaghan and Marino topping their wish list.

Marino's manager, Sam Ichinose, was also excited at the prospect of another showdown featuring his boxer. He was angling for a promotion in Hawaii but was equally happy to facilitate a rematch at Madison Square if need be. Ichinose had contacted Frank prior to leaving England to state that he would accept Twentieth's offer, providing the financial terms were acceptable. He even went so far as to promise to bring Marino to Belfast to fight, if he took the title from Monaghan in New York!

In an interview for the *Telegraph*, Sam said he would be 'delighted to guarantee' Rinty and Frank terms, though he would naturally prefer Hawaii to Madison Square. For the moment, New York was the live issue and Sam even used a little emotional blackmail, reminding Frank of the massive Irish population living in New York and Rinty's high profile status in the US thanks to *The Ring*. In other words, the fight would be easily sold to the public. Sam signed off his message by congratulating Rinty and his manager on their great win. Before Harringay he steadfastly refused to consider the idea of any return match taking place in Rinty's home city, but now it was Frank who was the manager holding all the aces.

Rinty was off limits for a while, despite the widespread speculating that surrounded him. It was reported that he would not fight again until the New Year because he was under doctor's orders to rest his hand for a couple of months.

Meanwhile changes were afoot for professional boxing. A few days after the Monaghan-Marino bill the Board convened and agreed on a range of key proposals that further dissolved regulation links with the former National Sporting Club. On Friday, 31 October it was announced that the old NSC rules would be replaced by a new code of regulations known as the 'BBB of C Boxing Rules', with the aim of improving safety for boxers. For the first time ever the corner posts to the ring would have to be padded. Under the previous regulations the padding of corner posts was not a stipulated necessity. A new three-rope design was also introduced, and to improve their strength, the ropes would be joined in the centre on each side of the ring. A unanimous decision was reached regarding the limit imposed on the duration of rounds for all professional contests. Optional regulations allowing the use of two minute rounds in certain contests were abandoned so that all pro bouts would feature three minute rounds.

There was also a change in the design of gloves for championship contests, with the minimum weight being increased. Gloves had been made mandatory for boxers when the Marquis of Queensberry rules were formalized and published by John Graham Chambers in 1867; they contained padding, usually made of lamb's wool or horse-hair, to soften blows and aid in the protection of boxers, insulating the myriad of small bones in a fighter's hands while curbing the damage a punch could inflict on his opponent.

Glove design had evolved from the 1700s. Jack Broughton, the 'father of English boxing', a pupil of James Figg's London Boxing Academy, had put his mind to this area of prize-fighting at his Tottenham Court Road base when he produced the first formal rule to govern bare knuckle boxing. His prototype glove was called a muffler. Initially this was used only for practice and not in contests. The first bout to feature Broughton's 'mufflers' took place at Aix-la-Chapelle in France in 1818.

When the Queensberry rules came into force, bringing bare knuckle fights to an end, a fairly skintight glove weighed no more than two ounces. These were in use until 1903 when the final contestants to wear them were Jimmy Briggs and Tony Daly, in Boston. When the illustrious John L Sullivan, the heavyweight champion at bare knuckle, switched to gloved boxing he fought the first World Heavyweight Championship contest under new regulations at New Orleans against James J Corbett in 1892. Sullivan had fought previously with made-to-order skintight mitts, made out of French kid, and two ounce gloves. The type worn for the fight with 'Gentleman' Jim weighed five ounces. The BBB of C's October 1947 meeting decided to raise the weight limit to a minimum of six ounces.

The week following these deliberations, Rinty was back in the news again, thanks to Jackie Paterson. His Scottish rival had been busy working in the background with legal advisors to secure support from the British top brass to ensure that Monaghan fought him next, and not Marino. News bulletins referred to Paterson's push for a fight with the Irish star in New York at Madison Square Garden.

As thrilling as the prospect looked on paper, the idea of bringing a boxer from Ireland and a boxer from Scotland, alongside consideration of the logistics involved, as well as the expense that would be incurred by supporters travelling to New York, did not look that viable. While the Americans were confident they could promote it successfully it made more sense for Rinty and Jackie to meet in Belfast or Glasgow, or at neutral venues in Liverpool, Manchester or London. 'Sad' Sam would have a canary but with the BBB of C on his side, Paterson was at the head of the queue to take Rinty on next.

Still, the latest twist to this US proposal had to be considered by Frank. He was engaged in tentative negotiations with Pat Collins, Paterson's manager. Movers and shakers on America's eastern seaboard were convinced they could facilitate the fight in the Big Apple. Part of the offer also included Peter Kane, the European bantamweight champion. As a spicy extra on the Monaghan-Paterson bill it was proposed that Kane challenge Manuel Ortiz for the world title. Reuters referred to the sponsors' intention for a double world title bill.

Paterson was able to nudge out the Hawaiians after a meeting with the BBB of C on 19 November, when the Board reviewed their earlier decision to strip him of his titles. That was one way of settling matters, but there was another: McAloran and Collins agreed that the most appropriate method to settle the issue was not by paying legal teams to fight in some courtroom, but by sorting out things in the ring. Madison Square was left smouldering on the backburner. Sol Strauss, acting on behalf of promoter Mike Jacobs, was putting together details for a New York deal. Paterson was keen on it, or so it was being suggested, and March or April suited him fine. Rinty's team was keen on the proposal too.

Within a couple of weeks, the goalposts had shifted. Frank had yet to receive anything in writing from Jacobs or Strauss. He wanted to read a concrete offer at first hand, not react to some snatch of cabled news from Reuters. By the end of October his patience had worn thin and he pushed the Americans to talk in figures. He wanted to know how much Rinty could expect to be paid, what the travel terms were, who was paying what, and where the training facilities would be. Strauss had offered a package for a rematch against Marino but nothing with regard to a Paterson bout, an altogether much bigger fish, given all the wrangling and the publicity generated. It was a matter of different fight, different promotion, and different sums!

On 31 October Frank contacted Mike Jacobs' representative, asking Strauss to define the exact nature of what they were proposing. At this point Frank knew no more than the media, which was that Collins had been approached in place of Sad Sam. The *Telegraph* interviewed McAloran about what was, or wasn't, happening. He informed them that two offers had been made. The Jacobs-Strauss proposal was the one he fancied more, as this would settle the question about who was the undisputed champion. Frank was confident the NBA's world title holder would prove too good for Ayrshire's hero, predicting that Rinty would 'beat Paterson at eight stone'.

If the fight was to take place at Madison Square, the Americans calculated that revenue would be close to US$100,000. It sounded tempting. This meant that the purse for Rinty and Jackie would be in the region of sixty percent of the overall revenue, with this split in whatever way the managers agreed. Was it all pie in the sky? Frank was not sure. He was bothered by the fact that the offer received by Collins made no reference to a guarantee about money, and he determined to hold out for definite word back from Jacobs or Strauss before reaching a decision. As more days passed without hearing from America he believed less and less that Rinty would meet Paterson in New York.

The devil is in the detail, and detail was the one thing that Frank lacked. What he did have was a range of options. The English were keen to see one of their own fight for the title: Peter Kane had been the last English flyweight to win a world title, gaining British, NBA, New York and European (International Boxing Union/IBU) recognition in 1938-1939. Apart from Liverpool veteran Joe Curran, who had lost a points decision in July 1946 to Paterson, England had produced no other challengers since then. The cogs in the machinery were now moving to secure an opportunity for Dickie O'Sullivan, who had just beaten Emile Famechon on points at the Royal Albert Hall on 1 November. Dickie's manager, Benny Huntman, was convinced that this result put his man in the frame for a title shot. In addition, the London media remembered the monotony of the Monaghan-Marino fight. Lainson Wood, a correspondent for the *Daily Telegraph*, attended the O'Sullivan-Famechon fight and believed the tiny Covent Garden scrapper to be the best flyweight in Britain. Everything depended on the outcome of the BBB of C's review hearing with Paterson. The money was on a third fight with Paterson.

The French authorities were also keeping an eye on the Paterson situation. Just as Huntman was flagging up O'Sullivan's credentials, the French federation was singing the praises of their top flyweight, Maurice Sandeyron, the European champion, whom they were pushing to be given a crack at Monaghan.

On 17 October, at London's Chancery Division, Mr Justice Romer granted an injunction that restrained the Board of Control from recognising anyone other than Paterson as World, British and Empire flyweight boxing champion. The BBB of C would now support Paterson's right to challenge Rinty, but there was a condition: Jackie was given until 31 March to meet Monaghan. If he had not faced Rinty by that date the forfeit would be all encompassing. Paterson would have to put his World, British and Empire titles on the line. If he fought and lost, he would lose every flyweight title returned to him after the court injunction.

Officials could not have been any more accommodating. An unusual period of four months was approved for Paterson to get his house in order. Frank wondered what was going on. Back in July Paterson had been told he would have no right to appeal, but now everything had changed. Frank failed to understand how officials, after an initial two hour meeting with Paterson's representatives, and several more locked in debate, had arrived at such an outcome. Rumours abounded that different medical opinions, including that of a psychiatrist, had been brought before the review hearing. For the first time Paterson had been allowed to bring in witnesses to support his claim of genuine ill health. The immediate result was that the governing bodies in Britain and America were now poles apart. The NBA was stubborn in its recognition of Rinty as world champion, while the Board of Control, who licensed Rinty, was forced to backtrack. They released a statement following the review hearing, issued by Secretary Charles F Donmall:

'The stewards, after reviewing all the fresh medical evidence, which had not hitherto been available, and which was at variance with that originally submitted, came to the conclusion that their previous decision as to the forfeiture of Paterson's flyweight titles be rescinded. The Board further decided that Paterson be given up to, and including, March 31 to defend the British, British Empire and World flyweight titles against Rinty Monaghan.'

Back in Belfast, Frank was not pleased. He made it clear to local reporters that he would be seeking legal advice on behalf of Rinty and would then consider their position. Rinty was the world champion, no matter what was going on in England. He reiterated that the NBA, the French federation and the Eire Boxing Board all recognised Rinty as such. Over in Hawaii the ears of Marino's manager stung when he heard the latest decision from London. He was pretty upset and, in an interview with the Associated Press news agency, demanded fair play from the British. He requested they revisit what had transpired in Glasgow during the summer. Marino had left Scotland disgusted by Paterson's failure to defend in July, and also by the fact that the stand-by boxer had been released from his position despite Paterson's obvious heath problems. Ichinose challenged Paterson to fight Marino, sending the following cable:

'Request B.B.B.C. take definite action concerning contracted and thrice postponed Paterson-Marino world flyweight title bout. Marino entitled to preference. Willing to fight Paterson anywhere at earliest convenience. We appeal for square deal.'

The only person truly happy with the proceedings was Paterson himself. Not only had he thrown a spanner in the works before Rinty and Salvador's fight in Harringay, but he had successfully fought, outside the ring, for his right to hold on to his titles; and now the British Board was bound to support him on a world title fight with Monaghan for which he had four months to prepare. He thanked the administrative stewards for their understanding. Of course he would not actually lose everything if things did not work out for him. He was still the British and Commonwealth titles holder at bantamweight, having knocked out Norman Lewis on the Monaghan-Marino bill.

For the moment politics had won out, resulting in another split within the flyweight division. At the end of 1947, out of the nine world championship titles available, only flyweight and light welterweight were in dispute over who was the rightful champion. For more than a decade the latter had been unsettled, ever since Barney Ross had vacated the championship in 1935, after switching back to welterweight and setting about wresting the title belt in this division from the legendary County Down-born Jimmy McLarnin, who had won the welterweight title twice. Canadian boxing authorities briefly backed the claim of Maxie Berger in 1939 but, for the best part of eleven years, the light-welter scene was in turmoil and without a linear champion to head up a division that produced 1930s stars such as Jack 'Kid' Berg, Tony Canzoneri, Ross and McLarnin, Johnny Jadick and 'Battling' Shaw.

The current situation between Rinty and Jackie was a throwback to 1931-1936 when there were more disputes over who was the lord of flyweight boxing than there were agreements. From the winter of 1927 to the late autumn of 1937 a total of thirty-two title fights were fought, with just one attracting unified approval. This contest matched American rivals

Frankie Genaro and Midget Wolgast in New York in 1930. However, even this failed to deliver a conclusive result when the bout finished with a ten-round draw. Title reigns by England's Jackie Brown and the ill-fated Scottish legend, Benny Lynch, featured in this period of disputed claims. Unity in the Championship had not been achieved since America's Fidel La Barba defeated Scotland's Elky Clark at New York in January 1927. It would take the Gorbals gladiator to unify flyweight boxing once more when, ten years after Clark-La Barba, the NBA's title claimant defeated rival New York commission claimant, 'Small' Montana (real name, Benjamin Gan from the Philippines) in London on 19 January 1937.

Rinty, the first Irishman to win a world flyweight title, had now joined the ranks with the best of the boxing heroes. In the next division up, bantamweight, he shared billing on the champions list at the end of 1947 with Manuel Ortiz. At feather, Willie Pep had healed the split between the NBA and New York authorities with a late knockout of Sal Bartelo. At lightweight the new boss was Ike Williams who, two months prior to Rinty's win over Marino, claimed undisputed recognition (the first since the 1941-1942 reign of Sammy Angott) by beating New York's claimant, Bob Montgomery. Meanwhile, the division between feather and light—'super featherweight'—remained inactive. Nothing had happened there since the fall of 'Kid' Chocolate to Frankie Klick in 1933.

Sugar Ray Robinson, Rocky Graziano, Gus Lesnevich and Joe Louis were the other champion names beside Belfast's famous fly. Sugar Ray held the welterweight title; Rocky, the middleweight crown, after a stunning sixth round kayo of Tony Zale in Chicago; Lesnevich ruled at light-heavyweight after wins over England's Freddie Mills and American Billy Fox; and the undisputed heavyweight champion was Louis, whose rematch that summer with Billy Conn drew an attendance of 45,000 in New York, before his subsequent defeat of 'Jersey' Joe Walcott.

Rinty hungered for the top position in his division: there was to be no lingering doubts from anywhere in the boxing community. The Americans and British needed to agree to a joint sanction. Obviously, the only satisfactory situation was that the division would champion one world title claimant; and so, another countdown to a major title fight was under way. Monaghan-Paterson, the third and final act, was now in the works. In effect, the upshot of the events at London's Chancery Division of the High Court was that Rinty and Jackie were on an unavoidable collision course.

The most incredible year in his life would end on another emotional high when Frances gave birth to another girl, Collette, on 10 December. Approaching the turn of another year, and with a new baby to feed and clothe, Rinty was looking for a fatter fee than before. Confident that a promoter would cough up the goods, he let it be known that he would not fight Paterson on the cheap. He also wanted to fight at home, his preference being for the King's Hall. It was up to the two managers, Frank and Pat, to finalise arrangements. For now he looked forward to spending the Christmas holidays with his wife and children, and celebrating what, for him, had been a spectacular few months.

14

JACKIE PATERSON WAS REPUTEDLY ONE OF the hardest hitters, pound for pound, to emerge in the 'hungry Thirties'. The Paterson story can be traced to the rural area of Ayrshire in the 1760s, a countryside that inspired Scotland's most admired and respected poet, Robert Burns, to pen his world famous poetry including 'Auld Lang Syne'. Jackie was born on 5 September 1920 in the coal excavation district of Springside where his father worked in the mines. In the early 1920s the family left Scotland to seek their fortune in North America. They settled initially in Canada before moving to the US where they spent the next eight years in Scranton, Pennsylvania before heading back across the Atlantic to the industrial port of Glasgow.

Jackie's earliest sporting interest was actually football. He became interested in boxing at the age of fifteen when he joined the Glasgow amateur club, Anderson. He shone as an amateur and was convinced that he should turn professional in the late 1930s, four months shy of his eighteen birthday, and a couple of years after Rinty took up paid boxing in Belfast. Pat Collins, a regular promoter of boxing bills at venues in Paisley and Celtic Park stadium, signed up as his manager. Jackie made his debut as a pro in Greenock, on 26 May 1938, when he beat Joe Kiely on points after a ten-round bout, winning for himself the tidy sum of £3.

By day he worked at John Brown shipyards on the Clyde, which allowed him to develop his muscular upper body through heavy graft. He did not stay too long at this job, however, giving it up for a position in the local butcher's.

His second professional fight brought him into contact with Rinty for the first time. What happened when they met in Belfast in 1938 established a decade-long rivalry. Monaghan was well established by the time, having reeled off seventeen victories in a row. He was steadily climbing up the Irish and British ratings, and being linked to box-offs for the first Northern Ireland Area Championship with Jim McStravick and Tommy Stewart. Two more victories were added when he beat Ivor Neil with a first round kayo, and then beat Joe Kiely over ten rounds. It was a little strange of Collins to put his young southpaw rookie in with a much more experienced Rinty, but this he did, and it paid off terrifically when Jackie, against all expectations, knocked Rinty out in the fifth round, on 23 July at Belfast's Oval stadium. This was the fight after which Rinty had woken up dazed and disoriented in the dressing room, wondering why he wasn't being prepped for a fight that was already over.

Jackie was a hard hitter, just like Rinty, and they were both plagued with hand injuries. In fact, Jackie was so prone to breakages that Scottish commentators speculated that he might be forced to retire when he was just twenty years of age. Yet he persisted, defying the critics to become one of the all-time greats in Scottish boxing, a worthy successor to Benny Lynch. However, he did not have an easy time. A much bigger problem than hand injuries faced him in the form of the scales. His fighting days at flyweight were few and far between as he found it almost impossible to hit the eight-stone limit. He found it easier, and more natural, to remain at bantamweight—eight stone and six pounds.

His most successful years in this division were 1939-1943. In May 1939 he claimed the domestic spoils, stopping Freddie Tennant in the eleventh round at Dundee. By the end of September that same year he was British champion, the fifth Scottish boxer to accomplish this feat. He also made domestic history as the first southpaw to win the British title. The eliminator was against Leicester's Eric Jones, for which Jackie finalised his training with two weeks in Portrush, Northern Ireland. It

Rinty delivers one of his trademark straight lefts to the body of Terry Allen.

Carrying on from his wartime experiences with ENSA, Rinty became an entertainer after retiring from the ring. 'Forces Sweetheart' Vera Lynn is in the centre of the photograph above.

Pete Murray (left) with his Television All-Stars. Skiffle supremo Lonnie Donegan is pictured shaking hands with a dignitary in the centre of the photograph, while said dignitary blocks Rinty from view.

Stanley Baker, with whom Rinty appeared in the film The Criminal. *The picture is signed by Baker 'To Collette, Best Wishes'.*

Garlanded with flowers and singing his heart out; Rinty after beating Marino at Harringay Arena in 1947.

Farewell to Harringay. Many great fighters assembled to mark the closure of the famous arena. Standing (left to right) are Randy Turpin, Jack Petersen, Dave Crowley, Harry Mizler, Bruce Woodcock, Ernie Roderick, Peter Kane, Rinty, Max Baer, Ronnie Clayton, promoter Jack Solomons, Arthur Danahar, Eric Boon, Tommy Farr, Len Harvey, Eddie Phillips and Don Cockell; front row (left to right) are Phil Edwards, Terry Downes, Henry Armstrong, Gus Lesnevich, Sammy McCarthy, Peter Waterman and Johnny Williams.

With co-star Shirley Diamond in Babes in the Wood.

Rinty and Collette take delivery of her first car outside their Little Corporation Street home.

Sean and Collette browse through a scrapbook of their father's cuttings as Rinty and Frances look on.

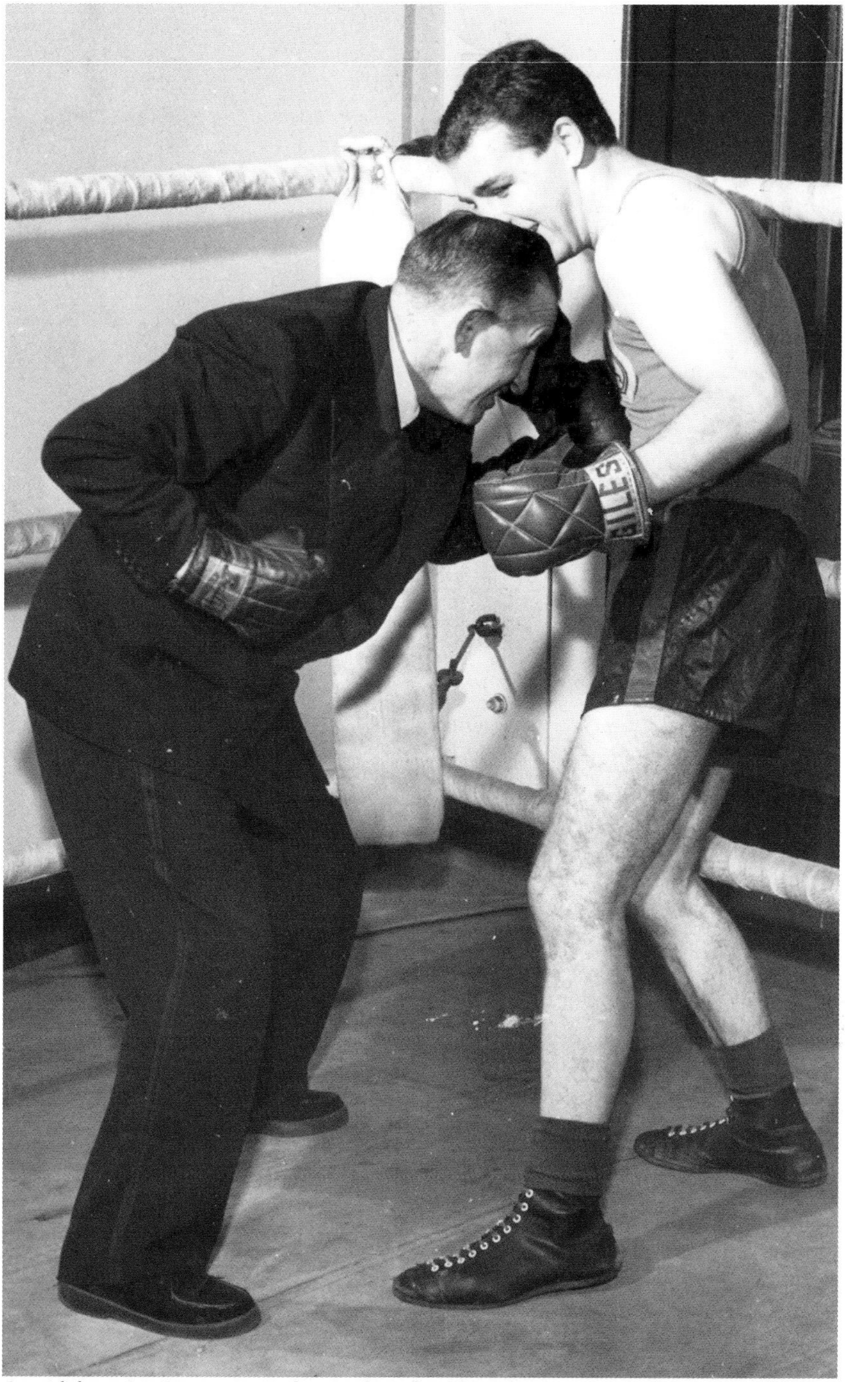

Scottish boxer Joe Gans receives a few tips from the old master.

Rinty enjoys a bit of banter with WBC light-heavyweight champ, and European, British and Commonwealth titles winner, John Conteh.

A few bars for the listeners of BBC Radio Ulster.

Nat Fleischer, editor of the bible of the boxing world, The Ring, *bestows that magazine's world title belt upon the new undisputed world flyweight champ as Frank McAloran, Bob Gardiner and Mrs Fleischer look on.*

Rinty pulls a face at a boxers reunion at the City Hall in Belfast. Among others pictured are Johnny Caldwell, Charlie Nash, Billy 'Spider' Kelly, Jim 'Spider' Kelly, Davy Larmour, John McCormack, Freddie Gilroy, and Lord Mayor William Bell.

Still slugging away. Rinty demonstrates that he hasn't forgotten the moves.

Rinty takes time out for a chat and a cuppa with train station officials in Portlaoise during a trip organised by the Northern Ireland Ex-Boxers'Association.

Rinty is carried shoulder-high to receive his induction into the Texaco Hall of Fame in 1969. The honour was presented by Jack Lynch.

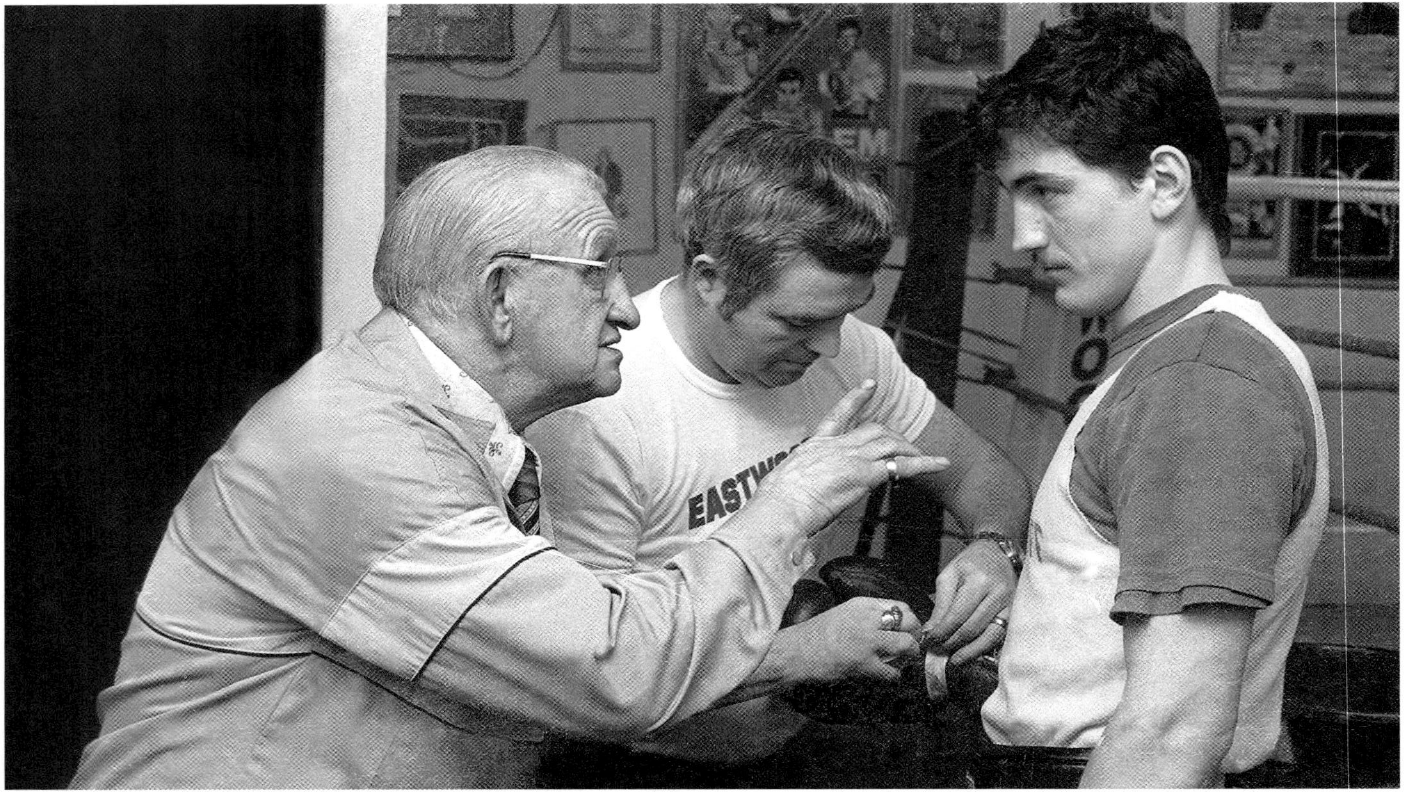

A few words of advice for future world featherweight champion Barry McGuigan at Barney Eastwood's gym in Belfast's Castle Street. Also pictured is Eastwood's main trainer, Eddie Shaw.

Rinty's daughters Martha (left), Marie (right) and Collette with his Ring *world title belt and Hall of Fame trophies at the King's Hall in 2007, on the day an Ulster Historical Circle plaque was unveiled in their father's honour at the Belfast arena.*

was worth it; he polished Jones off in less than half a minute with a right hook.

Then, on 30 September, Paddy Ryan fought him for Lynch's vacated title in Glasgow. The new Scottish sensation drew a crowd of eleven thousand who watched in triumph when he knocked out Ryan two rounds from the end of the scheduled fifteen. He was barely twenty, and the new British champion, but it had come at a cost. He had put away Ryan with a left hook to the chin and had fractured a bone in his right hand, the same hand he had hurt in a fight with Joe Curran. The injury scrubbed proposed non-title bouts against world top-rated Tiny Bostock in London and Rinty Monaghan at Newcastle in the north of England. This led to some friction when McAloran claimed his fighter was being avoided. Collins retorted that Paterson was genuinely injured; otherwise, there would be an imminent rematch. Who could have guessed that, despite two substantial offers in 1940 from Belfast promoter Nat Josephs, the rematch would not happen for another six years? In the meantime, Rinty fought Paddy Ryan at Newcastle.

With the increasing conflict throughout Europe, the British Board announced in the spring of 1940 that no trophies or belts for British and Empire title fights would be presented for the foreseeable future. This also included World and European Championship promotions. Paterson's world title plans would be kept on the long finger, until 1943, while he set about winning the Empire title, beating 'Kid' Tanner in Manchester after Tanner defeated Ryan. Thus began a run of fifteen straight wins for Paterson during which time Rinty's career was stalled more often than not, thanks to his war service.

Paterson and Ryan squared up again in 1941 in front of six thousand fans at Nottingham, this time for the British and Empire titles. Jackie scored an eighth round stoppage, then beat British bantamweight champion Jim Brady in a non-title contest on points, setting down a marker for when they would box for the crown. It was about this time that Salvador Dado Marino turned professional, making his debut in Honolulu on 20 June with a second round kayo of fellow rookie, Paul Francis.

Paterson's form continued to improve, as did his reputation for being arguably the hardest punching flyweight in British boxing in the early

1940s, enhanced by five wins, four of them reeled off in just over thirty days. He out-pointed Phil Milligan in front of eleven thousand at Manchester; forced Billy Hazelgrove to throw in the towel inside seven rounds in Bristol; stopped Ritchie 'Kid' Tanner during an Empire flyweight title bout in two rounds; and saw off Jimmy Lyden in nine and Runcorn bantam Jimmy Stubbs on points. His manager decided to put him in again with Jim Brady, this time for the British bantam title, on 5 August 1941 in Glasgow—a match which drew close to 21,000. Brady's experience and skill saw him box a clever fight to keep the title on points over fifteen rounds. It was Paterson's first defeat in seventeen bouts since his points loss at Earls Court to Charley Brown in November 1939.

No matter; he marched on to win thirteen out of fourteen fights, five by way of knockout—the one defeat, a sixth round stoppage at Nottingham by Frank Bonser, he avenged in style within two months. Jimmy Hayes, Milligan again, and Al Phillips lasted one, two and three rounds respectively to finish off this fourteen-fight sequence before the much anticipated showdown with Peter Kane. Queen's Park Football Club in Glasgow helped arrange the promotion for their ground at Hampden Park. Over 48,000 fans paid to see Kane defend against Jackie, making it the biggest boxing event in Scotland for a decade.

The hub of the country's shipbuilding industry was playing host to its third ever World Championship title fight. Benny Lynch had been involved in the previous two. Kane, aged twenty-five, had fought both Lynch and the American, Jackie Jurich, for flyweight titles before, losing and sharing the spoils with the Scot, while beating Jurich. The win was for the title, which had been taken from Lynch, who was losing his struggle with alcoholism. However, Benny was still involved as Pat Collins brought him in to help Paterson with his training and tactical approach.

All it took was a mere sixty-one seconds on a wet June evening. Referee Moss Deyong counted Kane out after a brilliant right cross, from the fist that Paterson broke winning the British title. The timing of the knockout had a certain symmetry as Jackie was nineteen days into his sixty-first month as a professional boxer.

The Glaswegian's career thus far resembled the plot of a typical

Hollywood rags-to-riches melodrama. If Jackie had ever entertained doubts about abandoning the beautiful game of football for a life in the ring, they could dispelled immediately. With the world title in Paterson's locker he was the top target for every genuine flyweight in Ireland and Britain, and all points on the fight game's compass led to him.

The same month that Paterson shattered Kane's title hold, Rinty drew with Harry Rodgers in Belfast. It was only the second time he had boxed since 1940. The gap between where Monaghan stood at in his career and the summit Jackie so superbly occupied was vast. It was up to James and Frank McAloran to plan and plot a route to where Paterson was at. Over in Hawaii, Dado had paced his way through eighteen professional contests. His record was an admirable 16-2; the second defeat took place a month before Kane's loss to Paterson. In a version of the bantamweight World Championship, as recognised by the Territorial Boxing Commission in the Pacific Islands, Dado was knocked out in the eighth round by David Kui Kong Young.

The next five years for Jackie were steeped in problems. Thanks to his battle with the scales he would succumb to illnesses that resulted from crash course diets and attempts to literally sweat off the pounds—which resulted in a court case.

The early weeks of 1948 were extremely difficult for many people. Major job losses were predicted with shipyards feeling the financial pinch. On 12 January, Jackie and his legal team were in London at the Chancery Division. It sat to review its determination on the action against the Board of Control brought before it the previous October. Mr Justice Jenkins listened to submissions from the boxer's advisor, Mr G T Hesketh, and from Mr Charles Russell, acting on behalf of the British Boxing Board of Control. The result was the ordered title fight between Paterson and Monaghan, to take place on or before 31 March. The judge announced an order to stay all further action by the boxer in the High Court, also discharging the interlocutory injunction granted against the Board of Control prior to Rinty's clash, for the World Flyweight Championship, as recognised by the NBA, with Marino. Another meeting between the Board and Paterson saw the boxer reinstated, much to the annoyance of the NBA and Rinty's management, as World

Flyweight Champion. Paterson was also given back his British and Empire flyweight belts.

The decision of the BBB of C to back down from their original position had resolved the matter and the Board's representative now requested the order be discharged and injunction lifted. This, Mr Justice Jenkins agreed to. Another bit of the jigsaw was in place, but no sooner had this been eased into position than a further problem arose in the form of televised access to the Monaghan-Paterson fight. The Board of Control felt television coverage by the BBC was having an adverse influence on certain shows, especially the small hall bills. These were the weekly matches throughout England, Scotland, Wales and Northern Ireland where promoters struggled to make ends meet after paying for the venue and boxers. Everyone lost out when fans watched the match for free at home.

The situation had been simmering for a while. For Rinty and Jackie, given the large sums of cash some promoter would have to stump up for the right to stage the fight, the problems between the Board and the BBC could not have occurred at a more inconvenient time. A few days after the High Court review gave the fight the go-ahead, the short-term future for broadcasting of professional boxing shows was on the Board's agenda. A statement by Charles F Donmall, the Board of Control's general secretary, drew attention to their concern about poorly attended promotions, about bills being cancelled, and the hardship caused to licensed boxers because of loss of work and earnings. Officials decided to dig in their heels, announcing that no further permission would be granted to the BBC before 20 February until talks had taken place, concerns addressed, and agreement reached.

Three promotions were granted permission for television coverage, beginning with the 26 January match between Vince Hawkins and Bos Murphy at the Royal Albert Hall for the Empire middleweight title. A title eliminator in Nottingham at the same weight, between Dick Turpin and Mark Hart, would also be broadcasted on 2 February, as would the 20 February bout in Manchester between European bantamweight champion Peter Kane and Italy's Guido Ferracin.

With promoters remaining undecided over the staging of the undisputed flyweight bout, the Board's dispute with the broadcaster was doubly troublesome. A spokesperson for the television company said they would be 'very glad' to attend a meeting at the earliest possible time.

Meanwhile, back in Belfast, the Northern Ireland Area Council of the BBB of C was looking at Rinty's tenure as the Area's title holder, duly deciding to arrange an elimination series and one at bantamweight. Five boxers were shortlisted for Rinty's old belt. Belfast's Jackie Briers was given a first round bye in the draw made by officials for box-offs or an elimination series, while bouts were made between Belfast's Ike Weir and Harry Rodgers of Derry, Frank McCoy of Portadown and another Belfast contender, Billy Birch.

In Scotland, Paterson was ready to turn over his next card. A week after the judicial review by Mr Justice Jenkins, and following lengthy negotiations with Bob Gardiner, Jackie and his manager Pat Collins signed up for a fight with Monaghan in Belfast with a provisional date of Easter Monday, 29 March. The contest would involve four titles—Rinty's NBA World Championship, Jackie's World Championship, as recognised by the British Board, and his Great Britain and Empire belts. Gardiner had scored the first World Championship promotion to take place in Belfast, and only the second to be held on the island of Ireland; the previous title bout had been the 1923 light-heavyweight clash of US-based Ennis native Mike McTigue and Senegal's world champion of that time, Battling Siki, at the La Scala Opera House in Dublin on St Patrick's Day. McTigue, raised in New York since his late teens, won the fight on points after twenty rounds. With Jackie signed, Gardiner now focused his energies on convincing Frank that he was offering the best terms going. Frank was not easily charmed, however, and was happy to play hard ball. Certain sums were bandied about with Bob constantly falling short of expectations. On the one hand, this was the biggest fight in the city's history, while on the other local news was full of unemployment on a wide scale.

Gardiner planned to support the main billing with a British bantamweight title match between Doran, the Northern Ireland champion, and Liverpool's Stan Rowan. To this end he secured a package with their two managers. Still Frank and Rinty remained aloft. A presumably tense Bob announced through the newspapers that the

King's Hall was his venue of preference and that Paterson had agreed to the contractual stipulations involving a financial forfeit of £750 to Monaghan if he scaled over the eight-stone limit along with another forfeit of the same amount should he fail to fulfill the contract for any reason other than medical.

The Monaghan team refused to bite. Street peddlers running the back alleys of Tangiers' souks, bartering and haggling prices with tourists for trinkets, might have found a couple of soul mates in Rinty's manager and the ambitious promoter. Negotiations over what constituted a fair and reasonable contract dragged on during late January without a compromise in sight. Gardiner was running out of time—with only eight weeks to the British Board's deadline for Paterson to defend his 'triple crown' of titles. There was a genuine fear that the fight would not happen at all.

Dublin's *Irish Independent* sent John Parker to ask Bob about the predicament. Mr Parker was informed that a couple more days of deadlock and Gardiner would be unable to meet the BBB of C deadline. Bob also confirmed that he had written to Rinty's manager, advising him of the seriousness of the situation, and urging him to respond positively and quickly.

As far as Frank was concerned, the solution was staring Bob in the face. He just had to dig deeper into his pockets; up the offer or there would be no fight. Therefore, the ball was in Gardiner's court. The promoter was forced to play his final card: if a deal was not hammered out between the parties by close of business on 2 February, he would wash his hands of the whole thing. Bob would walk away from Belfast's first World Championship and from a possible first undisputed flyweight title success by a Belfast boxer, and it would not be his fault!

An unflappable Frank, in response, made it crystal clear that there was no way Gardiner was going to get Rinty's signature by offering the NBA world champion almost £4,000 less than he offered Paterson. He dismissed the initial prize purse quoted as an insult and refused to consider a second offer that was still £3,000 lower than Paterson's. Frank admitted as much to John Parker, revealing that Rinty had initially been offered just £1,500, with five percent of the gate receipts thrown in.

'His [Gardiner's] second offer was £2,500 and that I also refused.

Provided we fail to agree terms it is difficult to say what will happen. Paterson has been instructed to fight before the end of March, but although Rinty has been nominated as a challenger there is no instruction that he must fight before or on any given date. Provided they do not meet on Easter Monday it is impossible at the moment to see the next championship move.'

Furthermore, Frank made it clear to Gardiner that he would settle for the BBB of C putting the contest up for purse offers, meaning that other promoters would be given the opportunity to stage the fight. The pressure was placed squarely on Gardiner's shoulders. Eventually he capitulated, to a certain degree. He made a final offer of £3,500, still £2,000 less than Paterson's purse, and far less than Rinty's original demand for £6,000.

Gardiner now had all his boxers lined up but there was yet another obstacle. Easter Monday was a non-starter. It clashed with traditional family holiday plans and the King's Hall was out of bounds since it was being converted into an ice rink for the Easter weekend. The promoter needed to name a new date or find a suitable alternative venue.

Poor Bob must have felt close to tears, but all was not lost, thanks to Sam Clarke, the general manager of the Royal Ulster Agricultural Society, who looked after the King's Hall, amongst other things. Clarke threw Bob a lifeline, telling him that the venue was available on 23 March. The promoter immediately contacted the two managers about bringing the fight forward. They agreed. Pat telegraphed confirmation, which was published in the local newspapers: 'Paterson agreeable to March 23. Kind regards to Rinty – Collins.'

Now Gardiner just had to obtain approval for what he hoped would be a massive turnout. It was suggested that such an event should comfortably attract a crowd well into five figures, twelve thousand people at least. This was the size of the crowd that had attended Jimmy Warnock's defeat of the then world flyweight champion Benny Lynch in a non-title bout. No doubt about it, it was a risky venture. There were still many people who continued to doubt that Paterson would make the weight or show up at all. Gardiner could only pray that his investment would not fall down around his feet.

He need not have worried too much. On 21 February, the European Boxing association met in Paris to discuss the Monaghan-Paterson fight. They made the crucial decision to appoint an official stand-by opponent for Belfast—one Maurice Sandeyron, star of French boxing and European champion. The Frenchman was requested to remain in training for the Belfast promotion. If either Monaghan or Paterson failed to make the weight, he would step in and challenge for the world title. Contrary to 1947, at Hampden Park, Sandeyron would not stop training until 23 March when he would be asked to make the eight stone limit. If it came to the bit, Sandeyron would defend his European title as part of the directive.

Everything was finally in place. There was nothing more to be done. In the run-up to the big day Jackie fought a lacklustre warm-up contest which ended with a poor and disputed decision over Al Chavez in Manchester. This cannot have been good for his confidence.

Whether he would make it to the King's Hall in fighting form was anybody's guess.

15

WHILE FRANCES LOOKED AFTER THEIR THREE kids and everything else, Rinty immersed himself in his training, running for miles every morning, and following his well-worn route that included the steep surface of Cave Hill. Each night found him at the gym, pushing himself under the supervision of chief coach, James McAloran.

Excitement was building as the days passed by. March was always a busy month for Irish sport, thanks to the final in the Nations Championship in rugby union and Aintree's Grand National. The month opened at Ravenhill, the main rugby venue in Belfast, which played host to the forty thousand spectators at the Nations Championship decider for the Triple Crown, who watched Ireland beat Wales, a magnificent achievement after nearly fifty years of failure to do. Then, seven days later, the Grand National saw Ireland's luck holding firm as a nine-year-old mare by the name of 'Sheila's Cottage', with County Carlow jockey A P Thompson in the saddle, claimed victory by beating favourites 'Dandies', 'Cromwell' and 'Happy Home'. It appeared to be a good year for Irish sport.

The big fight night at the King's Hall was now top of the local sports agenda. It was Rinty's turn to step up to the plate and try to deliver a substantial improvement on his performance against Marino, while doing so in front of his home crowd for the first time as world champion. He certainly put in the work and his training, by all accounts, was going according to plan. It could only be assumed that his opponent was working just as hard; assumptions were all that the pundits had since nobody knew where Paterson was or what he was doing.

Days passed without word. Rinty left the worrying to Frank, to Gardiner, to the media. For three weeks there was virtually no indication as to the Ayrshire man's well-being, and doubts about whether the fight would go ahead at all intensified on the eve of the event, Monday, 22 March. Paterson did not arrive to check into his pre-booked room at Belfast's Grand Central Hotel, a fact which sent alarm bells ringing throughout the boxing community. When Bob Gardiner was quizzed by excited reporters he remained calm and unperturbed. He assured everyone that a world flyweight title fight would take place at the appointed time with or without Paterson's involvement, reminding them of the French stand-by, Maurice Sandeyron. The only scenario that could prevent a fight going ahead was if Rinty was forced to pull out due to an injury or illness. The promoter went so far as to say that he did not 'care two hoots' if the Scotsman put in an appearance or not. He was confident Belfast's crowd favourite would make the limit, given that he was 'a natural flyweight'. Gardiner was equally confident that the fans would be treated to a great show. Furthermore, if it came down to it, Gardiner personally felt that a match between Monaghan and Sandeyron could 'provide a better contest'.

A telephone call had been made to the Scottish media when Jackie failed to show up at his hotel, instructing them to 'go on a manhunt'. News filtered back that despite an extensive search—a combing of the city that involved door-stepping Paterson's neighbours—he was nowhere to be found. The word on the street was that he had left Scotland for Belfast by air. This line was pursued and contact was made with airports at Prestwick and Renfrew to see if a plane had been chartered. All replies were reportedly negative. Not surprisingly, the phone at Jackie's house rang out while discussions with Pat Collins's wife, and with Paterson's trainer, failed to shed light on the mystery. If anyone knew where the boxer was, they weren't telling. The last time he'd been seen was when he was availing of the facilities at Glasgow's Ibrox Park ground, home of Rangers Football Club. Similarly, Belfast's soccer club, Linfield, at Windsor Park, offered their facilities should he decide to travel across a few days before the fight. He didn't take them up on their generous offer.

Under the terms of agreement signed in January, Jackie had agreed to be in Belfast twenty-four hours before the contest would take place. When reporters asked Gardiner about this he insisted that the fight would go ahead, as long as Paterson arrived at the weigh-in on time and made the weight.

The previous week Gardiner had made arrangements for local journalists to go to Glasgow's Anderson Athletic Club to report on Paterson's training and physique. They watched him spar with Norman Lewis, the Welsh champion. The *Irish News* was very complimentary about his fitness and sharpness for the upcoming battle. Their reporter dispatched an article stating that Jackie had turned on a 'sparkling display' for them at Anderson, adding that the Springside man's timing had 'improved immensely'.

Paterson made himself available for a brief interview in which he assured everyone he was in fine order and that he expected to make the weight comfortably. One observer at the gym was quoted as saying, 'There is every certainty, therefore, that the title fight in the King's Hall will be a spectacular and thrilling affair in view of the excellent condition of both boxers.' As if that wasn't enough to convince the journalists, a trial weigh-in was organised to prove his regime was on track: Jackie scaled four-and-a-half pounds over the title limit. This dry run on the scales was conducted five days before the scheduled contest, yet it failed to dispel all doubts regarding Paterson's ability to hit the eight stone mark in a healthy fashion, and on time.

Although Gardiner was putting on a brave face regarding the missing Paterson he had plenty more to be concerned about. Negotiations with the BBC about televised coverage of the fight were proving most unsatisfactory. Then, at the beginning of March, the promoter announced a serious setback for the public: despite lengthy discussions one of the most hotly debated fights would not be televised. He claimed the BBC offer put to him was unreasonable. It was a blow for those who could not get a ticket, especially for Paterson's fans back home in Scotland. The *Telegraph*'s John Caughey wrote that 'It is a pity that an amicable settlement could not be reached.' Gardiner realised this and set forth again to attempt a compromise of some sort. The demand to see the fight far outstripped available tickets and he felt personally responsible for the disappointed fans. With this in mind he approached the British Board and requested their permission to have the contest recorded by a reputable company for screening later at cinemas and theatres. The request was approved. It was better than nothing. Permission for media agency photographers to be at ringside was also sanctioned.

Meanwhile Gardiner's booking office at the Royal Hippodrome was enjoying a brisk trade. When it was confirmed that the fight would not be shown live the run on tickets was enormous. Business was further boosted when it was confirmed that another of the city's top boxers in the lighter weights, Jimmy Warnock, a non-title winner in the mid-1930s over the then world flyweight champion, Benny Lynch, would be on the under-card. Warnock was to be matched with Sandeyron, in a non-title bout, in the event of Paterson showing up, weighing in correctly and taking the fight. If Paterson did not fight, Sandeyron would box Rinty instead for the world title. In that case, Warnock would be matched with Jamaica's national flyweight champion, Pincie Thompson. The Shankill Road man's comeback and attempt to force an opening for a title challenge had hit bad luck on 9 March at the Royal Hippodrome. A cut to his right cheek from a clash of heads forced him to retire at the end of the fifth round against Brighton's Billy Hazelgrove. The retirement was precautionary to allow adequate healing time and ensure Jimmy would be ready for the Balmoral blockbuster event on the twenty-third.

While all of this was going on Rinty kept his head down, staying well out of the spotlight. The exaggerated focus on Paterson helped him keep a low profile in the weeks leading up to the bill. When called upon, his manager gave assurances that preparations were as good as they could be. Frank also expressed confidence in his fighter becoming the next undisputed title holder, whether it was the Scot or the Parisian standing between him and history. They would finish off preparations at Celtic Park.

The task of drumming up publicity for the King's Hall promotion was Gardiner's working brief. Although the health saga surrounding Paterson was generating plenty of debate, the ambitious Bob looked to land a colossal coup to hike interest further. Joe Louis, king of the world heavyweight scene, had some months before made known his plans to visit Britain. Accordingly, he and his wife were photographed some time later aboard the *Queen Mary*, leaving New York for England. As any promoter worth his salt would do, Gardiner tried to secure an agreement with Louis to attend the Belfast show. He told the press that he had sent an invite to Alabama's 'Brown Bomber', even suggesting to Louis that he might like to put on a sparring exhibition for the fans. If he pulled this off, it would be a massive feather in Bob's cap. Joe's advisor sent word that the 'Bomber' would love to come to Belfast, but would not make the trip for anything less than £1,500! It was more than Bob could afford. He tried to broker a deal, offering Louis a twenty-five-minute slot for an exhibition workout for a lower cash bond figure. However, the Americans were not interested in haggling and, sadly for the Belfast fight fans, the biggest star in heavyweight boxing decided not to travel over.

Gardiner had been successful in other matters. Despite there being no live television coverage, there would be live wireless coverage on the popular BBC Light Programme, going on the air from the venue at 7.45pm. The Corporation's leading sports commentator, Raymond Glendenning, with his exaggerated RAF wing commander handlebar black moustache and horn-rimmed spectacles, would be ringside. An accountant by profession, Glendenning had a reputation for being one of the fastest talkers on air. He could supposedly rattle off more than two hundred words every sixty seconds, which was certainly a help when he commentated on horse-racing events. He was also the main voice of the English Football Association's Cup Final. When he commentated on boxing matches he usually shared the microphone with former boxing referee, W (William) Barrington Dalby, who functioned as a sophisticated cigar-puffing inter-round analyst. Glendenning's 'Come in, Barry!' at the end of each round became a well-known catchphrase.

On the day of the fight, Rinty's brother Patsy finished shore leave in the industrial Portuguese port of Lisbon and was somewhere in the

Atlantic Ocean, on his way to Buenos Aires, as quartermaster of the *Highland Princess*. Fortunately for him, his ship's captain gave permission for the wireless to be rigged into the public address system:

'The sparky on board was allowed to link up the wireless to the Tannoy so we could hear the fight. This was the next best thing to being at ringside to see John. It was brilliant to listen to. I did not realize until I returned home that the fight was not televised for some reason, so the whole country was listening to what we heard on our way to Argentina. That was great. I watched a film of it afterwards. At that time the wireless was the big thing for people. Not every home had one. I heard that lots of people crowded into houses to listen to John's world title fight. That was the biggest fight ever to take place in Belfast at the time.'

Gardiner struck a private deal with Piccadilly Cinematograph Film Productions Limited to film the fight. Canada's Stewart MacPherson, who commentated for the BBC, and who would later present their popular *Twenty Questions* series in the 1950s, was secured to narrate the fight.

In the last few days before the fight Bob found himself with an added responsibility for the fans. With the mad scramble for tickets throughout the final week, the fraudsters were keen to take advantage. The promoter was informed that a large number of counterfeit tickets were in circulation which prompted him to use the media to get the message out about the potential of being sold contraband tickets for the balcony area.

Rinty's manager prepared the rest of his stable of boxers for the bill by matching them the night after St Patrick's Day at a show in the Ulster Hall. Bantam Eddie McCullough defeated Manchester's Billy Tansey, a cut to Tansey's right eye forcing a premature end to the contest. Alec Woods, Ulster's champion at cruiserweight, was in the wars for the second time in less than a month. After dropping a six-round decision to Scotland's Bobby Ogg he agreed to a fight with McAloran's young heavyweight Paddy Slavin. The piston left jab of Slavin earned a points win over eight rounds. On the night before the big fight, Lisburn's Jim Keery topped a bill at the Ulster Hall, scoring a points win over Bernard Pugh of Liverpool, the British army champion at featherweight. The same hall would host the official weigh-in for Monaghan and Paterson, if Jackie showed.

At long last, the day had arrived. The temporary ice rink had been dismantled and replaced with extra seating to cope with the crowd. At 5pm the King's Hall opened its doors to thousands of eager supporters, including five thousand Scottish fans, and VIP guests.

Rinty was looking well and rested, thanks to an early night. His weight was checked; he scaled seven stone and thirteen pounds. He was fit as a fiddle and ready for a tear-up. Official stand-by boxer, Maurice Sandeyron, was at the Grand Central with his Parisian manager Pierre Gandon. His weight was fine, also; it just remained to be seen what opponent he would be fighting.

Paterson had until 2pm to make his appearance, or he would forfeit everything: all his flyweight claims to a version of the World Championship, the British and Empire titles, not to mention the credibility problems he would have if, at this stage, he made a mug out of all those who had given him one last chance. Hundreds of onlookers crammed into the Bedford Street arena to see if he would turn up for the official weigh-in. The deadline came and went without any news from the Scot. Bewildered officials, for the want of something better to do, decided to give him a few more minutes, and a good job too. At four minutes past the hour a collective sigh of relief filled the venue when Paterson finally showed. His supporters greeted their hero with a massive roar. Jackie strode across the floor to the stage, removed his clothes and stepped on to the scales. The needle eventually settled and he was on the button.

Frances Monaghan turned off her radio and prepared to take her kids on a long walk, a sure sign that the first ever World Championship title clash at the King's Hall was about to begin.

***

Not sixty seconds after the bell rang it looked to be all over when Rinty's right hand landed a peach. James McAloran had spent years developing a stance which would allow Rinty to hit even harder. The focus paid off, and Paterson was severely rocked as he lurched backwards and staggered across the ring. Monaghan had successfully initiated an offence and Jackie's confidence shrank just a little. The home supporters were on their feet, sensing it could all be over in the next few minutes. Eager to make good on his punch Rinty prowled and pounced, rushed with his shots as he sought another opening for hard leather to thud into Jackie's jaw. However, he was much too anxious, too rash in his wild swings that failed to land, allowing his rival to settle, evade and see out the round. Chances for a first session kayo evaporated in a blur of missed punches. Then Rinty received his own warning when he was tagged with a crisp right hook, a powerful blow which made Rinty's knees buckle slightly. The bell signifying the end of the first was a relief to the mounting tension.

Glendenning and Dalby were given the opportunity to describe another clash during the break when fighting broke out between loyal supporters at the back of the hall. Amateur fists were thrown, as well as chairs, before security stewards managed to restore order just in time for the second round.

There was a pace to Paterson's boxing and gameness in the second which challenged harsh claims that he would be dead at the weight. His boxing was clean and crisp. Nevertheless, Rinty looked the bigger puncher. A couple of short rights argued a case that Paterson was really living on borrowed time beneath all the bold moves. Crouching with his devilish right glove on a hair trigger, a missed left brought the opportunity Rinty was on the lookout for. Paterson left himself wide open to attack and Rinty moved to make the most of the error. In flew the right again, catching Jackie flush just below the left eye. It struck with venom and Paterson's legs were taken from under him. He finished on his backside, blood seeping from a nick where the punch landed. The referee's count reached seven before Jackie managed to get back to his feet.

He was not happy and complained to Tommy Little that the punch was unfair, that Rinty hit him as the official was about to speak to them. Little was having none of it, waved away the protest, and back came Rinty, swinging both fists, aiming for closure. Again he rushed his shots. He was off target too often and Paterson weathered another storm to regroup and steady himself. The thrills had peaked for the time being. Much of the first two rounds were uneventful. The pace slowed in the third as both men displayed more caution, took fewer risks, and the quality dipped. Referee Little was not impressed and had a word with them, requesting more effort. The arena was restless and fans started slow hand clapping, demanding that the boxing improve. Monaghan remained the livelier through rounds three and four but, overall, the boxing from both opponents was sloppy, ragged and too wild, especially with attempted hooks and crosses. This trend continued in the fifth, Rinty in pursuit, Jackie back-pedalling and slipping punches.

The energy of Paterson's performance had so far impressed, at least. Whether he could keep the pace of his work at such a high tempo was anybody's guess. The first five rounds had fascinated yet lacked the explosive edge many hoped for, bar a couple of early incidents. The sixth round was relatively quiet, too, much to the frustration of the fans who wanted more quality punching. However, it must be said that Rinty was more comfortable working the counter-puncher routine. Perhaps the tactic was to see how much Paterson could actually do before the fuel gauge started to drop dangerously close to the red zone. Any hint of fatigue creeping into Jackie's boxing, and Rinty would surely pounce. Therein, however, lay his problem; he was much too eager to land a haymaker which resulted in him rushing his attacks, and his timing was off. He also knew Paterson had the capacity to leave this historic occasion in ruins. He was a big puncher who merely needed to unload a special right or left and Ireland's hopes for a first undisputed flyweight champion could crash and burn. Probably the toughest lesson Rinty ever experienced was the punishment Paterson had hammered out to him at The Oval in 1938. Rinty knew what his opponent could do if given the chance.

The bell rang for the seventh round and Paterson burst into action. He appeared to be bouncing on his very toes, staying frantically busy with neat moves and quick punches. Maybe he had fooled one and all, and lulled Rinty into a trap. He was increasing the pace instead of conserving the energy many doubted he had. He looked for a close quarter fight, swinging in the hope of finding a real corker of a hook. Anxious to follow up on his flurry of blows, he moved in close. This was to prove a dreadful mistake.

The cheering of Paterson's supporters was transformed into a collective sharp intake of breath. They saw it coming. Only Jackie remained oblivious, all his attention focused on trying to score a victory punch. Rinty showed him the left, stretched out the arm, measuring the next move, anchored himself, but then withdrew. Jackie took the bait. A swift jab nailed him and, crouched, Rinty let fly. A low trajectory swinging right hook straightened as Paterson stepped in with his guard open. Beads of perspiration darted off his glistening dark hair as the power of a hooked shot snapped his head to the right. It was the best punch of the fight, its ferocity crashed against jaw and flesh. The local fans went ballistic.

Jackie's knees gave away, his left leg jack-knifed beneath his torso and down he went. Flat on his back, arms outstretched, he refused to give in and courageously fought the referee's count. 'Four, five, six ... '

Unsteadily, he slowly got to his feet. The referee instructed Rinty to go to a neutral corner, allowing Paterson a fraction more time to recover; he was determined to recover. A dubious referee took a good look before he allowed the fight to recommence. Whatever was said about Jackie Paterson, he certainly did not lack guts.

Instinctively, he tried to block the next punch. Rinty, now demonstrating the composure and ruthlessness lacking in the earlier rounds, switched down to offload a terrific right hook into the ribs. It was brutal. Brave to the last, Jackie withstood the fierce onslaught for a few moments, head knocked right, then slammed left, nothing coming back as his sight was blurred from the blizzard of blows. The final act of the drama was a low swinging right cross. Paterson's jaw took the full force of it. He slumped to the canvas, buckled and spent, glancing briefly in the direction of his corner before his head sagged. The referee counted, without interruption, one through to ten.

The *Times* described the last few minutes: 'Right hooks, left hooks and right uppercuts crashed into Paterson's now defenseless jaw, and although the champion was game to the last he wilted under the terrific barrage of blows and crumpled up in a sitting position in the corner ... This fight will not go down as a great one but the thrill which accompanied the knockout will make it live in the memory of Ulstermen, at least, for many years.'

And again from the *Times*: 'Ten seconds of terrific punching by Rinty Monaghan of Belfast caused the downfall of World, British and Empire fly-weight champion, Jackie Paterson (Glasgow), at the King's Hall, Belfast, last night, the champion being counted out in the seventh round ... The knock-out, while not altogether unexpected, came at a stage when Paterson was actually showing some improvement. He had staggered Monaghan with a right to the jaw and two lefts to the body and, obviously thinking that his punches were hard enough to distress his opponent, went in rather wildly for the kill. This was his undoing, for Monaghan, strong as a lion and as lively, met him with a right to the jaw and Paterson fell flat on his back.'

It was a sad end for Paterson. He would never box at flyweight again.

But Rinty had won! He was now the proud possessor of a world title, recognised by the NBA and British Board—he was an undisputed champion. He was also the new British and Empire champion. The fans were beside themselves as an ecstatic Frank McAloran and the rest of his team chaired the winner across the ring. His triumph was celebrated in his customary style, with 'When Irish Eyes Are Smiling', his signature song, been given the heartiest of renditions amidst wild scenes of celebration. With Frank's arm draped across his shoulder, Rinty sang his heart out. The Governor, his Excellency Earl Granville, stepped into the ring to congratulate the boxer, as did Prime Minister Sir Basil Brooke, and Ireland's new British Open and British Match-Play golfing champion, Fred Daly. Paterson, a noble competitor to the end, hugged his conqueror before Rinty was propped up on someone's shoulders for a victory lap. He sang 'I'm Always Chasing Rainbows', and it would be a while before the fans would allow him to retire to the dressing room.

At the after-fight reception there was much slapping of the backs of winners while commiserations were made to Paterson and his team. Jackie stood up to say a few words and a hush descended. He congratulated Rinty on his win, recalling the night, ten years earlier, when, as a rookie professional, Paterson had beaten the Belfast man. It was a short, heartfelt speech, which finished with Jackie smiling at Rinty as he told him, 'Well, you made me; now I have made you.'

Immediately after the fight Jackie had been, understandably, in no fit state to talk to anyone. Media requests were rebuffed, though the local *Telegraph* man did manage to get through to his dressing room where Paterson ruefully reflected: 'What can I say? I have lost.' Pat Collins remarked that, just as Jackie had won his titles like a champion, he had lost them with dignity after fighting hard. Collins was now looking at a world bantamweight bid against Manuel Ortiz.

Speaking afterwards to the *Irish News*, Rinty said that he appreciated why the crowd broke into slow hand claps every so often but, as he reminded everyone, he was fighting the very best: 'If I was not as aggressive as some would wish, I would point out that I was fighting the world champion and I could not afford to take any risks.'

He was now one of boxing's elite professionals. In March 1948 his name was up in neon lights with heavyweight icon, Joe Louis, and light-heavyweight, Gus Lesnevich, who, eighteen days earlier, had retained his title with a first round rematch kayo of Billy Fox. (However, he would lose it again, in London, four months later, to England's Freddie Mills.) One of the biggest World Championship rivalries of 1948 was to be found in the middleweight division. This featured two Americans: Tony Zale and Rocky Graziano. Zale had lost his title to Graziano in July 1947 when he was stopped in the sixth in Chicago. Zale had previously knocked Rocky out in 1946, and did so again at Newark, resulting in Rocky never fighting again at world level.

Rinty's name was up there too with welterweight Sugar Ray Robinson. There was no undisputed ruler at light-welter, a division that had been in flux for over a decade, while the US claimed ownership of the lightweight, feather and bantam titles through Ike Williams, Willie Pep and Manny Ortiz. Williams scored a June kayo inside six rounds in Philadelphia over Beau Jack before the rivalry of Pep and Sandy Saddler, which would reach notorious levels during the next three years, kicked off in New York that October. Saddler deposed the champion with a fourth round kayo. They would meet four times for the featherweight title, and only once did the contest last the fifteen rounds scheduled.

Ortiz, in his second reign as bantam champion, returned to action that July with a knockout win in eight over Mexico's Memo Valero in Mexicali. Frank McAloran confirmed that one of several offers that poured in after 23 March was an invite to the USA in May to challenge Ortiz without risk to Rinty's title. Stateside promoters were rather keen to receive the new World Featherweight Champion. Domestic offers included a rematch with Bunty Doran, though not for the title, and Scotland's Norman Tennant. The main push was coming from France and the European authority. The name on their lips was a certain Maurice Sandeyron.

For now Rinty Monaghan could enjoy his status as a pioneer in Irish boxing. He was the only fighter outside of the US that could rightfully claim to be an undisputed world professional boxing champion at that time, an extraordinary feat. The future looked exceptionally bright.

16

SAM ICHINOSE WATCHED THE NEWSREELS ABOUT Jackie's final dethronement at his Pam Am club. Still seething over his luckless European tour, he became set on drawing Rinty to the tropical paradise as soon as he could. Salvador's hard luck story at Harringay had booked the islanders' passage back to the United States where, in April and May of 1948, Marino was kept busy with fights in Stockton, Sacramento, and San Francisco. He notched up four wins back to back before a ten rounder with New Yorker Cecil Schoonmaker (27-5-4) at Frisco's Civic Auditorium ended in a points defeat.

Once back in Honolulu he finished the year with four more wins, while Sam's chase for a third fight with Rinty resumed. It looked like a sure thing for a few days, at least. He sent a communiqué to Frank, promising to shell out $25,000, on top of covering the Belfast team's travel costs, proposing that the fight be staged in Hawaii, with a conditional clause on the table to try and clinch the deal: should Rinty lose, Marino would defend against him in Ireland, or anywhere in Great Britain, at a venue of Frank's choosing. There was one sticking point between the two managers in that they could not agree on a suitable referee for such a contest. Rinty's position would invariably be weakened by agreeing to up sticks and go to Honolulu, the backyard of the challenger, to defend his title in front of what would surely be a hostile crowd. The task of securing a decision to retain the championship under those conditions, if a stoppage was not accomplished, would be immense. After further debate a suitable referee was chosen in the form of Nat Fleischer, the editor of *The Ring*.

Now the offer appeared to be good enough, and Frank, confident in his boxer's ability to go over and do another number on the Hawaiian, informed Sam that he and Rinty were happy with the proposal. The fight looked to be on the cards for 1 March in Honolulu. Scratch the surface, however, and it can be seen that the deal was doomed to fail. The Monaghan team had underestimated the local response to the exotic location. Indeed, it was hard for his fans to comprehend how, after that incredible night at the King's Hall, and the ensuing local parties, the title could be risked in a place, thousands of miles away, that many of them had never heard of. They wanted to see Rinty defend his title for the first time in Belfast, back at the King's Hall. But business was business. It came down to who was prepared to offer Rinty the best financial terms. As Frank explained to the local media, the deal tabled by Marino's manager made the most business sense. Ichinose's offer equated to £6,250 for Rinty's share of the fight purse alone.

The fans need not have fretted. McAloran and Ichinose may have had a gentlemen's agreement for March 1949 in Honolulu, but it was not to be. Both the British and European boards were not interested; in other words, the chances of Rinty being granted a permit were nil. A BBB of C licensed boxer required a permit to fight abroad from the British Board. This became more difficult if the boxer in question was the holder of a world title. Rinty was one of only two BBB of C licensed boxers at the close of 1948 to be in possession of a World Championship belt in any of the eight contested weights. The other was 'Fearless' Freddie Mills who, on 26 July, dethroned a badly cut Gus Lesnevich at the White City Stadium in London.

Without official blessing the Hawaiian event could not go ahead. To ignore the BBB of C's position regarding a permit would be very costly and the last thing Rinty needed was to be hit with a barrage of Board of Control sanctions. One of the arguments put forward in nipping the

Honolulu match-up in the bud was that Marino, the NBA's own nomination, had already been given his chance at Harringay in 1947.

Mounting pressure on the British Board from Europe's governing body resulted in an announcement that they wanted Rinty to put the undisputed championship on the line against the French European champion, Maurice Sandeyron. Promoter Jim Rice's offer now looked the smart money deal: a £5,000 pay day for Rinty to fight Sandeyron and, if terms could be thrashed out, Rinty would have all the trimmings of a Belfast city venue. There would be no travel involved, no jaunt halfway around the world, and he would fight in front of a huge home crowd.

However, Rinty's manager was not finished with the Hawaiian offer just yet. In the first week of January, Frank stated that it was his intention to contact the Board of Control and ask its secretary 'to secure for me the British Board's formal permission for Rinty to fight outside their jurisdiction'. He reasoned that, in the circumstances of having agreed to the best offer, the Board should not withhold a permit allowing his boxer to defend his title on foreign soil. He outlined his position to the *Telegraph*:

'I am now writing to Mr Ichinose to that effect and when I receive the BBB of C permit for Rinty to fight in Honolulu I shall notify the Hawaiian promoter to go ahead with his arrangements, which will include the deposit of the guaranteed purse in a British bank to Rinty's credit.'

The papers were full of the debate. While the sum offered by Ichinose was an incredible amount, staying to fight in Belfast meant a drop of only £1,250. Hawaii involved a lot of travel, and maybe up to three weeks away from family and friends. Hitches and hold-ups had to be factored into the pros and cons of a trip to Honolulu. Frank was also wary of sharing Ichinose's dreadful disappointment of travelling for weeks at great cost only to see his boxer lose. In fact, the risks were big, financially as well as emotionally, when considering the long journey, the different climate, the possibility of injury and delays, even cancellation. Manager and boxer needed to calculate all this against the $25,000 offer Ichinose was trying to entice them with.

On the other hand, the French powerbrokers determined that should Rinty fight their star Sandeyron and beat him, then the European title would be his. This was a hugely seductive offer. Holding four titles at the same time, the World, British, Empire and European, would be quite something. For one thing, no Irish boxer at any weight had ever managed to accomplish such a feat. In fact, no boxer licensed by the BBB of C had won a European flyweight title for more than a decade, a state of affairs the Board were doubtlessly keen to see rectified by Monaghan.

A European title caught the imagination of Rinty's supporters. This belt, with its robust and sometimes contentious history, had proved elusive for many top notch flyweights. Jim Rice's prospect was definitely growing in appeal, so much so that, on Tuesday, 11 January, it was formally disclosed that Rinty's first defence of his title would take place in Belfast against Sandeyron, who had agreed to put his EBU title on the line in his quest to become the first Frenchman to claim the undisputed world title.

Two fellow countrymen had claimed versions of the World Championship, but not the undisputed title. 'Young' Perez was last to secure a version of the Championship, the same one that Rinty had finished up with after Jackie Paterson's legal challenge to the British Board, and a title recognised by America's influential National Boxing Association. Perez achieved his success in 1931 with a second round knockout of the NBA's sanctioned world champion, Frankie Genaro. He would lose his grip of it a year later in Manchester when he was beaten in his first defence by the same Jackie Brown that Benny Lynch had taken the European title from in 1935. The original French world champion was Emile Pladner. His success was also a disputed claim, recognised by the NBA, after a 1929 win in Paris against Genaro.

There was one catch with the European title; the end of January was much too soon for Rinty. Backed into a corner on this, and with the Hawaiian deal scuttled, Frank looked to delay the date as he was keen for Rinty to shake off the post-Paterson ring rust. His boxer would need a good warm-up bout to prepare for a fighter of Sandeyron's seasoning. Luckily, a compromise was thrashed out and the world title bout was set for 5 April with the proviso of a warm-up contest for Rinty. The EBU accepted this and the deal opened the way for McAloran to fulfill an agreement for a non-title contest in London against Dickie O'Sullivan on 7 February.

Frank was especially keen on the O'Sullivan encounter since a previous engagement with the top London flyweight had had to be called off the previous October after Rinty had fallen ill. He'd been troubled by a chest condition that stubbornly refused to clear up, and was forced to cancel the fight to undergo a period of rest and recuperation. Unfortunately, this was a pressing issue. He was at the top of his game as a professional fighter but, health-wise, things were not what they should have been. Specialists were working with him to try to alleviate a bronchial problem. Although they were able to manage the condition, progress to cure him was not significant.

Rinty was struggling. Ten months on from pummelling Paterson, things were still not right. He knew it, Frances knew it, and Frank knew it. His lungs were under pressure and the doctors had yet to find an answer. Perhaps the toxic trails that snaked across Belfast's skyline from the mill and factory smokestacks had left an invisible mark. Maybe the Spartan training conditions were a contributory factor. It was difficult to pinpoint the culprit source of Rinty's respiratory discomfort.

O'Sullivan's people had kept their man busy. A stocky, aggressive character, he had fought Sandeyron and Les Johnson. His manager then decided to pit him against another top Londoner, Islington's Terry Allen. They had exchanged blows, briefly, for the South East title ten months earlier when O'Sullivan had been disqualified in the second round. This second meeting was promoted by Jack Solomons for the British Board's South Eastern Area title at the Royal Albert Hall. Jack promised the winner a fight against Rinty at his next big tournament to be held at Harringay Arena on 7 February 1949. Terry had suffered a catastrophic first round knockout defeat to Monaghan in London in the spring of 1947. If he could get the measure of O'Sullivan, a return with Rinty might propel him up the British ratings and put him in line for a shot at the biggest prize of all.

With so much at stake O'Sullivan and Allen fought a torrid battle. Allen won a fight that earned high praise from leading sportswriter, the London *Daily Telegraph*'s Lainson Wood, who described it as 'one of the fiercest and grandest 12 round battles between little men seen for a long time'.

Since Allen's defeat to Rinty he had gone from strength to strength in the division, winning fourteen of his last fifteen contests. He shared with Rinty a preference to counter attack. When they met at Solomons' promotion in Harringay, Terry was initially able to keep out of harm's way. It was not until the fourth round that Rinty's aggressiveness started to catch him. However, the champion was soon feeling the effect of his lingering chest problem, coupled with his sabbatical from fighting. Despite a solid fifth round, Rinty was having problems finding his range and, in the sixth, Allen sent him to the canvas. He'd left himself open to a terrific right. Taken straight to the jaw, the blow floored Rinty. Down on one knee, the referee's count reached five before Monaghan rose to his feet. Seconds later, his senses foggy, a right hand cracked against his head and down he went again, this time not rising until the count of seven. Luckily the bell sounded and saved him from further punishment, or from being stopped for only the second time in his career. The *Daily Telegraph* reported that the world champion was well off his game. The execution of his punches was ragged, ability to judge distance completely off, and Allen was making him pay. Rinty had not experienced this kind of hammering since his thrashing at the hands of Jackie Paterson in 1938. He gathered himself together, grateful that the contest was made for eight, and not ten, rounds. Allen kept the pressure on but could not finish it early and had to settle for a points win.

Rinty's timing was all over the place, naturally enough, given the months he had been forced to take off because of poor health. That was the only excuse offered. Of course, the show must go on, and the shaken champion crooned a rendition of 'I'm Always Chasing Rainbows'. It failed to impress the London journalists. He had hit the canvas with alarming regularity and they did not like it. Allen's ability to tag him almost as he pleased had the media doubting Rinty's ability to handle the fine skills of the Gallic star. The review in the *Daily Telegraph* did not cut him much slack: 'If indeed this was true form the championship is as good as in France, for Maurice Sandeyron has an easy job on hand when he goes to Belfast.'

Yet, for all the negativity, the Allen contest was only a basic eight-rounder with no title on the line, and made at four pounds over the championship limit. Rinty had not put in his usual training and was returning from a period of ill health. He knew what he had to do to get back on track. It involved weeks of dedicated training, including nights of sparring with top British bantam, Eddie McCullough, as well as Jim Robinson and Billy O'Neill, and resuming his morning runs, which would trim him back down to eight stone. He would make the critics eat their words. Admittedly, the criticism had been fair enough. People who knew their boxing were shocked by how poorly Rinty had performed, but there was still time to prepare for Sandeyron.

Perhaps the only people more driven than a boxer focused on a title were the promoters. They always had to think about the big picture, always on the lookout for the dream pairings. Bunty Doran was hoping for a shot at the European bantamweight belt, to be held in the King's Hall in April. Bob Gardiner had been working for weeks to sort out a deal for Bunty to take on the Italian, Guido Ferracin. Despite a good win over the champion of France, Theo Medina, the European Boxing Union refused to reward Doran with a crack at Ferracin, preferring to have Ferracin defend the title against Spain's Luis Romero. Bunty was matched instead with tough English bantam, Stan Rowan, whom Doran knew well as he had lost to Rowan in a British title eliminator, extinguishing any chance of challenging Jackie Paterson at that stage in the process.

Rowan and Paterson were scheduled to meet in March at Anfield in Liverpool. If Rowan came through that unscathed, Gardiner was keen to bring him to Belfast. Meanwhile, the BBB of C's Northern Ireland Area Council announced details of its purse deadlines for its Area title bouts, which included a match between Doran and Tommy Madine.

Gardiner wanted Terry Allen to fight on the Monaghan-Sandeyron under-card. His idea was to put Allen in against Northern Ireland's flyweight title holder, Jackie Briers. For a bantamweight bout he was hoping to have Edinburgh's Jimmy Stewart take on young McCullough.

Jack Solomons was pushing for a world bantam title shot for England's Danny O'Sullivan, managed by Benny Huntman, the target being Manuel Ortiz. But a still smarting Sam Ichinose was waiting in the wings. He was bitterly disappointed when Rinty was prevented from defending his title in Hawaii. A talented opportunist, Ichinose worked the angles in the US to block O'Sullivan's bid and landed the catch of a world title fight for Marino, who would step up from flyweight and meet Ortiz in Honolulu on 1 March. Ortiz, with 101 contests under his belt, and twenty world title bout wins from twenty-one, proved too good and retained his title on unanimous points.

Would the world flyweight champion, after such a poor show against Terry Allen, retain his title against the brilliant Maurice Sandeyron?

17

FOR MANY, MAURICE SANDEYRON WAS THE favourite to win. Terry Allen's punching Rinty to the floor had, quite frankly, tarnished the champion's reputation. Even the Irish media were not too positive about Rinty holding on to his title, while correspondents in London had absolutely no faith in him. They reminded their readers how former world title challenger, Elky Clark, had disagreed with the referee raising Rinty's arm after the unexciting match against Marino. Others began to dismantle his win over Jackie Paterson. There were whispers about Paterson spending the entire night before the fight sitting beside a boiler in order to sweat off the last couple of pounds. As far as some were concerned Jackie had not looked too well; therefore, beating him had been no great shakes. Once again Rinty was going to have to prove himself. He had two months to prepare and could not afford to waste a minute.

His opponent, who ran a small café in his native Paris, was a late arrival to professional boxing. Born on 21 March 1921, Sandeyron was prevented from concentrating on his talent thanks to the war. He finally decided to try his hand at fighting professionally in 1944. The initial phase of his career did not give any indication that he would amount to much. He triumphed in only one of his first seven contests, losing five and drawing one. However, it must be remembered that there were not many opportunities under the Nazi regime in France for athletes to practice, and professional boxing events were few and far between. When one was organised, France was found to be short on flyweights, which explained how Maurice, as a novice, ended up boxing for the French Championship three times in those first seven pro bouts. Among those he faced was future EBU bantamweight title winner, Theo Medina, as well as a future opponent of Rinty's, Emile Famechon.

Sandeyron arrived in Belfast two days before the fight, taking a room at the Grand Central Hotel. He completed his training at the Athletic Club in High Street along with French flyweight champion, Louis Skena, who was matched against Northern Ireland title-holder, Jackie Briers. Jackie had taken the Area Council's title with a sixth round stoppage of Frank McCoy the previous November in the first domestic flyweight scrap since Monaghan's 1945 knockout of Bunty Doran. The French team must have been aware of the media's view that their man was favourite to trounce the highly criticised Monaghan. It was felt that Rinty's best chance was a stoppage, mid-match at the very latest. If the fight was to go the full fifteen rounds, Sandeyron could wear the champion down and secure a points win. The two boxers were familiar with the other's style. Maurice had watched Rinty beat Paterson, while Frank had made at least three trips to London, and had observed Maurice fight Dickie O'Sullivan. He had drawn in his defence of the EBU title, and lost a non-title contest on points, before getting the decision at Harringay. The showdown with Rinty would be his eighth title fight since meeting Medina in 1945; that defeat, alongside a domestic title loss to Famechon in Nice in April 1946, had been his only setbacks. Medina had the distinction of being the only opponent to have ever stopped him.

Maurice was not noted as a big hitter. Outside of an eighth round technical stoppage of Mario Solinas in Paris in June 1947 he had not stopped anyone in eleven bouts. His only victory by way of an anesthetic shot had been a fourth round kayo of England's Johnny Summers at Nottingham in April 1947, his first contest following a shock win over Famechon in Saint Etienne for the French title. His core strengths were his speed and his craft, and he was widely regarded a skilled boxer who was quick on his feet.

On 5 July the fans began to file into the King's Hall at Balmoral. There was an edge to the night, with Rinty's supporters uncertain about what to expect. A big interest in the fight was evident from the scarcity of the tickets, and from the fact that an extra train had had to be laid on from Derry for the travelling fans. Of course, this was the first time that an Irish boxer would be defending a world flyweight title in Belfast. Even the weigh-in at the Ulster Hall attracted a big crowd. Rinty was looking in fine form, scaling a drum-tight 7st 12lb 2oz, a few ounces lighter than his opponent. His training had gone very well despite his discomfort with his lungs.

To date, no Irish boxer had managed to win the Championship of Europe at eight stone. In fact, no British licensed fighter had claimed the flyweight title since Scotland's Benny Lynch, who held the title intermittently over the three years after 1935. Since his heyday, the title had been the periodical property of two Belgians, two Frenchmen, and an Italian. 'Kid' David of Belgium secured it between part of 1935 and 1936. Ernst Weiss of Austria and Valentin Angelmann of France also held the crown for part of 1936. Lynch retrieved it until 1938 when it changed ownership again to Italy and Enrico Urbanati. For the next five years Urbanati was Europe's flyweight champion, after which the title was put on ice until 1946 when Raoul DeGryse of Belgium claimed it. The following year he lost to Sandeyron. The King's Hall might see Monaghan become the twenty-fifth flyweight to win the European Championship since it was introduced in 1913, and first won by England's Sid Smith.

On that score, Rinty was aiming to establish his claim as the eleventh British Board/NSC licensed boxer to win Europe's title at this weight. Apart from Smith the others were England's Bill Ladbury in 1913, Percy Jones of Wales in 1914, England's Joe Symonds in 1914, Scotland's Tancy Lee from 1914 to 1916, and Jimmy Wilde of Wales. Wilde enjoyed two spells as champion, first of all between 1914 and 1915, then for an undefeated reign from 1916 to 1923. For this latter period Wilde was also undisputed world champion. Elky Clark of Scotland succeeded Wilde, winning the title in 1925 and holding on to it until 1927. Another Scot, Johnny Hill, was champion from 1928 to 1929, and then England's Jackie

Brown ruled for almost four years from 1931 before Lynch emerged on the scene. At this point Wilde and Lynch were the only British licensed boxers to simultaneously hold the European and undisputed world titles.

This was Rinty's big chance. If he beat Sandeyron he would become a four-titled champion. For the moment only the fearless Freddie Mills, England's star light heavyweight, had managed the extraordinary feat of holding the four titles at the same time. Freddie, who won the European title in 1947, had beaten the great Gus Lesnevich in a world title rematch in July 1948 at White City Stadium in London.

Maurice Sandeyron had fought some top class men in his short career—Medina, Famechon, DeGryse, Honore Pratesi and O'Sullivan. If he were to win the world flyweight title it would substantially boost French morale. Gallic flyweights had not figured too prominently in the world order since Emile Pladner was at the height of his game in 1929, when he beat Frankie Genaro in Paris. However, his world title claim was 'disputed' as it was only recognised by the Americans.

Title fight promotions rarely run without a hitch and this one was no different. Welsh official C B Thomas had been appointed referee. This did not sit well with Sandeyron's manager, Pierre Gandon, who argued that Thomas was not neutral enough. He demanded that someone else be appointed, threatening to pull his fighter otherwise. European Boxing Union officials became entangled in the row, taking Monsieur Gandon's side. Poor Bob Gardiner needed this eleventh hour distraction like a hole in the head. As it turned out, a French official saved the day. Monsieur Gremaux, the president of his country's Boxing Federation, held emergency talks with Maurice's manager. Pierre agreed to let his boxer fight despite his continued reservations about Thomas.

The fight opened with Rinty's left hand immediately jabbing and piercing at the French man's guard. Rinty, the aggressor, worked every inch of the canvas, developed openings and delivered his shots with terrific timing. The precision of his punching amazed those at ringside. He had been criticised so much over the last few months, and had arrived at the King's Hall as very much the underdog. Within minutes he had blown away the doubts. This was nothing like the cautious display that had edged Marino in 1947, or the blizzard of blows that had rained temporarily down on Jackie Paterson. He was not content to wait and counter and look for the big punch, the feared right hook that had dropped so many previous opponents. Instead he was determined to prove that there was more to his game than a kayo strike.

His boxing was beautifully controlled over the initial twelve minutes, flawless almost. Sandeyron could only wait and hope for Rinty to make a mistake by exposing his chin, as he had with Terry Allen, which would allow him to try for a kayo. The Frenchman refused to lose heart, was quick and clever, paying due care and attention to staying out of reach of Rinty's right hook. Bunty Doran and Jackie Paterson had come to grief after falling victim to it. Unlike the Marino fights there was little grappling or clenches which meant that the referee had little need to interrupt the action.

Sandeyron weathered the early storm impressively, demonstrating excellence in defensive work, and showing no signs of distress. When the fight moved into short range toe-to-toe flurries, he tried all he could to rip at Rinty's stamina with short arm hooks that carried fair snap and bite. However, Rinty coped and was light on his feet, staying clear of any harmful hooks aimed at his temple and jaw line while countering with rights over Sandeyron's guard and rapier jabs.

The first five rounds were marked down to the champion. In the sixth, Sandeyron's battery of right hooks at close quarters earned him a share of that session. Rinty responded by turning up the heat in round seven, sending the crowd wild as he nailed Maurice with a powerful right cross. The Frenchman wobbled slightly, but he regrouped and came back strongly. He was taking a lot of punches, and at the close of round nine his face was flushed and bruised and looking the worse for wear.

The bout had reached an interesting stage. Questions about Rinty's durability had to be addressed. He had boxed fewer than fifteen rounds in thirteen months, and much of his training had been restricted as doctors treated his chest complaint. Six rounds were left. Was he able for them?

Maurice stepped into the tenth round sporting a large swelling around his left eye. Unperturbed he remained steadfast, pressing the fight as much as he could, knowing that Rinty could find this stage of battle difficult to maintain his tempo. Unfortunately the champion continued to be elusive and his jab was catching Sandeyron on the way in repeatedly. Three rounds to go and Maurice knew he needed a knockout, a punch he had thrown just once, at Johnny Summers, in 230 rounds of boxing. He needed to summon another now, and fast! Then Rinty began to give him hope. In the twelfth round he visibly slowed; tired for the first time in the contest, he looked to hold and spoil. Maurice's sapping body shots were beginning to hurt a bit more. Nevertheless Rinty finished with a flurry just before the bell. He finished the next round well and, with the King's Hall going wild, Rinty dug as deeply as he could to give the last two rounds one hell of a whirl. At the final bell he knew, Maurice knew, and everyone in the arena knew: he was still the world champion.

The performance was well above the ordinary, in a different class to the historic Marino and Paterson spectacles. He had proved a point. The reporter for the *Independent* was delighted with Rinty's quality boxing: 'He used the straight left in the classic manner of Wilde and Driscoll.' For the first time in Ireland's boxing history, the country had produced a European flyweight champion.

The *Telegraph* described the ensuing scene: 'Upwards of 10,000 spectators rose to their feet and rousing Irish cheers conveyed mass congratulation to the happily dancing champion who was enthusiastically embraced by his manager-trainer Frank McAloran and other handlers. Sandeyron sportingly shook hands with the champion and the pair was photographed by a battery of cameramen. Monaghan's father also climbed into the ring and proudly embraced his son, the crowd all the while yelling lustily for Rinty to sing his victory song.'

There was further celebration in the family when Bunty Doran, on the under-card, claimed a points win over another Frenchman, Georges Mousse. Injury had forced Stan Rowan to cancel. Northern Ireland flyweight champion Jackie Briers, however, dropped a decision to the French champion, Louis Skena.

Frank McAloran told reporters that he believed Rinty had clearly shown his critics that he was a talented boxer: 'My boy won well. Rinty and I were out to show the critics that it was not only a dig which had sent Rinty to the top but that he could box as well.'

Maurice Sandeyron had no complaint with anyone afterwards,

including the Welsh referee. When asked about losing his bid to become the first French world champion for twenty-three years, his manager translated his sporting reply: 'The fight went to the better man. Good luck to Rinty.'

Over the next couple of days, speculation was rife about Rinty's next move. The Board of Control authorised a British and Empire flyweight title eliminator between Terry Allen and Dundee's Norman Tennant at Dens Park in Tennant's home town on 25 May, and they were keen that the winner challenge Rinty for the domestic belts he'd ripped away from Paterson in 1948.

So, what had Frank in mind for the champion's next task? The manager was still keen to go to America and showcase Rinty to the huge Irish community in a place like New York, though not to defend the flyweight title. He had a bigger dream; he was thinking of switching Rinty up in weight, to bantam, the end game, to force a title challenge against Manuel Ortiz, the world champion of that division. Rinty's cousin was also being linked to a move for Ortiz, with the possibility of a showdown that summer. Rumour had it that Ortiz was keen to make a tour of Europe and was looking at possibly defending his title in England or Ireland, depending on the terms. Frank confirmed that Rinty had been invited to the US for a number of non-title bouts with flyweights from the New York area, as well as to challenge Ortiz for his crown. There was even an offer to see if Rinty was interested in taking a break from boxing, by singing his way around a string of American gigs.

Bernabe Gutierrez, a promoter in the US, made his pitch. A communiqué to the flyweight champion's management outlined a raft of interesting ideas and options. Gutierrez wanted the Irish star to headline at least two promotions in New York. Another offer arrived all the way from the Philippines from the team behind top Filipino bantam, Tirso Del Rosario. Basically they had the money to shell out for a non-title fight in Manila, with no strings attached. This approach from the Asian Pacific quarter testified to Monaghan's standing in the sport. Del Rosario, a popular boxer, had, just sixteen months earlier, unsuccessfully challenged Ortiz for his world title. No matter, McAloran had no interest in travelling to the Far East. The big prize was Ortiz and a chance for

Rinty to add a world title at bantam to what he owned at flyweight. Even if he were to lose to Ortiz he would not risk the flyweight crown. It was very tempting indeed, offering Rinty an excellent opportunity to test and further himself. No boxer since the inauguration of the professional fly and bantam divisions had ever held both titles at the same time.

Only two former flyweight champions, Emile Pladner of France (NBA-recognised in 1929) and 'Small' Montana of the Philippines (New York-recognised in 1935), had previously gained a world title opportunity at bantam. Both had suffered early defeats, Pladner by a third round kayo to Panama Al Brown for the undisputed title in Toronto in 1932, and Montana by a third round stoppage for the NBA title to Lou Salica, in Toronto also, in 1940.

Meanwhile, 'Sad' Sam Ichinose was trying every which way to persuade the Belfast men to head for Honolulu, but there was just not enough money on the table. Gutierrez's offer was certainly the most generous, and definitely the less complicated.

The Reuters agency dispatched a reporter to Los Angeles to interview Ortiz's manager, Tommy Farmer. The reporter asked whether the world bantam and flyweight champions would clash that summer in what would be a novel battle. Farmer replied that he not yet been formally approached by Gutierrez, or anyone else, proposing such a match. He expressed a degree of surprise that the story had been carried by the media. This was a little peculiar.

Five days later, a story ran back home in the sports pages of the *Belfast Telegraph* about the latest offer from Hawaii. Ichinose had tabled an improved bid in an attempt to follow up Marino's failed challenge to Ortiz with a move back to flyweight seeking a third match-up with Monaghan. Once again Rinty was offered $25,000, and the package also included round travel tickets. Ichinose proposed 2 August for Rinty to defend his title in Honolulu. McAloran responded negatively, feeling insulted at Rinty being offered the exact same money despite now holding four titles. Sam tried again but McAloran was having none of it. Not enough money and too much risk. The offer was nowhere near what he felt such a venture was worth. In sterling, it amounted to approximately £5,000, plus travel. He made it clear to Ichinose that he would have to put his hand much deeper into his pocket just to be considered.

'This is just a repeat of Mr Ichinose's offer. He would be required to raise it considerably before we would think of undertaking such a trip. As you know, we were interested in Mr Ichinose's efforts to stage a title fight in Honolulu but when we studied what our hotel and training expenses out there might easily run to, we dropped the 25,000 dollars offer like a hot brick.'

There was absolutely no objection to fighting Marino again but the terms had to be right for Rinty. Frank wanted to see how far Ichinose would take it. If he was truly serious he would have to double his offer to $50,000 (£10,000), though if he raised the bar to $40,000, plus travel expenses, it might be feasible. Frank called Ichinose's bluff, at least for media and public consumption, since the BBB of C were not overly supportive of any such deal. The following day the Associated Press reported back from Honolulu: Sam declared that he was ending his pursuit of Rinty.

While the newspapers clamoured for details about Rinty's next opponent, doctors were issuing him with orders to rest for the next few months. The only exercise he could perform was walking. The Sandeyron fight had taken a lot out of him and there was still no solution to his discomfort. Frank soothed worried journalists, telling them that the condition was not too serious, something he genuinely believed. If the lung problem could be sorted out by rest, then Frank thought it made better sense to seek approval to fight in the United States. If the money was right, an historic showdown against Ortiz was too good to turn down. As usual, nothing was as simple as it seemed. The BBB of C had different ideas about Rinty's next fight, preferring to see him defend his newly acquired European title; in other words, they did not want him to go to America. However, all was not lost. The summer schedule was free and Frank still hoped to be able to accept Gutierrez's bid, providing that the promoter secured the support of Ortiz's manager, Tommy Farmer. But it was not to be. Ortiz's management organised a European tour of non-title bouts for the summer. And that was that.

When Ortiz arrived in England he fought British featherweight champion, Ronnie Clayton, in Manchester at catchweight. He also travelled to Paris to meet French title-holder, Theo Medina. All this time, Rinty was resting up before kick-starting his training once again. Instead of fighting Ortiz in New York, Rinty was lined up for a non-title bout in Belfast. Italian champion Otello Belardinelli, who in January had beaten Guido Nardecchia for his National Championship, was signed up to bring Monaghan's four inactive months to a close. Otello was coming off a points loss in Brussels to the rated Belgian prospect Jean Sneyers. The fight, a warm-up for Monaghan's next world title defence, was fixed to take place in the King's Hall on 19 August 1949. The long rest had been exactly what he needed and his doctors permitted him to return to the skips, punch-bags, sparring and early morning runs. The Italian domestic title holder did not overly extend him and Rinty eased through the ten rounds, gaining a points win.

Rinty appeared more than ready for his next challenge. He was about to perform another first—a defence of not one but all four titles simultaneously, something never done before by a British Board boxer. Although the BBB of C supported the European authority's push for Monaghan to defend their title against Pratesi the following January, a deal was thrashed out to fit in a defence in September 1949. The opponent would be none other than Terry Allen, who was presumably delighted at finally being allowed a crack at the title.

18

SEPTEMBER 1949 STARTED WELL FOR RINTY and Frances, with the birth of their first son on the fourth of the month. Sean was their fourth and last child, brother to ten-year-old Martha, seven-year-old Rosetta, and toddler Collette, not yet two. Rinty did not have too much time to spend with the new arrival as he was training hard for his battle with Terry Allen on Friday, 30 September. This would be his third meeting with the Londoner and would be a battle for the World, European, British and Empire titles, a quartet of prestigious eight-stone division crowns, making the match an historic one.

Leading bantamweight contender, Eddie McCullough, who was on the brink of challenging for the British title, was a reliable sparring partner, as was Rinty's brother-in-law, the well-rated featherweight Harry McAuley. Other partners included Peter Robinson, Bertie Todd, leading lightweight Jim Robinson, and Billy O'Neill. Frank McAloran promised everyone that Rinty would not be repeating his last performance against Allen. This was a much improved fighter who was determined to retain his position as the number one flyweight. Frank accepted that Allen was a dangerous and gifted opportunist but he predicted that victory would be Rinty's. Frank's claims were probably unnecessary as Rinty was the favourite, thanks to his performance against Sandeyron. According to the *Telegraph*, Rinty was 'expected to rout his London challenger'.

However, the boys at the gym knew things were not running as smoothly as McAloran suggested. His stellar fighter was struggling with the training. The morning runs were becoming increasingly arduous, putting him under serious strain. His bronchial-infested lungs were struggling to cope and, if anything, the condition was deteriorating. Rinty perhaps sensed that the Allen fight would be significant for him at another level, and that his fighting days might be numbered. On 19 August he fought, and defeated, the Roman, Otello Belardinelli, at the Royal Hippodrome in Belfast for an international ten-round contest made at 8st 4 lbs. The Italian had won his domestic flyweight title seven months earlier against Guido Nardecchia.

The Monaghan-Belardinelli bill was chiefly supported by Northern Ireland's middleweight title-holder, Jackie Wilson. He defended the Area Championship over twelve rounds, unfortunately losing a points decision to Freddy Webb. In the other under-card bouts, Belfast flyweight Billy Barnes extended his unbeaten record to 4-0 with a points win over Dublin's Chris Hardy, the fight being made at 8st 2lbs; while Belfast lightweight Billy O'Neill out-pointed Jamaica's John Hazel.

Two days before Rinty's son was born, Bob Gardiner put on a show at the Royal Hippodrome headlined by an international heavyweight contest between Irish champion, Paddy Slavin, one of Rinty's roadwork partners, and Canada's Don Mogard, chief sparring partner to world top-ten-rated American prospect Lee Savold. Several Belfast boxers were on the bill: leading welter Tommy Armour, featherweight Charlie Neeson, lightweight rivals Gerry Smyth and Tommy McMenamy, and Rinty's chief sparring partner, bantam Eddie McCullough, who was matched against Pierce Ellis of Manchester. McCullough was tipped to challenge for the British title, which was at the time held by Stan Rowan, who had taken it from Jackie Paterson the previous March. On the home front the Irish title was held by Bunty Doran. Great things were predicted for the twenty-one-year-old and it was a ferocious shock to the community when news of his sudden death was made public. He died in the Mater Hospital on Saturday, 24 September, following an operation for a perforated appendix.

Eddie had first walked into McAloran's gym as a fifteen-year-old kit carrier for a couple of professional fighters who were staying at his sister's guest house in the New Lodge Road area. These were heavyweight Frank Hayes from Kildare and his friend, the middleweight, Freddie Price, from Dublin. Frank was also a fine fiddle player and encouraged the boy to play the violin. Soon Saturdays were filled with music competitions at the Alhambra Picture House and Molly's Hall, down the country at Dunloy, while week nights saw Eddie cheerfully carrying the boxers' gear to the gym. It was not long before he wanted to be a boxer too. It was inevitable really. Boxing had always been important factor in the McCullough household. Eddie's father Richard had enjoyed amateur boxing and, when he joined the Irish Army, he'd fought in various tournaments around the country. Eddie's brother Paddy was a booth fighter at Ma Copley's tournament in Chapel Fields during the 1930s alongside Rinty. Younger brother, George, a featherweight, had the distinction of being the final amateur opponent of the future British, Empire and Northern Ireland professional champion, Billy 'Spider' Kelly, at Derry's Guild Hall. Jim 'Boxer' Hall took Eddie under his wing at the gym and encouraged him to stretch himself. George remembers the turning point.

'This one time Ted arrived home without one of his front teeth. "Boxer" Hall had him under his wing at the gym, but this night Ted had his front tooth knocked out. That did not deter him. Eddie continued to go to train at McAloran's place, really loved it, and it was not long before he was recognised for having a bit of talent. He had a great straight left, was a natural at the boxing, so quick about the ring and very accurate with the jab. Ted soon established himself as a brilliant prospect, fighting at bantam. That straight left of his, which was the punch he became noted for, it was like a piston. Ted could hit you a few times before you realised what was happening.

'In the family home he was known to us as Ted. He was one of nine and all of us were there at his beside, at the Mater Hospital, on Belfast's Crumlin Road, when he died. Only a few days beforehand he asked his girlfriend to marry him. Ted's death was a terrible, terrible shock to the family, to his fiancée, to everyone who knew him. It is still difficult to talk about, even after all these years.

'Ted died a few days before Rinty's title defence against Terry Allen. He was to fight on that bill, on the under-card against Johnny Boom. At the time people were saying that Eddie was British title-winning material, he was that good, and maybe was good enough to go even further than that. Unfortunately, we never got the chance to see how good he really was. Rinty was badly shook up by what happened. I do not know how he managed to get himself ready to defend all his titles against Terry Allen a few days after Eddie died. That must have been very difficult. Eddie was his main sparring partner at the Hardinge Street gym. They trained for years together, ran the roads in the mornings with Paddy Slavin and a few others. They would run the Sheep's Path, the Cave Hill and Bellevue steps.

'Eddie would get me out of bed at six in the morning to go with him, so I joined the gym as well to learn the boxing, and I remember we would put on these heavy sweaters and big heavy boots, run up the Antrim Road, up the Cave Hill and back home, go the Shore Road and Bray's Lane the next day. Eddie was so fit. He would run Bray's Lane backwards. That was hard on the legs but that is what Eddie and Rinty went through every morning before going to their work. They were so fit and strong.

'Something I think was working on him before that. After Ted died I was talking to Jimmy Webster. They fought shortly before he became ill. Jimmy told me that when they fought he could hear Eddie groaning every time he hit him with a body punch so maybe the condition with his appendix was working on him then.

'Boxing was important to the local communities around Belfast; both amateur gyms and professional gyms were all over the city. It gave you something to do, kept you off the streets, and you were trained and kept fit and some of the boxers at the Hardinge Street gym, which was an old wreck of a place, were really very good.'

Bill Rutherford, from the *Ulster Sports Gazette*, spent many nights watching the Hardinge Street boys being put through their paces. He recognised Eddie McCullough as a talent very early on: 'Rinty's sparring partners are numerous, but they are all heavier than himself. He is not likely to find many lighter. The usual ones are Eddie McCullough, who at 18 years of age is already showing all the attributes necessary for a future British bantam champion.'

Eddie won thirty-three of his pro fights, losing only three. His most memorable win was at the King's Hall against Hawaii's Tsuneshi Maruo, sparring partner to NBA flyweight title challenger Dado Marino. Maruo was coming off a win over top English hope and future British bantamweight champion, Stan Rowan, when they met in 1947. Eddie recovered from a knockdown, the only one of his career, to see his hand raised by referee Neilly Thompson.

'It finished in a points win for Eddie,' recalls George, 'and at that time that was a great victory. Neilly told me afterwards that it was the punishing work with that straight left of his that won the fight. That was his best punch. I remember that so well.'

Eddie's opponents over the years included former Empire champion, 'Kid' Tanner, the vastly experienced 'Fighting Jockey' Jimmy Gill (who lost a decision to Rinty in 1940), and English Area champions Gus Foran, Tommy Proffitt, Owen Johnston, Jimmy Webster and Ron Draper, with only Webster and Draper managing victory. Eddie's other loss was to Belfast rival, Jackie Briers.

John Caughey wrote about Eddie McCullough's death for the *Telegraph*, describing the 'drama and pathos' that had marked the young bantam's last fight. After speaking to some of Eddie's colleagues, Caughey understood 'the cloud of gloom that now envelopes his club mates'. Both Frank and Rinty had visited Eddie in hospital, and Rinty had held the youth's hand and sang to him during his final hours. Caughey quoted Frank: 'His death was a tremendous shock to his family, myself, and his countless friends. He was a grand, clean living sportsman and I am convinced he would have gone to the top.'

The tragedy cast a dark cloud over the King's Hall promotion. Eddie's passing was a dreadful blow for Rinty and he sank into a depression. There was some talk of postponing the match but Bob Gardiner decided to press ahead, hoping that Monaghan would be able to focus on the contest when he took to the ring. The event was sold out, so it seemed only right to keep going. It can only be presumed that Eddie would have agreed with this. Gardiner dedicated a page in the programme to Eddie. A portrait photograph, taken by Royal Avenue studio photographer, Jerome, was reproduced alongside Bob's tribute to the 'prince among boxers', a craftsman he respected, and a talented fighter regarded as 'a great bantamweight of the future'. Bob reflected:

'Eddie had already made much progress in the game with victories over such worthy foemen as Jim Berry, Rory Pritchard, Tsuneshi Maruo, Jimmy Gill and Jackie Briers. Determined to reach the top of the boxing he was fired with other ambitions too. Talented in many ways, he had a particular taste for music and was a violinist of considerable competence. A life of rich promise seemed to be opening up for him. But it was not to be.'

Rinty's already precarious emotional state was further rocked when, the morning before the fight, he received a letter from the Inland Revenue demanding that he make payments at super tax bracket rates. The world champion was being sorely tested—his consuming grief, his struggle with his lungs, and now this. There was another financial blow for everyone involved in the sport when sterling was seriously devalued, a huge issue for promoters and boxers alike. Jack Solomons reacted to what was described as a 'bombshell' by stating that, in his opinion, the financial agreements he had made would have to be reassessed and purse offers hiked by approximately thirty percent.

Nat Fleischer, the esteemed editor of *The Ring*, was in England on business and decided to delay his return to New York to attend the King's Hall promotion so that he could present one of *The Ring*'s prestigious World Championship belts to the winner. With one eye on a possible future title challenge to world bantamweight champion Manuel Ortiz, promoter Gardiner had sent invitations to Ortiz and his manager, Johnny Rodgers, to attend the Belfast show.

There was a setback for boxing fans who had failed to get tickets. As with the Paterson fight in March, Gardiner had been unable reach a settlement with BBC executives. Therefore, the King's Hall top of bill, and possibly Monaghan's last contest, would not be shown live on television. Unlucky fans would just have to make do with their wireless. Bunty Doran's bout with Danny O'Sullivan would provide the chief support to the bill and then Monaghan and Allen would come on at 9pm.

The night before, Allen and O'Sullivan had relaxed by going to the Belfast Empire theatre to see the show *Miles of Smiles*.

Amateur and professional analysts wondered what sort of entertainment lay ahead. If the champion opted to go for the jugular early, then the crowd would be in for a potentially dramatic and possibly short night. However, the more popular opinion was that Monaghan would be exercising caution. Allen had floored him too many times in February to decide on a risky all-out attacking strategy.

On the night, the bout lasted every minute of the scheduled fifteen rounds but the result caused a bit of a stink. It was not the most eventful of world title bouts. It was bloody and something of a yawn for the sell-out crowd, devoid of thrilling moments, the blood mainly coming from Allen, who sustained four cuts. His corner claimed they were all the result of clashes with Rinty's head. There were too many untidy phases for it to be exciting with much of the contest fought at close quarters. Rinty had decided not to do too much chasing. He wanted it tight and awkward and with plenty of in-fighting. Allen's tactics complied. This allowed the champion to dictate most of the rounds, fight the fight he wanted to, and with more accurate short-hooking and uppercuts, it was thought that he piled up the points.

The referee did not see it that way and surprised everyone present when he announced a draw. Ortiz's manager Johnny Rodgers had watched the fight at ringside and later spoke to the *Telegraph* about his disgust: 'For the life of me I cannot understand why the London referee Sam Russell made the fight a draw. I thought Monaghan had won.' He also fuelled the prospect of Rinty and Ortiz meeting for the world bantamweight title by saying that he felt Monaghan 'would make a better opponent for Manuel than Allen'. His overall opinion of the fight echoed everyone else's: 'a dull world title scrap'. The *Telegraph* argued that Monaghan had done enough to win by a safe points margin. Obviously referee Russell attributed more to Allen's effort. If the fight inside the ring had lacked spectacle, events outside the ring livened up when a couple of rival fans broke into a brawl as the boxers came out for the fourth round. Police intervened quickly to defuse the squabble.

Laison Wood, writing in the *Daily Telegraph* and *Morning Post*, also disagreed with the referee's scoring, admitting bewilderment that it ended in a draw. He believed Allen 'never did enough to deserve to take the titles from the Irishman' and rated the fight a poor one. He remarked that it did 'neither credit', and 'as a championship contest it was farcical. It was all flurry and fret and precious little do.'

A frustrated Frank McAloran agreed with Ortiz's manager that Rinty should have been named winner. He outlined his intention to bring Rinty to the US for a title showdown that did not involve risking his flyweight status. The Board, however, supported the European governing body who wanted him to defend next against Pratesi. Not only that, but they wanted a rematch with Allen after the Pratesi match took place. Ortiz's manager confirmed that the International Boxing Club, based at Madison Square Garden, was interested in staging Ortiz versus Monaghan if the two parties could agree on a deal. This, Frank McAloran stated, was their preferred option. Because a draw had been called, Allen remained the number one contender and was entitled to a second challenge some time in 1950.

It was not a good night for Bunty Doran. Nevertheless, this contest was hailed as the best fight of the night. O'Sullivan's speed caused Doran problems all the way through and his body was smudged with bloody smears. Bunty's cleverness had him ahead on points in what was a final British title eliminator until disaster struck. Five seconds into the twelfth he was sparked out by a barrage of punches. The kayo sparked a ring invasion and the referee C B Thomas required police protection. Doran suffered temporary paralysis to his arms and legs when one of the final cluster of punches struck a nerve. He was taken to the Mater Hospital and kept in for observation. O'Sullivan visited him the following morning.

The rest of the bill saw Lisburn's Jim Keery stopped in one round by 'Kid' Germain of Barbados; former Irish amateur flyweight champion, Billy Barnes of Belfast, retired in the fourth round of his scrap with Glasgow's Joe Murphy due to a hand injury; and one of Rinty's former opponents, Dubliner Joe Collins, defeated the Strafford bantam Johnny Boom, who was originally to box the tragically deceased Eddie McCullough, on points.

The fifteen rounds with Allen took its toll on Rinty. Anyone near to ringside at the King's Hall could not fail to notice his struggle to breathe freely. It was most unfair. He should have been enjoying his reign as champion and looking forward to lucrative deals to support his family. If the deal with Ortiz worked out, along with the Pratesi and Allen fights, it would have meant more than £20,000 for the Belfast slugger. Instead, he was wheezing like an old man, thanks to the amount of catarrh infecting his lungs. Unable to train as he needed to, he was finding it more and more difficult to stay fit and make the weight. Meanwhile, the thirty-one-year-old had never been in more demand. There were challengers queuing up in Europe to take pot shots. Apart from the no-risk invitation to America, there were British and Empire title fights on the backburner. Promoters in the USA were screaming out for him, along with promoters in the Far East. The British Boxing Board of Control and Europe's governing body were planning who he would defend against next, and Sam Ichinose was making renewed efforts to attract him to Hawaii. Local newspapers were brimming with excitement over each offer as it was made. The Board announced its decision on 15 November that, on 31 January 1950, Rinty would defend the European Championship against Honore Pratesi of France.

It was a difficult enough time for the boxer but nothing compared to what came next. His youngest daughter, two-and-a-half-year-old Collette, woke up one morning to discover that she was unable to move her legs. The toddler was diagnosed with 'Infantile Paralysis', or polio, as it is more commonly known today. There had been a recent outbreak in Northern Ireland. As Collette says today, 'There was no vaccine then, so I was just born too soon. I do not remember too much of that period of my childhood, only that I used to sleep in the parlour because with the polio I could not get up the stairs.'

Rinty was pushed to breaking point and had to make a decision. Accordingly, on Saturday, 25 March 1950, the local press ran the story that, for medical reasons, Rinty Monaghan, undisputed World, European, British and Empire Champion, was retiring from boxing. The deadline for his European title defence with Pratesi had come and gone, prompting lots of gossip and whispered speculation. The March announcement simply confirmed what many had already feared to be the case.

Monaghan revealed that he had met with the Northern Ireland Area Council of the British Board the week before to outline his position. Just twelve months earlier, Area chairman Alex Dalzell had hosted a gathering of the great and the good in local public life to congratulate Rinty on his knockout of Paterson. This was a very different meeting: Rinty detailed the ailment that was forcing him to quit the sport. He brought his x-ray plates with him as proof of his condition but the Area Council chiefs refused his resignation. Grasping for a more positive alternative they drafted a recommendation, asking that Rinty try returning to the gym to see how he fared. This was a ridiculous outcome, as Monaghan was clearly not in the best of health, and his doctors had warned him not to undertake anything more strenuous than walking. Unable to convince the officials of the seriousness of the situation he felt his only option was to go public, which he did a few days later. When the British Boxing Board of Control served him with a written notice, on 30 March, Rinty's boxing career was officially at an end.

The notice was publicised the day after promoter Jack Solomons moved to secure the signature of both Johnny Sharpe, Terry Allen's manager, and Pratesi. He planned to match them for the World and European Championship titles, proposing a Harringay Arena show for Rinty's vacated belts, on 25 April. Officials were notified that Solomons had verbal agreement from the French champion's management and added their support—the fifth England versus France clash for the world title was on. This contest would also be the first undisputed title bout between the two countries since Jackie Brown had fought 'Young' Perez and Valentin Angelmann three times in NBA-recognised title fights in 1932 and 1934. Brown won three and drew one, and all matches were 'disputed', lacking universal recognition. Allen and Pratesi met in London in May and Jack's gamble on Allen paid off. Terry earned a points win to become the first English undisputed champion at eight stone since Peter Kane in 1938.

Unlike Monaghan, the success did not elevate the Islington boxer to world one number in *The Ring*'s ratings. A few months later, Allen agreed to comply with the demands of 'Sad' Sam Ichinose by embarking on the journey to Hawaii to defend his newly-acquired title against Rinty's old rival, Salvador Dado Marino. Hopefully, Terry had enough time for sightseeing since, when it came down to business, he lost to Marino. The Islington hotshot's reign had lasted a mere ninety-eight days.

Marino's run included a return match win over Allen in Honolulu and three bouts with Japan's Yoshio Shirai. Shirai stopped Marino in their first fight, a non-title bout in Hawaii, which was followed by two world title contests fought in front of a crowd of 40,000 at the Korakuen Baseball Stadium in Tokyo in 1952. The little Hawaiian pushed Shirai all the way in two fifteen-round battles but Shirai proved the master, winning on points each time. The second Korakuen Baseball Stadium clash would also be the last time boxing fans would see Marino fight. Following the rematch Dado decided to call it a day and hung up the gloves two years and eight months after Rinty's ailing health had forced him to quit.

Rinty did not take very well to his premature retirement. As a kid he'd set out to be a boxer, to entertain crowds, with ambition no higher to begin with than securing a spot on the Labour Hall shows run by Mr Gilmore and matchmaker Harry Hanley some twenty years before. He duly followed his doctor's advice and took it easy for two years, staying away from the gym and resisting any kind of strenuous exercise, which led to an overall improvement in his health. As his old rival Salvador bowed out of boxing in Tokyo he gave in to the pressure to try and give it one more go. Rinty wanted out of retirement and, in 1952, attempted to resurrect his career, albeit against medical advice. He felt he needed the boxing bug back in his life. He missed the training and the comradeship that accompanied the sport at which he had so excelled.

At thirty-three years of age, Rinty was full of enthusiasm, back in training, and did not for one moment consider that his comeback would be denied him. He applied to have his licence released from medical suspension by the British Board. However, the sport had moved on with lots of new names and faces. Japan's Shirai ruled the eight-stone world arenas. In Europe, the Belgian Jean Sneyers was top dog, and domestically Terry Allen, Teddy Gardner, Jimmy Pearce, Eric Marsden and the emerging Welsh star, Dai Dower, were the main players on the scene. Flyweight did not interest him. Making that weight was overly ambitious and unrealistic. Rinty had his eye instead on Jackie Paterson's old stomping ground of bantam. John Kelly was the emerging talent in Ireland at the weight and Scotland's Peter Keenan was British champion.

Rinty's brother Patsy was home on leave from Merchant Navy duties in Trinidad, South America and Africa at the time. He remembers Rinty's excitement at the prospect of being a part of the boxing scene again. Patsy had boxed for years as well, fought in ports all round the world. He understood where his brother was coming from. Boxing was like an addiction that Rinty was finding it increasingly hard to withdraw from. He convinced himself that he could turn back the clock and perhaps be a champion again. The illusion was soon shattered when the British Board's letter of refusal arrived.

'It was about 1951, maybe 1952, I think,' recalls Patsy. 'I am not quite sure of the exact date, but it was around that time because I was home on leave and John trained with me at the gym at night and was in pretty good shape. John said he was feeling a lot better, a lot stronger after a long rest and break from training. He wanted to have another go and he did not think the Board would turn him down.

'He was back working with James McAloran at the gym and hoped to make a return at bantamweight. He did not think he was too old to give it another go, so he decided to apply for a licence to fight from the Board. We talked about what we would do if he got the licence and he just kept training away until this day a letter arrived from the Board. They wrote back and stated there was no way John would be granted one.

'The Board refused to give him a licence and told him that their decision was on medical grounds. He was very disappointed about that, very disappointed. John found it very hard to take in. It was a big setback for him but he said to me sometime afterwards that at least he had tried. John never talked about it again.'

By the early 1950s Jackie Paterson had also left boxing. His stubborn decision to go through with a world title fight against Rinty in Belfast in March 1948 was the beginning of the end. He failed to win six of his next eight contests, all at bantam. One of the defeats was on points at Anfield Football Ground in Liverpool to Stan Rowan, which cost him his British and Empire titles. In fact, that contest was his last major fight for a title. He did cross jabs and hooks with the then world champion, Manuel Ortiz, over ten rounds during a European tour by Ortiz in October 1949. This was a non-title match that drew a crowd of 23,000 in Glasgow, and which Jackie lost on points. Defeats followed to Vic Toweel in Johannesburg, Eddie Carson back home in Scotland, and Willie Myles, on 7 February 1951, at the Cairn Hall in Dundee. Myles was Paterson's final opponent in a career that spanned ninety-one traced professional fights.

On 4 November 1952, the same month that Salvador Dado Marino had fought his fifth and final flyweight title fight against Yoshio Shirai, Honore Pratesi was matched in London with a highly-rated South African contender, Jake Tuli (real name Jacob N'tuli). Two months earlier Tuli had created history by beating Teddy Gardner to become the first black South African to win an Empire title. Unfortunately, the greatest risk every professional boxer takes when he enters the competitive ring befell the Frenchman. After Tuli won a split points decision, Pratesi collapsed and died in a London hospital from a ruptured blood vessel in his brain. He was just thirty-one years of age.

19

SEAN 'SPIKE' MONAGHAN NEVER KNEW HIS father as a world flyweight champion.

'I was born a few weeks before his last fight, the world title defence against Terry Allen, so I did not know my father for his boxing. That is a part of his life that I knew nothing about. I probably did not know anything at all about it until I was well into my teens. All through my life, until he died in the early Eighties, my father was just a song and dance man to me. I did not know him as anything other than for his singing and the bands he was involved with.

'He had a dance band, called "Rinty and the Rintonians", in the early part of the Fifties, and I remember all these musicians and famous singers, like Ruby Murray, a great friend of my parents, being about the house all the time. There was always singing and music in our house when I was growing up and I followed my father in that way. I tried out the boxing when I was young for a while but it was the music that really interested me, and I played drums for years in country and western and dance bands in England and at home.'

Sean remembers how, as a teenager, people would approach him to ask if he was Rinty's son. When he confirmed that he was they took great pleasure in explaining why his father was such a hero to the working class community of Sailortown and the York Street district. After several conversations with Rinty's old fans, Sean decided to learn more about his father's career.

'Some time in my teens it dawned on me he was not just the song and dance man I knew. Once I started to read about what he did I started to ask him a lot about that part of his life and it was fascinating to listen to him describe what he remembered about the fights, the great boxers he fought like Jackie Paterson, what Belfast fight nights were like in the Thirties and Forties. He was an amazing man really and it is great that he is remembered so fondly as this legendary world champion boxer.'

Sean remembers that little house in Corporation Street was forever entertaining visitors. For instance, the veteran broadcaster Richard Dimbleby was a regular in their front room.

'I think any time Mr Dimbleby was in Belfast on business he would drop in to see Rinty. I remember him visiting many times. Television people were about the place all the time from the BBC and from Dublin, and people from the radio and the newspapers. There were always reporters calling to interview about something. Frank Carson lived around the corner from us and was friendly with my father.

'Lots of people involved in shows in Belfast would call and there were famous boxers in and out of our house all the time. There was always something happening, somebody calling to see him and have a chat over tea. Dad loved a cup of tea and was very fond of gravy rings. He had a sweet tooth, as they say. There was always a quarter of sweets in his pocket. When I was a wee boy I did not take much notice really of who was in the house. You don't when you are young. You are more interested in playing about the place, but my mother told me many times about the wonderful people who would call at our house. Years later I got to know some of them, and why they were such friends with my father.'

When Rinty retired from boxing, he cast around for another way to support his family, turning to his second love, music and entertainment. He had saved quite a bit of money and decided to invest some of it by putting together a band of musicians. Naturally he took into account that his name would be a good selling point for securing bookings and gigs. The music scene was thriving in the early 1950s with new bands being formed on a weekly basis, or so it seemed. A friend from west Belfast, Billy Burns, was a professional musician who travelled the world, playing on ocean liners with various artists. Rinty determined to visit Billy the next time he was home. Burns lived at Springfield Drive, off the Springfield Road, in an area known as Mackie's Height, due to its proximity to Mackie's engineering works. His son Liam, who also grew up to be a musician and a member of top traditional folk group, The Freemen, recalled the scene.

'Rinty's car was like a big tank. I was in awe of him. Here was Rinty Monaghan in our house. Everyone knew how famous he was. I was about fourteen at the time. He came in and sat down with my father and says, "Billy, you know, I always loved show business and I would like to get a band around me." They talked for hours. At the end of it all they agreed to form a band. My father agreed to be part of it and they decided they would go on the road and tour the country. They would call themselves "Rinty and the Rintonians". It was catchy enough, I suppose. Being Rinty's band was the big thing. It got them known right away. It was an interesting time for bands in Ireland—Rinty and the Rintonians were one of the first bands of the Irish showband era. While they did not last too long, the fact they were part of that initial showband scene in this country adds a lot to the story. From what my father told me about it, they really enjoyed themselves while it lasted, and had a great time touring here, there and everywhere.'

Initially the gigs were plentiful for the ill-clad band, and they were booked to play in halls, pubs and clubs as far flung as the counties of Tipperary, Galway, Sligo, and Dublin. They played at various Belfast nightspots and, in County Down, they were a regular attraction.

'To look at them all dressed up they were more like a football team than a showband,' continues Liam. 'The dress sense was not great but they did not care too much about that. They wore what looked like yellow goalkeeping jerseys with black dress pants. When they decided to go on the road I was a kitchen boy on the railway and I remember the Great Northern line was running a Knock Special, taking all the pilgrims down to Knock.

'My mother asked me to bring back some holy water as she wanted to bless the band before they left for their first tour to County Tipperary. I forgot all about the holy water and knew my ma would kill me. There were these bottles in the tiny kitchen on the train so I decided to fill them from the Great Northern Railway water tap.

'The boys were going to a place called Borris-in-Ossory. They were booked to play in a big marquee and, because there were so many in the band, they used two cars to travel and transport all their instruments. My mother was as proud as punch. They had received loads of publicity as Rinty Monaghan's band. They were very good too. My father brought together a lot of the top musicians. I will never forget the day they left our house for Tipperary. I was terrified to tell my ma that the bottles were filled with tap water from the train. Anyway, out goes ma with the hair scarf on to bless the boys and the cars and everything else. She sprinkled the cars with it. All the boys blessed themselves and off they went. I never did tell her what was really in the bottles and sure they all arrived there and back safely.'

Rinty was well placed to belt out the Rat Pack hits of Sinatra, Martin and Davis. He was already an experienced entertainer thanks to his ENSA days, when he had drawn inspiration from one of England's top showmen, George Formby. During the 1930s, when Rinty was sweating his guts out at McAloran's gym, Formby was the highest paid entertainer in Britain with his ukulele act. During the 1940s, while in ENSA along with Rinty, George was a regular visitor to Belfast. He was also an avid boxing fan and liked nothing better than sitting ringside on fight nights in the Ulster Hall. The Rintonians incorporated some of the city's finest trumpet, sax and trombone musicians, guitar players and drummers, and the band went down a treat. The original band included trombonist Ted Darragh, alto clarinetist Gerry Denvir, pianist Freddie Deeney, trumpeter Danny Campbell, drummer Bobby Regan, alto-sax player Sammy Morgan, tenor-sax and clarinetist Jimmy McAlea, with Sammy Lowry on trombone, Jimmy Regan on bass, and guitarist Mal McKeown. For a time they packed out arenas. Liam recalled the performance:

'Rinty would sing and halfway through the show they used to do what they called "a skit". They did all the dances and all the rest of it but there was a part where Rinty would say something over to my father, all rehearsed you know, and they would show their chins and the crowd would call out, "Go on Rinty, hit him." It was very funny. They used to spar, shadow-box, pretend to throw punches. Sometimes they would clip each other and probably the last time Rinty was put on his backside was during a performance back in the Fifties. At least that is what my father told me. One night a phantom punch was not timed right and Rinty had to take it.

'I did not see that much of them. They were on the road most of the time. I think they were probably on the go for about eighteen months to two years, but what I do remember clearly is they hit the showband scene in a blaze of publicity. They enjoyed it for as long as it lasted. The fact they were all top notch musicians made it so enjoyable and worthwhile. Unfortunately, it did not really pay. That was the problem with it; the band was too big and the wages were not enough to make a good living. They had fun but eventually they decided to stop touring and split up.'

When the band broke up, Rinty featured in an array of the popular music spots throughout the 1950s and 1960s. He played and performed at the Empire, where Ken Dodd was a regular and where, in one show, a young Welsh singer was profiled as an exceptionally talented singer prospect—a sixteen-year-old girl by the name of Shirley Bassey. There were stints at the Gaiety Theatre, the Clarence Palace, the Trocadero, where comedians Frank Carson and Roy Walker held court, and the Rock Town in Great George's Street, which later became Molly Maguire's. The Spanish Rooms in Divis Street was a popular hangout, as was the UTA Club and Clifton Street's RAF club. He played on shows at St Mary's Hall with Frank Carson, Josef Locke and Jackie Wright, who, in later years, worked with the top English comedian Benny Hill. The Talk of the Town at Bridge End was another popular spot, while there were cabaret nights at the Abercorn and Club Orchid in King Street. Rinty's good friend, Ruby Murray, was one of the biggest stars around. She even made the *Guinness Book of Records* when she had no less than five songs in the charts at the same time, a feat only equalled in British music by The Beatles.

Sean remembers his father as an 'old fashioned entertainer. He loved entertaining people. He sang all over the place, in all sorts of venues. In later years, when asked to come along to an old people's home and sing a few songs, he could never say no. I do not think he ever refused anyone. That was just the way he was.'

Much later on, Rinty was interviewed for a radio series that focused on famous Northern Ireland personalities. The programme, *People in Profile*, was presented by Alf McCreary, who asked the former champion about his musical favourites. Rinty recalled that the first vinyl record he ever bought was 'Gloccamora', a favourite with Latin jazz combos. Frank McBride recorded Rinty's musical choices for a various artists' compilation entitled *When Irish Eyes Are Smiling*.

Intermingled with his boxing memories Rinty recalled how his parents enjoyed impromptu sing-a-longs with the kids. They particularly loved Al Jolson's 'When You Were Sweet Sixteen'. Jolson, like Rinty, worked with ENSA during the Second World War when he entertained the Allied Forces in London with Vera Lynn. 'Sally' was another song that had special significance for Rinty. This was a big hit for English vaudeville star and comedienne, Gracie Fields. Rinty first heard it when he went with his mother to see Gracie's big box office movie hit, *Sally in Our Alley*. But perhaps the most important song for him was Frank Sinatra's 'My Way'; Rinty explained that he always felt the lyrics summed up his boxing career.

Life after boxing was not a bed of roses but he refused to blame anyone, not even the tax man, who took so much of his hard-earned income away from him. The band had cost him a lot financially and he liked a wee flutter most weeks on the horses. He even invested in breeding racing greyhounds. Rinty was also very generous to a fault, coming to the aid of anyone who asked for his help. For instance, he once loaned a man £1,500 and failed to get a single penny back. The cumulative effect of all of this was that his boxing earnings, about £30,000, just about disappeared inside six years. It might have turned out differently. In the final year of his career, 1949, he had wanted to invest a large portion of what he had in city property schemes. As he himself recalled:

'I had it all sized up to put it into property. A gentleman was going to do it all for me, a real gentleman, and I was giving him £15,000 to put into property, which was good money. The man took ill and died and I could not get anyone else to look out for a business for me. I did try but there was nothing suitable so I just kept the money in the bank. I took ill, then the income tax came, took nineteen and six in the pound off me and they did not leave me with an awful lot. But I kept smiling, working, going out singing, making people laugh and happy ... and I had a marvelous family.'

He tried to build up a taxi business and drove a cab for a long time, but this too was unsuccessful. Then he managed to pick up a job back at the docks; however, it was only temporary. By the mid-Fifties he was broke and forced to sign on at the dole. Fortunately this too was temporary. He picked himself up and contacted some friends in the music and theatre business, making the big decision to leave his family behind and go to London. One of his old boxing fans was a theatrical agent and he promised to help him. Soon enough a spot at a London nightclub was secured. Word got about that he was back in business and drawing in the crowds. More gigs followed and, before too long, he was working on the big shows with the likes of Frankie Vaughan and Bernard Bresslaw.

With his name back in lights, he left London for Scotland, starring in various shows in Glasgow for a time. He also became involved in pantomime, working with Shirley Diamond in *Babes in the Wood*. He toured theatres up and down England and Scotland. It was not ideal to be separated from his wife and family but it certainly was an enjoyable way to make a living. This was his biggest break since working with the Rintonians and it led to others. Producers of a new show for television featuring Pete Murray, the star of *Juke Box Jury*, approached him to manage a touring All-Star soccer team.

In 1959, he was offered a small role in the film, *The Criminal*, starring Welsh actor, Stanley Baker. In those days plenty of boxers, with their scars, flat noses and cauliflower ears were taken on by film producers to play the roles of background villains, henchmen, and silent enforcers or, in Rinty's case, a getaway driver and jailbird. Released in 1960, *The Criminal* was cited as the hardest British film of its day. Baker played a ruthless Irish hood, Johnny Bannion, who was to be sprung from prison to mastermind a racetrack robbery. The actor was schooled in the part by real-life underworld figure, Albert Dimes.

When the acting jobs dried up Rinty returned home to Belfast. The next few years were spent in a series of jobs that were usually short-lived. Then, in 1976, Rinty took a job at the nearby Shamrock Service Station in Great Patrick Street. Phil Moley ran the garage and parts business and had got to know Monaghan after he'd bought a Volkswagen from him.

'Rinty would call in regularly and any time he did we would stand and talk for ages about all sorts of things and maybe have a cup of tea. Rinty liked his tea. One day he called and I said to him that I was looking for someone to do the early morning shift. Somebody had left and I had a vacancy going. So I started talking to Rinty about it. He was always an early riser. I suppose it was a habit of his going back to when he was training at the boxing, getting up at dawn to go running and all. At the time Rinty was not up to much and agreed to come to the garage every morning and work the early. He was with me for years after that.'

Phil also had a contract for newspaper distribution, and distributed the local morning editions of the *Irish News*. Rinty would be found most mornings down the back of the *News* enjoying a chat with both printers and management. It would also give him a chance to check the paper for the racing cards and sort out a bet at his bookies. Phil remembers his customers queuing up patiently on Great Patrick Street for petrol as well as the opportunity to talk to a former world champion.

'It was hilarious out there in the mornings. People used to come in to me and say, "Is that Rinty Monaghan out there?" and I would say to them, "Yes, it is; sure go over and say hello", and away they would go. He was a great storyteller. One story he used to love to tell was about when he was boxing and about the Vaseline they used to put over their eyes, which the referee would usually then rub off. Rinty used to say that he put this Vaseline under his arms and he clenched them, his opponents that is, early on in a fight to get it on their gloves. How that helped, I do not know, but it was a story he told often and it was always very funny the way he would tell it. You just had to laugh.'

Rinty's boss also shared his passion for boxing, a passion that took them all over the place to watch the top local fighters.

'We had quite a few trips in our time. Rinty loved getting along to the fights. He tried to get to as many shows as he could and not just local events. He would travel all over the place to see the fights. We used to go to watch Charlie Nash a lot and the big heavyweight, Dan McAlinden. One trip we made to see Dan was to the Burlington Hotel in Dublin. That was just hilarious, Rinty all dressed up to the nines, very dapper in his tartan waistcoat and all. That was another thing I remember about him. Rinty always presented himself so well, even when he was pumping petrol at the garage. It did not matter to him what he was doing, or where he was going, he always turned himself out really well every day.

'Another boxer he liked to go to see was a young fella who would later become a world champion, too. The fella was Barry McGuigan. Rinty would go round to see Barry at Barney Eastwood's gym in Castle Street; he'd go to see all the fighters there regularly.'

His years at the garage crossed over briefly with a short comeback on the cabaret circuit. His old pal and associate, Charlie Tosh, who had been in ENSA with him during the war, ran a recording studio called Hawk Records in the County Down village of Kircubbin. He invited Rinty to come in with some musician pals to cut a few songs. Spike played in a band on the drums, and he was asked to be part of the backing group at the recording session. There could only be one choice for the main single—Rinty's theme tune, from small hall bills to the world title fight nights of Harringay and the King's Hall, 'When Irish Eyes Are Smiling'. The proud singer brought his records to the garage to sell them in the shop, and they sold quite a few.

Many of Rinty's evenings were taken up with his good friend, the amateur boxing coach at the Holy Family club, Gerry Storey, who, as a kid in the 1940s had ran alongside him when Rinty was out training. Gerry was heavily involved in community work linked to the Holy Family club. (Just before his seventieth birthday he was presented with the international Laureus Sports award, in recognition for his contribution.) He would frequently turn up at Rinty's door looking for his help and was never refused. He remembers that Rinty even made a short return to the ring for a fund-raising event at the harbour in Ardglass, County Down. He was supposed to sing a few songs, do his impressions of Popeye and Olive Oyl, play the harmonica and sign autographs. Gerry also invited their mutual friend, another former world champion, American heavyweight, Floyd Patterson, whom they had got to know through his promotional work for Holy Family club tours to the USA. The Ardglass gig turned into a 'title bout' with another 'Yank', Frank McCann, who worked with Gerry at the boxing club. Ireland's former Tokyo Olympic Games coach, Harry Enright, was enlisted to act the part of the referee.

'It was one of the funniest things,' Gerry recalled. 'Rinty was about sixty-two or sixty-three at the time. Not that I knew, but things with him were not too good. His health was in a poor way but he never said anything. That was one thing about him. He was an extraordinary man and never complained about anything. As usual I called at his door for him. I told him what I was thinking about, that I wanted to know if he was up for a trip to County Down for a special fun-day thing the club was running for the kids in Ardglass. It was for charity and we had a ring put up and wanted him to take part in a fun bout for a bit of a laugh for the children.

'The idea was he would be matched with "Yank", who'd earned the nickname from us because he could tell a story, spin an old yarn. Frank and Rinty were very good friends, knew each other really well, and Frank always referred to him as John Joseph, never Rinty. Initially we did not tell "Yank" what we were up to. It was announced that former world champion Rinty would top the bill for a boxing bout with Willie Clyde, a big amateur who was twice the height and size of him. When we arrived, we were shocked to see so many people. There were thousands there.

'I thought, "My God, what have I done now?" We announced the plane had been delayed at Aldergrove and that big Clyde would be late. Rinty and Yank were over in the bar, Rinty was not drinking, and Yank was in there getting in a couple of vodkas. I explained to them then what I wanted. Harry would referee. Basically Yank was to push Rinty, Rinty would push back, the referee would disqualify Yank, declare Rinty champion and he would sing a few numbers.'

Nothing could possibly go wrong, or so Gerry thought. Unfortunately, Frank forgot that he was supposed to hit Rinty, while the referee lost the run of it altogether. By the end of the round Rinty was as white as a ghost from the effort. Gerry made it through the crowd to find out why the bout was taking so long. Rinty, breathless but laughing, told him that the referee had forgotten to disqualify Yank, and so on.

'I moved round to where Yank was and, at the start of the second round, tripped him up as he moved away from the stool. He thought the referee had done it, hit him a dig, and everyone is laughing, Harry disqualifies him at long last. Rinty takes a few minutes to get his breath back and starts entertaining the crowd with songs and impressions. It was a real farce, hilarious, but that's the kind of things we would get up to.'

In 1969, Rinty's fantastic contribution to Irish sport was celebrated in sharp-suited style when he was presented with a lifetime achievement award by the then Taoiseach, Jack Lynch, at the Texaco Awards ceremony. The annual Texaco Sportstars Awards were first presented in 1958, and were the brainchild of two Texaco (then Caltex) employees. The men went to see Kirk Douglas in the 1949 boxing movie, *The Champion*, about a middleweight champion whose achievements are publicly acknowledged at the American Boxing Writers' Association Awards, and were thus inspired to set up an Irish equivalent. An important factor of the award would be the judges, who would have to be recognised experts within the sporting community and impartial from the outset. This resulted in a panel of distinguished sports journalists from the main national newspapers. One of the original judges was *Belfast Telegraph* journalist, Malcolm Brodie, who was a strong advocate for Rinty's induction into the Hall of Fame. The 1969 judging panel also included Mitchel Cogley (*Irish Independent*), Paddy Flynn (*Evening Press*), Kieran Kenealy (*Evening Herald*), George King (*Sunday Independent*), Paul McWeeney (*Irish Times*), Maurice O'Brien (*Irish Press*), Tom O'Hara (*Irish Press*), and Willie Cotter (*Cork Examiner*).

The inaugural winning boxer in 1958 had been another great Belfast pug, Freddie Gilroy, who was also recognised by the awards committee in 1959 and 1962. Johnny Caldwell won the award in 1960, and again in 1961. Immaculata ABC amateur, Jim McCourt, won in 1964 for his Olympic Games lightweight bronze medal success in Tokyo, and again in 1966, after winning Commonwealth Games gold in Jamaica. Other boxers to be honoured included Mick Leahy (1963), Gus Farrell (1965), John McCormack (1967), and Mick Dowling (1968).

Shortly after the Texaco award, RTÉ television chiefs sought to arrange an interview with Rinty for their *Sport in Action* series. Producer Jim George was anxious to send a film crew to the Belfast docks area to film him but nobody could find his home address. As George remarked in 1970: 'If you want to contact Rinty any time, do what the film crew did; address your letter to Mr Rinty Monaghan, Champion of the World, Ireland.'

Ten years later, on 7 December 1979, Rinty was inducted into Northern Ireland's equivalent of the Texaco Awards, the Sean P Graham Sportstars scheme. The Northern Ireland accolade was particularly significant to Rinty as he interpreted it as recognition and thanks for what he had achieved for Belfast in the 1940s. The televised awards were hosted by Ulster Television's sports presenter, Jackie Fullerton. Legendary footballer, George Best, presented the Hall of Fame Award to a beaming Rinty in front of an enthusiastic audience that included guest of honour, Gerry Fitt, a leading political figure at the time. Fitt had actually attended the same primary school as Rinty, St Patrick's Christian Brothers' School in Donegall Street, and he'd also worked alongside Patsy Monaghan in the Merchant Navy during the 1940s.

When interviewed by the *Daily Mail* about his lifetime achievement award, Rinty was in fine form: 'This is a wonderful moment but I shouldn't really be here. A Belfast newspaper pronounced me dead after all a few years back. I enjoyed my obituary but the report was, of course, terribly exaggerated. I was an ambulance driver at the time and when a man collapsed in the street I gave him the kiss of life. Unfortunately the paper got our names the wrong way round.'

20

IN EARLY JANUARY 1984, DOCTORS BROKE the dreadful news to Rinty and his family. Over the years his ill health was a constant companion and something that just had to be endured. Since giving up boxing Monaghan was a frequent patient, enabling doctors to keep an eye on his troubled lungs and chest.

When he hit his mid-sixties, however, there was an avalanche of new problems. For one thing, he started to lose weight steadily during the summer of 1983, and his throat began to cause him problems. He developed nodules on his vocal chords, small, hard growths that are sometimes called singers' nodules. Today, a diagnosis of nodules would be tackled with a rigorous session of voice therapy which would see them off over a twelve week period. Failing that, they would be surgically removal. Vocal chord nodules are a typical complaint in singers, especially those, like Rinty, who had been troubled with chest infections. Meanwhile, the cause of Rinty's weight loss was discovered to be diabetes, which further complicated the weakened condition of his chest and throat.

Rosetta, his second eldest daughter, remembered the day the test results came through.

'It was in July that daddy was diagnosed with diabetes. Shortly after that he was sent to see about his throat again. He had to go regularly for check-ups because daddy suffered from nodules, the throat problem singers can take. The last check-up was about January and the last time they looked it must have been cancerous. The end was quick enough.'

A benefit night was held in February for the family at the Steeple Inn in Antrim town, thanks to fellow Belfast man Billy Wilson, and Charlie Tosh's record company. It assembled an all-star cast of local singers, personalities and boxers, including former Miss England, Donna Mayers, hostess of the popular television quiz show *Mr and Mrs,* and singers Eileen Donaghy and Tom Lambert. It was a fine tribute to a man who loved nothing better than to entertain others.

Five weeks later, on Saturday, 3 March 1984, the announcement was made: Rinty Monaghan, the Undisputed World Flyweight Champion, was dead at the age of sixty-four.

Rinty said once in a radio interview: 'I have been written off for dead three times. The first time was in 1976, the second time was in 1978, and on a Monday broadcast, it was reported that I was dead. The first time a gentleman collapsed and I gave him artificial respiration and brought him round. People were saying, "That's Rinty Monaghan", but they did not say that it was Rinty Monaghan who was helping the man. In 1978 someone collapsed in York Street. I was not even near the place. It was a false alarm.

'I was reported dead in 1981, but I knew nothing about it until I came back up to the house to find two reporters standing at my door. One of them said to me, "Are you dead, Rinty?" and I said to him, "Yeah, do I look dead?" I have never seen as many friends in all my life, and I'm the first dead person to see that.'

On Tuesday, 6 March, thousands of friends, including many former boxers, gathered with the Monaghan family in Upper Donegall Street to pay their final respects to a larger than life character and one of the all-time greats of Irish sport. Rinty's coffin was carried over the threshold of St Patrick's, the church where he'd married Frances forty-six years earlier, on Boxing Day in 1938. Floral arrangements and messages of condolence were stacked outside from his many friends in the boxing and show business community. One of the wreaths had been fashioned in the shape of a boxing ring from white carnations, with two red carnations signifying gloves. Frances received telegrams of condolence from the likes of Frank Sinatra, Dean Martin, and boxing hero to millions, Muhammad Ali.

Father Myles Murray officiated at the funeral mass to a congregation comprised of the biggest names in the boxing world. There was his former training partner from the Cave Hill runs, Paddy Slavin; two of Belfast's legends of the Sixties, Johnny Caldwell and Freddie Gilroy; Peter Keenan, the former British bantamweight champion, who flew in from Glasgow to attend the service; Billy and Johnny Warnock, who represented one of the most famous boxing families from the Shankill area of Belfast; Jackie Briers and Jimmy Ingle; Davy Moore, Billy Barnes, Gerry Hassett, Desmond Marrinan and Garnett Denny; Manuel Quinn from Ma Copley's Chapel Fields; Peter Sharpe, Paddy Maguire, and John Kelly; Dan McAllister and Jackie Mussen; and his cousin, Eddie 'Bunty' Doran, the fighter who 'gave' Rinty his first title.

Father Murray spoke affectionately about the man who had always been such a popular figure in the neighbourhood: 'He brought good news … a gentleman, a man loved by many. That is what life is all about; touching people, bringing joy and bringing happiness, making friends.'

After the mass, the cortege passed by the hundreds of mourners who had lined the streets along Carrick Hill and the Falls Road, all the way to the City Cemetery. The atmosphere was largely one of nostalgia, with plenty of talk about the fight nights at the Ulster and King's Halls, Rinty's great triumphs over Doran, Sandeyron, Paterson, Marino and Allen, along with his battles at The Oval and Solitude with Tommy Stewart and Ike Weir.

On Monday morning, the *Irish News*, *Belfast Telegraph* and *News Letter* carried extensive tributes in their sports and news sections, as well as the obituary columns. The front page of the *News Letter* featured a short tribute entitled simply, 'Irish Eyes':

'Rinty Monaghan was one of Ulster's few sporting legends. The whole community will mourn his passing. His achievements in the boxing ring from which he retired in 1950 as an undefeated champion have been an inspiration to generations of young people at clubs the length and breadth of the Province. He contributed in no small measure to the growth of boxing as one of Ulster's leading sports which, with the recent successes of Barry McGuigan, Hugh Russell and Davie Larmour, has helped regenerate Belfast. Whenever and wherever "When Irish Eyes Are Smiling" is played people will remember Rinty Monaghan with affection.'

The *Irish News* dedicated the following tribute to Rinty's life and achievements: 'Back in the austere days of the post-war years, boxing, under the skilful direction of promoter Bob Gardiner, reached what many regard as its zenith in Belfast. We had a score of good lads—ambitious, determined, and with the skills necessary to succeed to high honours in the sport. But the game then was tough, the benefits of the welfare state had not fully been implemented and to be unemployed or in a low paid occupation meant living within or just above the poverty line.

'Boys with hope in their hearts saw the opportunities in the regular boxing shows in the King's or Ulster Halls as one way to supplement their incomes. Rinty was not, of course, one of those starry-eyed newcomers. He had come through the poverty-laden days of the 'thirties, but his success and the way in which he personally handled that success, lit a torch which gave light and example to the Kellys and the Gilroys and the Caldwells who followed him to championship honours. He was, however, much more than a professional glove fighter.

'His personality gained him the love of rich and poor alike. Not for him the hard word about others, not for him the regretful talk of what might have been, just an acceptance that life had much to give all of us if we have the verve and the willingness to grasp at it. Today in Belfast, Catholic and Protestant, Nationalist and Unionist, will be a little sadder. But they will be represented in person or in spirit as Rinty is laid to rest in his final resting ground... the tears will eventually dry, but the memories will live forever.'

Jack Magowan, in the *Belfast Telegraph*, wrote: 'Monaghan was the most lovable of men. Not from him the dour, often cranky gravity that so many champions seem to bring to sport. He sang and laughed his way through life and liked to see others laugh with him. As Popeye, he was a riot, and he could play the mouth-organ and tap dance with equal dexterity. He was a one-man vaudeville act and could have made more money in show business, I always felt, than he ever did in the ring.'

Denis O'Hara, a former boxing writer with the *Irish News*, and leading correspondent of the *News Letter* and *Sunday News*, made the following tribute in the *News Letter*: 'Rinty Monaghan was much more than a successful and famous fighter. The chirpy, wise-cracking champion brought instant sunshine to every person that had the good fortune to meet the former world flyweight champion ... his tragic passing on Saturday and following a six-month illness will be mourned by generations of post-war fight fans, mums, kids and grannies who had merely a remote interest in boxing. Rinty was something special.'

A boxing historian, Fred Heatley, commented in an obituary for the *Irish News*: 'He was a small man, but one who made up in heart and warmth for what he lacked in height. His passing will be missed and by none more so than by those who recognized in Rinty Monaghan a magnificent fighting machine and a unique individual who never broke his links with the ordinary people.'

***

Rinty outlived the man he'd beaten to become the undisputed flyweight world champion. Jackie Paterson's life had spun out of kilter in the 1960s. A successful businessman in Glasgow, he fell under the spell of gambling—like Rinty, he had a particular passion for greyhound racing. He eventually moved to South Africa where, aged just forty-six, he was fatally injured, allegedly by a drinking associate, in November 1966. Initially it was claimed he had been murdered. The other big name in Rinty's life, Salvador Dado Marino, retired from boxing in 1952 and lived to the ripe old age of seventy-four. He passed away on 28 October 1989.

On 27 August 1990, a new play opened to the public at the Group Theatre in Belfast. Entitled simply *Rinty*, it was written by the well-known Belfast playwright, Martin Lynch. Michael Liebmann and Joe McPartland took the roles of young and old Rinty respectively. The play was also staged in the US, with the Macalla Theatre Company staging a production in the Bronx, where Rinty was played by Declan Mooney. It only had a short run but the reviews were excellent. One reviewer in particular praised the poignancy of the scene where the older Rinty tries in vain to warn his younger self about the hard times ahead. Rinty would surely have laughed at seeing his life being depicted in a country he had been invited to so many times, but had never got to visit. Martin Lynch summed up the story in an interview: 'The play is not just a celebration of Rinty, because he had his troubles as well as his good times. But I hope audiences will have a good laugh as well as a cry.'

***

On 2 May 2007, sixty years after Rinty's NBA world flyweight title win over Marino, a crowd of family, friends, fans and media gathered at the King's Hall for a very special event. The Ulster Historical Circle, after three long years, and with the approval of the King's Hall administrators, was unveiling a commemorative Blue Plaque in honour of Rinty Monaghan's career and the huge contribution he had made to Belfast's history. The plaque would be a permanent reminder of a great little fighter who, in the late 1940s, had become the best flyweight boxer in the world at this very arena.

More than twenty years after his death, Rinty was headline news again. The unveiling ceremony included a beautiful rendition of the song Rinty was so associated with: 'When Irish Eyes Are Smiling'. His three daughters, Martha, Rosetta and Collette stood proudly in front of the plaque for photographs and interviews. There was a little sadness in that the girls' brother Sean was not there to see it, or their mother Frances. They had passed away in 2004 and 2005. Sean had been only fifty-two, whereas Frances had lived to the fine age of ninety-one.

Patsy Monaghan said: 'Rinty would have loved the occasion, loved all the attention, and I thought the tribute the Ulster Historical Circle made about him was lovely. The family is so delighted that he has been honoured in this way. It was great to see that he was remembered and the King's Hall is the perfect place for the plaque.

'This was where he enjoyed many of his greatest triumphs. As world flyweight champion he was never beaten at the King's Hall. A lot of people of my generation remember the night he knocked out Jackie Paterson there. That was probably Rinty's most famous fight of them all. He beat Sandeyron there, drew with Allen, then retired as the undefeated World and European champion, undefeated British champion and undefeated Empire champion. That was some record to finish his career with and it finished at the King's Hall, so there was no better place in Belfast for the historical people to put up this plaque to commemorate Rinty.'

Marie, Rinty's only sister still residing in Belfast, also enjoyed the ceremony. She said: 'It was beautiful, a lovely occasion for all the family. It's just a pity Sean was not alive to see the tribute to his daddy. Pity too that John's wife Frances was not alive to see it either. The family are very pleased that this has happened, though it would have been nice had something like this taken place when John was alive. But it is something to be very proud of and the commemorative plaque is at the King's Hall for all the visitors to the hall to see and that is very nice. It is the right location for it. John achieved so much in boxing at the King's Hall. He would be so pleased.'

Rosetta said: 'It was great to have so many of the family together and so many of daddy's friends there for the ceremony. He was a sporting icon. I think it would be great if the sporting personalities Northern Ireland have produced over many years, those who excelled, were celebrated more. They should not be forgotten. Belfast should have a sports museum dedicated to all these great people.'

Martha said: 'He was famous all over the world. It was very nice to see this honour taking place at the King's Hall where daddy fought as the world champion and was never beaten in world title fights. I do not understand why this recognition did not happen years ago.'

Collette, the youngest daughter, said that the occasion was very emotional for all the family: 'It was a wonderful ceremony, lovely to see so many of the family there, the boys coming all the way from America to be there for it. It could not have been a nicer day. Sean not being there was really very sad. Something like this would have meant so much to him. Every one of us is so pleased that the Ulster Historical Circle commemorated Rinty's life in this way.'

Rinty was the seventy-seventh person to be honoured in this way by the Ulster Historical Circle. Others include Samuel Beckett, who won the Nobel Prize for Literature in the same year that Rinty was inducted into the Hall of Fame; former President of Israel, Chaim Herzog; *Titanic* creator, Thomas Andrews; United Irishman Henry Joy McCracken; pneumatic tyre inventor, John Dunlop; painter Sir John Lavery, and wireless pioneer, Guglielmo Marconi.

***

From 1947 to 1949 the biggest names in boxing were Joe Louis, Gus Lesnevich, Rocky Graziano, Tony Zale, Sugar Ray Robinson, Willie Pep, Manuel Ortiz, and Rinty Monaghan, a kid from Belfast who loved raw eggs, swore by the benefits of goat's milk, soaked his fists in brine to harden them, and ran up Cave Hill of a morning.

The Boxing Record

John Joseph 'Rinty' Monaghan fought more than sixty times as a professional—sixty-six, according to generally accepted records; but sixty-seven times, if the archives of The Ring Stadium from 1932 to 1935, which were made available to me by the late Belfast boxing enthusiast and writer, Alex Maskey senior, are to be scrutinised. Thanks to Rinty's daughter Collette, another mystery was cleared up regarding her father's birth date. The story goes that Monaghan started boxing professionally for Frank McAloran in 1934, a month after his fourteenth birthday. This was slightly wide of the mark. He was, in fact, just past his sixteenth birthday, as the year of his birth was 1918, and not 1920, as has been previously stated elsewhere.

His sixty-seventh, and final contest, was at the King's Hall against Terry Allen of Islington. The resulting draw saw Rinty make history as the first British licensed flyweight to defend four major titles—the Undisputed World Championship, European Championship, British and Empire Championship—simultaneously and successfully.

The fights listed below are only those that have been traced; the overall total is more than likely closer to three times the number of what has been actually recorded. The great man himself claimed to have fought 178 times in a career that started when he was just eleven. He fought at all the big arenas of the late 1920s and early 1930s before his listed professional debut in September 1934, against Sam Ramsey, at The Ring. Unlike many kids at the time, who dabbled in boxing and trained at local gyms and clubs like John Bosco ABC, Rinty did not box any amateur contests for a club or compete in any amateur tournaments.

Alex Maskey senior trained for a time at McAloran's gym during the 1940s. In early January 2007 we met at his home in the Andersonstown area of west Belfast. Sadly, there would not be a second meeting, as he passed away a couple of weeks later. Mr Maskey's painstaking research occupied his retirement years; he loved delving through old papers at the library. He compiled tremendous information about The Ring Stadium, in Thomas Street, where Rinty grew up. The stadium promoted shows from 1932 to 1935, and one of its headline fighters was Derry's future British champion, Jim 'Spider' Kelly, who was an inspiration to the young boxer billed as 'Boy' Monaghan. Rinty last fought at The Ring a month before it closed down. Fortunately for me, Alex had made notes of all the bills—who fought who on what night, and who promoted and made the matches. His research was invaluable, particularly his information about the 119th professional bill held at the former bus depot, dated 5 December 1934. On that night, Billy Smith of Belfast beat Liverpool's Peter Clarke by fifth round retirement, and there was a draw between Belfast rivals, Johnny Basham and Jackie Campbell. And then there was this:

'"Boy" (Rinty) Monaghan (Belfast) drew 4x3 "Boy" Ramsey (Belfast).'

Rinty's first contest was against Boy Ramsey, as was his second, a little-known fact. Previous records list his second opponent as Jim Pedlow. Alex's once blue, now faded, cardboard file, entitled 'The Ring Thomas St, July 1 1934 to Dec 31 1934', had provided a surprise find. Rinty fought six times with Sam Ramsey, and not five, making Jim Pedlow opponent number three. Pedlow is also significant in that the young Monaghan recorded the first of his fifty-one professional wins against him on the under-card of contests involving Jimmy Warnock and Patsy Quinn on Wednesday, 19 December 1934.

RINTY MONAGHAN'S BOXING CAREER

Total Contests: 67
Won: 51 (KOs 20); Lost: 9; Drew: 7

1934

28 SEPTEMBER: drew over four rounds with Sam 'Boy' Ramsey at The Ring Stadium on a promotion by Jim Edgar in Belfast;

5 DECEMBER: drew again on an Edgar Promotion at The Ring in a rematch with Sam 'Boy' Ramsey over four rounds;

19 DECEMBER: beat Jim Pedlow on points over four rounds in Belfast.

1935

17 FEBRUARY: stopped Vic Large by fourth round KO in Belfast;

29 MARCH: stopped 'Young' Finnegan, again by fourth round KO, in Belfast.

1936

13 JANUARY: beat Sam 'Boy' Ramsey on points over six rounds in Belfast;

22 FEBRUARY: beat 'Young' Josephs on points over six rounds in Belfast;

20 MARCH: draws for the third time in four meetings with Sam 'Boy' Ramsey, their second six-rounder, staged in Carrickfergus;

28 MARCH: beat Sam 'Boy' Ramsey on points to take his record against Ramsey to 2-0-3, after a six round contest in Belfast;

8 APRIL: beats 'Young' Kelly on points over six rounds in Belfast;

16 MAY: stops 'Young' Josephs in rematch on a technical knockout in round three in Belfast;

20 MAY: just four days later, has his first ten round contest and scores a draw with Jack McKenzie in Belfast;

24 JULY: third fight with 'Young' Josephs in five months is scored a draw after six rounds in Larne, County Antrim;

18 SEPTEMBER: defeats Joe Duffy on points over six rounds to end the year unbeaten in Larne.

1937

1 APRIL: loses for the first time, out-pointed by Jim Keery, over six rounds in Belfast;

10 APRIL: defeats Mick Gibbons over six rounds on points in Belfast;

21 JUNE: rematches Mick Gibbons, wins again on points over six rounds in Belfast;

7 JULY: sixth contest with Sam 'Boy' Ramsey, earns a six-round points win in Belfast;

13 JULY: first of three contests with Ted Meikle in two months ends in a fourth round stoppage win in Belfast;

9 AUGUST: wins rematch with Ted Meikle on points after eight rounds in Belfast;

18 AUGUST: defeats Frank Benson by sixth round technical knockout in Belfast;

17 SEPTEMBER: beats Ted Meikle for a third time with a points decision over eight rounds in Belfast;

1 OCTOBER: stops Paddy O'Toole by fourth round technical knockout in Belfast;

17 NOVEMBER: first win by straight knockout, defeating George Lang by KO in round one in Belfast;

2 DECEMBER: defeats Tommy Allen by fifth round KO in Belfast.

1938

21 JANUARY: third straight KO win in-a-row, defeating Alf Hughes by ninth round knockout in Belfast;

4 FEBRUARY: beats Pat Murphy on a fourth round technical knockout in Belfast;

1 MARCH: knocks out 'Spider' Allen inside two rounds in Belfast;

3 MARCH: first time to fight outside of Northern Ireland ends in victory over 'Cyclone' Kelly after a ten round contest in Liverpool, England;

15 MARCH: wins a return with 'Cyclone' Kelly on points over ten rounds in Belfast;

6 MAY: defeats Joe McCluskey on points over ten rounds in Belfast;

27 MAY: knocks out Peter Peters in the first round in Belfast;

18 JUNE: knocks out Ivor Neil, again in the first round, in Belfast;

1 JULY: defeats Joe Kiely on points over ten rounds in Belfast;

23 JULY: suffers second defeat of his career, first by stoppage, when knocked out by a Glasgow novice contesting only his second pro fight—a certain Jackie Paterson—in the fifth round at The Oval in Belfast;

11 AUGUST: beats Joe Curran on points over ten rounds in Liverpool, England;

2 SEPTEMBER: loses a title eliminator for the Northern Ireland Area Championship to city rival Tommy Stewart on points after ten rounds in Belfast.

1939

27 FEBRUARY: knocks out Joe Curran in fifth round of rematch in Newcastle, England;

20 MARCH: defeats Sammy Reynolds on points over ten rounds in Newcastle, England;

28 JUNE: wins a rematch against Tommy Stewart, who, since their Northern Ireland Area title eliminator, claimed the inaugural Northern Ireland flyweight title against Joe McStravick, winning a non-title bout on points over eight rounds in Belfast;

20 JULY: defeats Billy Aston over eight rounds in Liverpool, England;

8 NOVEMBER: defeats 'Seaman' Chetty on points after ten rounds in Newcastle, England.

1940

10 JANUARY: loses for the third time when beaten by Paddy Ryan on points over ten rounds in Newcastle, England;

4 MARCH: wins third contest with Tommy Stewart on points over eight rounds in Belfast;

20 MARCH: beaten for the fourth time in forty-four contests by dropping a points decision over ten rounds to top-rated Jimmy Gill in Newcastle, England.

1942

26 DECEMBER: defeats future Northern Ireland bantamweight title challenger, Joe Meikle, on points after an eight-round contest in Belfast.

1943

6 JUNE: draws with Harry Rodgers, who had lost to Ed 'Bunty' Doran for the Northern Ireland flyweight title seven months earlier, over eight rounds in Belfast;

13 JULY: loses to Ike Weir, a future Area flyweight title challenger, on points after ten rounds in Belfast.

1944

4 OCTOBER: wins a rematch against Joe Meikle by first round KO, the tenth straight knockout win of his career, in Belfast.

1945

9 JULY: defeats Dublin's Joe Collins over ten rounds in Dublin, a fight claimed to be for the Irish title;

13 SEPTEMBER: defeats Tommy Burney on points after ten rounds in Liverpool, England;

18 OCTOBER: loses to Joe Curran, who was competing in his 143rd pro fight, on points over ten rounds in Liverpool, England;

6 NOVEMBER: knocks out defending champion Ed 'Bunty' Doran for the Northern Ireland Area crown, stopping Doran in the fourth round at the Ulster Hall, Belfast.

1946

4 APRIL: rematches Tommy Burney and wins on points over eight rounds in Liverpool, England;

7 JUNE: in his first fight in front of his home fans since winning the Northern Ireland title, avenges his 1938 knockout loss when he KOs Jackie Paterson, by now the world flyweight champion, in the seventh round of a non-title bout in Belfast;

11 SEPTEMBER: defeats Alec Murphy on points over eight rounds in

Glasgow, Scotland;

24 SEPTEMBER: wins rematch with Sammy Reynolds when Reynolds is disqualified in the eighth round at Belfast.

1947

11 MARCH: knocks out leading English prospect, Terry Allen, during the first round of their contest in London, England;

1 JULY: defeats French star, Emile Famechon, after ten rounds on points in London, England;

16 JULY: steps in for ill world champion Jackie Paterson to fight Hawaii's NBA-nominated title challenger, Salvador Dado Marino, at catchweight in a non-title bout and is disqualified in the ninth round in Glasgow, Scotland;

20 OCTOBER: wins the vacant World Flyweight Championship title against Hawaii's Salvador Dado Marino, the fifteen-round points victory at the Harringay Arena in London being recognised by the National Boxing Association (NBA) and Ireland's governing body, but not the British Board, after Jackie Paterson wins a court injunction to prevent the BBB of C from recognising the status of the bout.

1948

23 MARCH: knocks out Jackie Paterson in the seventh round of the clash of NBA- and BBB of C-recognised world champions to become Ireland's first linear, or undisputed, world flyweight champion, and also win the British and Empire titles from Paterson at the King's Hall in Belfast;

28 JUNE: defeats Charlie Squire by seventh round KO in Birmingham, England

1949

7 FEBRUARY: loses a non-title return match with Terry Allen on points over eight rounds in London, England;

5 APRIL: claims the European title with victory over Maurice Sandeyron of France on points after fifteen rounds in a contest that was also a first defence of the World Championship title at the King's Hall in Belfast;

19 AUGUST: defeats Italy's Otello Belardinelli in a non-title bout over ten rounds on points in Belfast;

20 SEPTEMBER: draws with Terry Allen in defence of the World, European, British and Empire flyweight titles in what was to prove the last fight of his illustrious, history-making career at the King's Hall in Belfast.

1950

MARCH: retires on medical grounds (chronic bronchitis) and does so as the undefeated World, European, British and Empire flyweight champion. His decision is ratified and made official by the British Boxing Board of Control on 30 March.

Rinty's brother Patsy received this from Mollie Hare, of Foxleigh Grange in Birkenhead, where to this day there is a pub called 'Rinty Monaghan's'. The identity of the poet is unknown.

RINTY

The hips they were slender, the shoulders wide,
With a wee bit of weight that he couldn't hide
But still erect and jaunty of stride
'Twas yesterday's hero, Rinty.

Tight-fitting jerkin, zipped to the chin,
Pressed pants, shiny shoes, everything neat and trim,
Little changed from the time he had battled to win
The World's crown for Belfast—and Rinty,

Ask the young ones—they may not know,
But ask their elders, 'Who, years ago,
Stole the thunder at every show?'
They'll tell you—'It was Rinty!'

Good men and brave men, men of skill
Tried hard for his flyweight title, until
They were handed a ticket to 'Sleepyville',
A fourpenny one from Rinty.

The best at his weight all had their chance
But rings around them he would prance
To win, and then we'd a song and a dance
From the inimitable Rinty.

His fame blazed forth like a beacon lamp
With a legion of fans to cheer and stamp
For Belfast's own world flyweight champ
The one and only—Rinty.

He quit the game whilst he still wore his crown,
Took his leave from the ring he had graced with renown.
Even hard-bitten fight fans choked the tears down
When we said 'Goodbye'—to Rinty.

From sports page headlines he has sunk,
Didn't stay too long and become punch-drunk.
Why lie in boxing's yard of junk?
'That's not for me'—said Rinty.

'My song and dance act will still be the same,
I'll still have some fun at the old snooker game,
And if you face me at poker, you've only to blame
Yourself—if you're skinned—by Rinty.'

The years may roll on, but time can't erase
The memories you've left, of the ring and the stage.
On behalf of the fans who belonged to that age,
Many thanks for the memories—Rinty.

REFERENCES

A variety of materials were used to source the road that Rinty took throughout his career; I have separated them into their appropriate groupings.

Bibliography

Burrows, John; *Benny, The Life and Times of a Fighting Legend*: Mainstream, 1982

Callan, Gerry; *Barney Eastwood's Irish Boxing Yearbook*: Gerry Callan, 2001

Campbell, John; *Once There was a Community Here: A Sailortown Miscellany*: Lagan Press, 2001

Harding, John; *Lonsdale's Belt*: Robson, 1994

Hugman, Barry J; *British Boxing Board of Control Boxing Yearbook:* Mainstream, 2007

Lynch, Martin; *Pictures of Tomorrow & Rinty*: Lagan Press, 2003

Morrison, John; *Triumph to Tragedy*: MacGhille Mhuire, 2000

Myler, Patrick; *The Fighting Irish*: Brandon, 1987

Magazines/Newspapers

Andersonstown News

Belfast Telegraph

Daily Mail

Honolulu Star Bulletin

Irish Independent

Irish News

London Evening Standard

London Times

News Letter

Northern Whig

The Ring Magazine

Ulster Sports Gazette

Weekly Telegraph

Miscellaneous

Alex Maskey senior, for The Ring Stadium Years 1932–1935
BBC Timeline, for information on the Belfast Blitz
George McCullough's archive, for the career of Eddie McCullough
International Hall of Fame
The Newspaper Library at Central Library, Belfast

Web Sites

Boxrec.com
First World War.com
Irishclans.com
Galeuk.com
Localhistories.org
Sailortownbelfast.org
Texaco.ie
Videovista.net

Index